D1879436

Crisis in Higher Education

CRISIS IN HIGHER EDUCATION

Role Analysis of Teachers in a University System

Dr. Rani Mehta

Publications

KALPAZ PUBLICATIONS

DELHI - 110 052

Crisis in Higher Education
Role Analysis of Teachers in a University System

Rs. 790
© Dr. Rani Mehta
ISBN : 81-7835-305-9

All rights Reserved. No Part of this book may be reproduced in any manner without written permission.

Published in 2004 in India by
Kalpaz Publications,
C-30, Satyawati Nagar,
Delhi-110 052
Email : kalpaz@hotmail.com

Lasertype Setting by: Tact Computer Graphics, Delhi
Printed at: Mehra Offset Press, Delhi

Contents

Foreword

In this era of information society, or better still knowledge society, education, especially higher education, has acquired a crucial significance. The concurrent trend of globalisation has shot higher education into sharper prominence due to the reliance of the former on structures of competence and the role of the latter in competence production. Higher education can enhance self reliance of a nation in the emerging scenario of globalized interdependence by producing competent manpower required for accelerating the pace of development.

A teacher in the embodiment of competence as well as an agent of its transmission to the young generation. For the same reason, a teacher is the pivot of the educational system. The performance of higher education is likely to be as good as the performance of the teacher. The performance of the teacher depends on three Cs; competence, communication and commitment, among other things.

What is happening to the role perception and performance of a teacher in the system of higher education in India? Is it measuring upto the expectations of students? Does it give good evidence of teacher's competence, communicative ability and commitment? How is the role performance of a teacher affecting the performance of higher education? Is it producing crisis in higher education? These are some of the questions that the book seeks to answer on the basis of an empirical study of the role perceptions, expectations and performance of the teachers in select teaching departments and affiliated colleges of the Panjab University in Chandigarh. The study is based on three systematic samples, i.e. of teachers, students and educational superiors.

The study brings out some revealing findings. Most of the teachers, for example, prefer instrumental roles such as teaching and research over expressive role like cordial relationships with colleagues and communication with colleagues and students. This is indicative of the declining social role of teachers today. The study also discovers a gap between teachers' self estimate about their performance and students' perception of teachers' performance. In the students' perception, the performance of teachers falls short of their expectations and leaves something to be desired. The teachers are found wanting on attributes such as clarity of thought and expression, sensitivity towards students needs and hardships, sincerity of purpose and above all dedication and commitment.

On the comparative analysis, it is further observed that the university teachers confront more of professional problems in their role performance, while the college teachers encounter more of organizational problems due to bureaucratic inter-central and management politics. Most important of all, the study highlights that irrespective of the gender, status and academic achievements of teachers, they overwhelmingly maintain that the higher education is in crisis. The three most important factors identified for such a crisis are: increasing politisization and bureaucratization of higher education, teachers' tendency to give precedence to their self-interest over the good of students and faulty examination system and evaluation procedures. The increasing politisization and bureaucratization undermines the level of teacher competence and commitment because of its contaminating influence on the recruitment process. This often results into demoralization of teachers and their demotivation in respect of academic excellence.

On theoretical front, the book advances a three point conceptual frame for the teacher role analysis. It comprises the socio-politicial structure as external system, organizational milieu as internal system and the teacher-centric attributes including his role perceptions and motivations as well as expectations of his supervisors and students as the core system.

Dr. Rani Mehta, the author of the study deserves our appreciation for the commendable work done by her. Her study is a welcome contribution in the field of sociology of education and educational administration. The real meat of the study lies in the discovery and exposition of the students' perspective on the teacher role performance which makes its extremely relevant for all those concerned with educational planning and administration. The scholars would find the book as engaging and valuable as the policy planners and educationists

Preface

Education has two basic functions to perform in society. One is historical while the other is cultural. In the historical context, education plays an important role in the perpetuation and transmission of knowledge from one generation to another while in the cultural sense, it transforms the relationship between the individual and society by developing the personality structure of individuals. This can facilitate them to identify themselves with their changing culture and find constructive roles in society through educational pursuits for self-understanding, better knowledge of the choices available to society and for a critical view of the culture.

As a professional, a teacher is expected to transmit knowledge, develop skills and build up personality structure of students so that they are better equipped to face the challenges of life in their later years. But, whether a teacher is a professional or not, has been debated for long. The esoteric knowledge which he or she has acquired through hard learning, exposure and experience to develop the necessary competence in order to influence the behaviour pattern of his or her students, is often questioned.

His or her role performance as a professional is mainly constrained because of the compelling undesirable influences of the external socio-political system impinging adversely on the functioning of the university. Moreover, he or she has to confront the complex organsational milieu of the internal university system full of conflicting interests of the significant others. Besides, some teachers by their personality pre-dispositions are inclined to have more of political, bureaucratic and non-professional value orientations than academic. These knotty and complex issues prompted me to examine the role analysis of teachers in a university system so as to make it more effective for diffusing the crisis in higher education.

I was initiated into this research work by my worthy supervisor Professor Sherry Sabbarwal, Department of Sociology, Panjab

University, Chandigarh. I benefited a lot from her valuable suggestions as I received her able guidance at every step of the research work. Moreover, her pleasant temperament always encouraged me to have an easy access to her. I owe her a special sense of gratitude.,

I am also extremely thankful to the previous chairperson, Professor (Mrs.) R.M. Sethi and the subsequent chairman, Professor K.C. Kaistha, Department of Sociology, Panjab University, Chandigarh, for their support and cooperation in carrying out this study. My special thanks are also due to Professor S.L. Sharma, a renowned sociologist and Dean, Faculty of Arts, Panjab University, Chandigarh, for sparing valuable time from his busy schedule to write a foreward to the book. Infact, his outstanding work on Modernising Effects of University Education, inspired me to undertake the present research work.

I would also like to express a deep sense of gratitude to my parents (Mrs. Saroj Mehta and Professor S.R. Mehta) for supporting and encouraging me to complete this research work. I would like to make a special mention about my father who motivated me a let and gave his valuable guidance throughout my research endeavors. My elder sisters, Ms. Rashmi Mehta and Ms. Deepa Dutta, were also a big source of inspiration for me to take up this research work.

I am extremely grateful to my respondents, both the teachers and the students for willingly co-operating with me in providing the relevant data. Without their help, it would have been difficult for me to complete this research work.

Last but not least, I am thankful to Kalpaz Publications, Delhi for making special efforts for publishing this work carefully and quickly.

Rani Mehta

1
Introduction

"The future destiny of the world rests with the teachers and the students. If the teachers train their students in the right direction in the path of righteousness, the world will be filled with citizens who are Yogis and *Jivanmuktas* and who will radiate light, peace, bliss and joy everywhere."

Swami Sivananda
Divine Life Society

It is a well recognized fact that teachers have a significant role in shaping the personality structure of students. Besides, there are always certain sets of expectations related to their functioning. They also have certain perceptions of their role as teachers and often their performance gets affected by their perceptions of and expectations from their role. Thus, the focus of the present study is to make explorations in the role-analysis of teachers along the above lines in the university system.

The present chapter is divided into two parts. The first part will highlight the problem of research, historical aspects of growth and development of education in India, review of studies and objectives of the study while the second part will focus on the theoretical framework, hypotheses of the study and methods of data collection.

(I)

1. The Problem of Research

Man through his creativity and various kinds of sensibilities has generated a wealth of knowledge related to himself and his physico-socio-cultural environment. He has the power of knowledge to bring in transformation in the social and economic life of the humans. As man advanced in his journey to the development of society, the collective knowledge built by him in association with his fellow human beings, got institutionalized into an educational system. The sole objective of this system was to impart intellectual and moral training to the young persons. This system was also instrumental in bringing about social change in our society through scientific inventions and discoveries. The basic objectives of education have been two-fold. As a historical function, its thrust is on the perpetuation of culture from one generation to another in a given society. However, at the psychological plane, education helps in developing the personality of individuals.

No doubt, during the last few decades, developing countries have achieved tremendous progress in education, but in qualitative terms, the achievements are far from satisfactory. The enrollment ratio of students at all levels has increased at an unprecedented rate. However, enrollment in higher education has taken place at a greater rate than at the secondary and primary levels, both in the developing, as well as, in the developed countries. But the enrollment ratios at the secondary and tertiary levels in the developing countries are still lower than those of the developed ones. It has also been pointed out that in some of the developing countries, investment in higher education has been too rapid and perhaps at the expense of meeting some of the other societal needs (The World Bank, 1980).

Education, besides satisfying some of the basic human needs also acts as a means of meeting some of the other needs necessary for the development of human culture and social life. As such, its expansion is largely determined by the prevailing socio-economic and political order. Quite recently with the concept of egalitarianism introduced in the development of developing nations, that is, "Growth with Social Justice", there is now a greater concern shown in favour of democratization of educational resources at all levels.

In the Indian context, we had a rich tradition of "Gurukul" teaching, where an evolved person, either spiritually or mentally, would impart moral and intellectual training to the young. This is now a lost phenomenon. Our present system of education is a legacy of the British regime and our school, college and university educational system has been mainly determined on the same pattern. At the time of independence of our country, the planners and policy makers realized that illiteracy and ignorance, were the stumbling blocks for the development of our nation. As such, in the post-independent era, education was considered as a main instrument of social change. Efforts were made to expand education at all levels through the Five Year Plans. However, in spite of the best efforts made to eradicate illiteracy from our country, we still have nearly 34.6 per cent of our population above the age of 7 years as illiterates (24.1 per cent Males and 45.8 per cent Females; 2001, Census). The earlier efforts of our government have been in the expansions of the enrollment ratios of students rather than changing the nature and character of education. This quantitative approach, to a limited extent, was helpful in providing self-reliance and national identity to our citizens. Subsequently, certain qualitative objectives such as social equity, development of teaching of science, relating education to our national needs and building a national capacity for planning and administration of research in education were added to the national agenda. Despite heavy drop-out rates of students at the primary level (nearly 60 per cent), our progress in modernizing education is well recognized by the fact that we are ranked among the first 10 technically educated countries.

As of now, we have as many as 229 universities and 7199 Arts and Science colleges all over the country (Xavier, 2000). This has still not kept pace with the rise in the population. Moreover, most of the students entering into these institutions are drawn from the upper strata of the society. Research evidence suggests that the majority of the students going in for higher education belong to upper castes, urban areas and are having convent/public or private school background (Jayaram, 1979). This elitist approach to higher education could not be rectified despite the appointment of various Education Commissions by the Government of India. Even after more than fifty years of Independence, our pattern of higher education is run on western lines without changing of syllabi for various courses suitable to our present needs and goals. Gore (1994) in his analysis has highlighted various crises in the university system such as outdated course syllabi, lack of funds, faulty examination and evaluation, politicization and bureaucratization of the university, stress on liberal arts rather than on vocational courses, non-involvement of teachers, especially from the colleges, in the decision-making bodies and lack of adequate incentives for the committed and dedicated teachers. Even the opening of certain unitary universities specially at the central level, having a focus on campus teaching, has not helped in tackling the above stated crises in higher education effectively.

Apart from these problems, what stands out as a sore thumb is the limited role of the teachers both at the university and college levels. This is mainly due to lack of influence of teachers on the students because of the structural constraint of a less number of teachers to a greater number of students. Besides, organizational constraints and lack of autonomy to teachers, also affect the higher education adversely. As such, there is a need to re-organize the pattern of higher education and a system needs to be evolved in which the teacher plays a more creative role than performing routine activities.

The role of a teacher has various dimensions such as teaching, research, administration and consultancy. Therefore, it may be worthwhile to examine the role of teacher in the university system. Gore (1994) remarks that a teacher is expected to rise above his self-interest and develop a concern for the common good of the students in particular and of the society at large. By virtue of his status, he is also in a position to influence the character of students and build up their personality structure for their effective roles in the society. However, a teacher has to operate within the university prescriptive system. As such, there are sets of expectations related to his functioning. Besides, he also has certain perceptions of his role as a teacher and acts as a guide in transmitting appropriate knowledge, developing suitable skills and building up necessary attitudes among the students so that they may come out with distinction and competence in their later life.

Thus, it becomes imperative to analyze the role performance of the teacher in terms of how he or she perceives his or her own role as well as how he or she tries to relate it to the set of expectations from him or her by others, that is, the administrators, the colleagues and the students. The present study is an attempt in that direction.

2. Historical Aspects of Growth and Development of Education in India

The journey of education in India is a long drawn one. We have moved on from Gurukuls of 200 B.C. through the ancient

Buddhist Viharas, the medieval maktabs and Madarsas to the modern education system, which is a direct result of the British rule.

Ancient Indian Period— In the epic period the "Gurukul Parampara" established "Guru-shishya" relationship purely along altruistic lines. The "Guru" not only imparted knowledge to his students on their duties (Dharma) and actions (Karmas) but also acted as a "Marg-Darshik" (One who gives direction to his followers). A wholistic approach was followed to impart physical (military), moral and intellectual training to the young persons. Nehru (1946) refers to these as forest universities as they were located in forests, to avoid the influence of urban centres. However, with the advent of Buddhism, the Gurukuls were relegated to a less significant status and the Buddhist monastries (Viharas) started influencing the minds of people. The focus was on following the middle path which avoided attachment to passion and worldly pleasures on the one hand and the practice of self-mortification and asceticism on the other. Buddha started monastries (Viharas) where monks lived and spent their lives, praying and preaching Buddhism. The Viharas were also used as schools attended by people from all strata of society. Some of the more famous were at " Nalanda" and "Vikramshila" in Bihar and "Valabhi" in Gujarat.

Nehru (1946) also refers to Benaras as a centre of learning and according to him even in Buddha's time, it was known as such. Although, it was not anything like a university, yet there were numerous groups there, consisting of a teacher and his disciples who held fierce debates and arguments on various subjects. However, in the north-west, there was a famous university at Taxila known for science, especially medicine and the arts. People used to go there for education from distant parts of India. During the Buddhist period, it also became a centre of Buddhist scholarship and attracted Buddhist students from all over India and across the border from the central Asia and Afghanistan.

The Mughal Period— During the Mughal period, Persian was the official court language. Thus, a number of 'Madrasas' were opened to promote both the Persian and Urdu languages. As the majority of Muslims in India were converts from Hinduism, partly because of their long contact with the Mughals, they developed numerous common traits, habits, ways of living and artistic tastes in music, painting, architecture, food and common traditions, especially in Northern India. A large number of Hindus wrote books in Persian while at the same time, a number of Muslims scholars translated Sanskrit books into Persian and wrote in Hindi. For example, Abdur Rahim, a Mughal noble in Akbar's court, was a scholar in Arabic, Persian and Sanskrit and his Hindi "dohas" (couplets) are still recited. A number of poets had begun writing in Urdu and in the 18th century, Delhi and Lucknow became the centers of Urdu poetry. Besides, many Muslims scholars were attached to the court or were incharge of theological and other academies.

The Colonial Period— The Colonial origin of modern education system is traced back to Indian Act of 1813 of the education policy promoted by the East India Company. A provision was made to spend a lakh of rupees on education. This was, later on in 1833, increased to ten lakh rupees. However, the commitment of the government towards this task was inadequate (Basu, 1982). The East India Company was expected to provide good education necessarily through the medium of English to only a few persons who may or may not be from the upper castes. It was expected that these persons would educate the masses through modern Indian languages (Nurullah and Naik, 1951). There was an implicit caste and class bias in this elitist policy of education, which was further strengthened through the adoption of Macaulay's minutes of 1835, favouring English as the medium of learning. This, in effect, destroyed the old indigineous system of education and set aside the new western system of education decisively beyond the reach of the masses (Heredia, 2000).

Later on, the East India Company in its education dispatch of 1854, introduced a system of grants-in aid to privately managed institutions. This made the expansion of education dependent on the private agencies who were willing to carry the burden which the government expressed its inability to bear (Heredia, 1981). As a consequence of this grants-in-aid code, it is observed that about a third of cost was borne by the private agencies whereas two-thirds was provided by the government. Although, this provided a relief to the government of some of the financial cost and much of the organizational initiatives in education but it resulted in the laissez-faire policy enunciated by the Indian Education Commission

(1882), popularly known as Hunter Commission (Basu, 1982). No doubt, the rapid expansion of education as a result of this, caused serious concern to the government. Lord Curzon tried to bring some order in the educational system, with an emphasis on quality over quantity but in spite of Indian Universities Act of 1904, the Calcutta Universities Commission (1917) found the system, "fundamentally defective in almost every aspect". The demand for education, especially Western and English education, motivated a large number of private agencies to go in for it, with a desire of upward mobility for their respective caste and religious communities. It was estimated by Naik (1967) that about 85 per cent of colleges and 65 per cent of our secondary schools were in the private sector. Following the footsteps of missionaries each new group, that is, Brahmins after 1882, Non-Brahmins after 1921, the Dalits with Ambedkar in the 1940's and Adivasi Seva Mandals in the 1950's, asked for government recognition and grants, not on the basis of performance and quality but on the principle of equality and non-discrimination (Dickinson and Appasamy, 1967).

No doubt, the official education policy in British India had strict religious neutrality but this religious neutrality was simply a matter of historical accident. It is argued that diversity and depth of religious affiliation in India was a pragmatic political necessity (Naik, 1965). In short, higher education in India turned out to be extremely elitist in content and form representing a small tip of the pyramid with a very inadequate base. The focus here was on the transmission of knowledge and not on its creation and more so in the Arts than the Science, producing more generalists than specialists and more liberals than professionals (Heredia, 2000).

The first three universities of modern India were established in the year 1857 in Calcutta, Bombay and Madras. These were affiliated universities having certain colleges attached to them. The pattern was to hold examinations, charge fees and award degrees at under-graduate and post-graduate levels (Gore, 1994). Before the establishment of these universities, the East India Company supported the opening of the Calcutta Madrasa and the Benaras Sanskrit College in 1781 and 1791, respectively. Both these institutions were providing a regular supply of qualified Indians to help the administration in the courts of the company. It is also reported that the Fort William College was started in Calcutta in

1801 and a few of Indian scholars under a British Principal were engaged to acquaint the British civilians with the languages, history, law and customs of India.

Post Independence Period— At the time of independence of the country, the educational situation was not encouraging. Due to a long colonial rule, the basic task was to restructure it radically and rapidly with a view to provide a system of national education suitable to our social needs. The thrust had to be on providing universal, free elementary education, reduction of adult illiteracy, adoption of Indian languages as media of instruction, a rational language policy for effective communication, restructuring secondary and higher education through vocationalisation and diversifications, making course contents socially relevant, modernization of methods of teaching and examinations, promoting research facilities and putting special emphasis on the education of weaker sections of the society such as women, scheduled castes and tribes and other backward communities (Kamat, 1972).

It is observed that during the period from 1950-51 to 1975-76, the total number of educational institutions increased by about two and a half times whereas the number of students enrolled went up by four times. The number of teachers correspondingly also increased four-fold whereas the total outlay on education rose from about 1.2 per cent of the national income to a little over 3 per cent (Kamat, 1980). Subsequently, there has been expansion of higher education during each of the Five-Year Plans. As on 1999-2000, we have as many as 229 universities (Xavier, 2000). These include institutions deemed to be universities but exclude other institutions of national importance. Besides, we have as many as 9278 colleges including professional colleges (Medicine, Engineering, Agricultural and Teacher's Training). The number of students enrolled with these institutions is 6425000 whereas the number of teachers is around 311000. We have 39 institutions deemed to be universities as well as 11 institutions of National importance. It is also observed that the share of higher education expenditure during the eighth Five Year Plan (1992-97) was around 7 per cent (Tilak, 1999).

Not more than 6 per cent of the students in the age group of 17-23 years are enrolled for higher education. The corresponding ratio in developed countries is above 40 per cent while in developing countries, it is around 7 per cent. In our context, a large proportion of enrollment of students in higher education is at the under-graduate level whereas students in post-graduate and research studies are few (Source: UGC, Annual Report, 1995-96).

Further, it is observed that the majority of students (90.07 per cent) are enrolled in general courses while a few (9.93 per cent) have gone in for professional studies in higher education. The male-female ratio for general studies as on 1996 is 1.69:1 whereas in 1947 it was 8.29:1. Again, in 1996 the male-female ratio in professional courses was 3.12:1. The above statistics are indicative of an increase in female enrollment in higher education (Powar, 1997). During the course of planned development, efforts have been made by the respective state governments (since education is a state subject) to structure the educational system, in a way, as to outreach the areas previously unserved. Further, attempts have also been made to improve the quality of education by relating it to the indigeneous life and culture of people and to the different needs of regional areas within the country. In order to improve the relevance of education to our cultural ethos, efforts have been made to re-activate our national languages and to impart instructions to students through them during the early years of formal schooling.

However, these efforts have created more disparities among students in this competitive world as most of the students trained through local languages cannot have higher rate of occupational achievements than those trained through English medium. This elitist approach to higher education has not been rectified despite various commissions appointed by the Government of India, that is, by the University Grants Commission, the apex body at the national level to guide the central as well as state universities from time to time.

The University Grants Commission (UGC) was set up in 1953 on the recommendation of Radha Krishnan Commission on Education (1950). In order to promote quality research works in various subjects at the university level, the UGC went ahead in establishing centres of advance study in selected universities in the country, as there was a growing fear that the university departments were being reduced to mere teaching shops (Deshpande, 2001). However, these centres have not yielded the desired results. In many cases, they have been performing below standards and in some cases these have been closed down. Quite lately, the functioning of UGC has been questioned in various quarters both by the professionals and the non-professionals. Despite the UGC being innovative in launching programs such as autonomous colleges, examination reforms, semester system, merit promotion scheme, academic staff colleges to organize refresher and orientation courses for college teachers and academic accreditation of an institute, there is no visible lasting impact of these schemes in improving the standards of teaching and research in higher education.

The situation of educational standard at the college level is more alarming than at the university level. In one of its recommendations, the Kothari Commission in 1964 suggested the idea of conferring autonomous status on some colleges with a view to provide them freedom to devise and adopt their own curriculum, courses of study and syllabi, methods of teaching and evaluation and admission policy. However, this could not be implemented before 1986. The National Policy on Education (1986) translated the concept of autonomous colleges into action and the UGC decided to give autonomous status to 500 colleges throughout the country by 1990. Unfortunately, this target could not be achieved for various reasons. In 1994, there were only 114 autonomous colleges spread over seven states. Tamil Nadu, Andhra Pradesh, Rajasthan and Gujarat have 112 of these 114 colleges whereas Orissa and Madhya Pradesh each have one autonomous college. The performance of these colleges is normally reviewed to ensure accountability (Sundaram, 2000). Presently, efforts are also being made to promote autonomous colleges in the Northern region. However, the privately aided colleges have expressed doubts about this program due to acute financial crunch. Further, it is feared that due to information revolution and liberal economic forces promoting privatization of education, the college and universities may not be reduced from centres of learning to centres for earning. We have already not more than 6 per cent of our youth going in for higher education and in the event of its privatization, not even 1 per cent of youth will be able to receive it. The privately aided colleges will find themselves in a difficult situation to go in for autonomous status in view of the irregular grants-in-aid, the 5 per cent cut, a freeze on the sanctioned posts, a steep hike in the fee structure and due to hints of further cuts in grants (Sharma and Kapoor, 1999).

One of the main contributing factors for deterioration in higher education is the poor allocation of funds. Since independence, our education expenditure has never touched the 4 per cent mark of the Gross Domestic Product (GDP). No doubt, the Kothari Commission (1964-66) had recommended that it should not be less than 6 per cent. This was accepted in principle but could not be implemented despite repeated promises made by successive governments. In fact, a large number of newly started universities and colleges on account of paucity of funds and facilities turned out to be "academic slums". The major share of benefits of higher education during the last 50 years has gone to the elite sections of the society (Pillai, 2000). However, efforts were being made by the government to raise the expenditure on education to 6 per cent of GDP during the Ninth Five Year Plan.

Recently, the UGC has recommended introduction of certain new courses at the university level such as astrology and Vedic rituals to revive our past cultural heritage but this has led to controversial debates on the issue. However, the Radha Krishnan Commission Report, (1950) advocated that there should be a detached atmosphere of an academic institution where one can study, analyze and eliminate the prejudices and misunderstandings disfiguring inter-religions, to promote its secular character (Visvanathan, 2000).

3. Review of Studies

An attempt to examine the available literature reveals that most of the studies on this topic in India and abroad have focused either on students or on teachers in the school and college set-up. The review that follows is divided into two parts. Some of the studies conducted abroad will be reported first, while the studies carried out in India will be taken up next.

Studies Done Outside India—The following studies describe the changing role of teachers, teaching beliefs, ethical dilemmas faced by teachers, faculty-chairperson relationship and a shift in attitudes of teaching assistants.

Knapp (1962) pointed out in his study a long term trend in the changing role of the teachers. Historically speaking, the teacher had been expected to contribute to the character development of students through counselling and other personal contacts. However, this aspect has become less important now and a greater emphasis is being laid on his research role.

Mizuno et al. (1990) examined the relationship between teaching beliefs and behaviour of elementary school teachers of Japan, Australia and Korea. The parameters used to show this relationship were classroom organization and management, curriculum instructions, test and evaluation and motivation. The relationship between teaching beliefs and behaviour was found most congruent among Australians, most incongruent in the case of Koreans and most vague for the Japanese teachers.

Gunnel (1991) carried out a study of ethical dilemmas among Swedish teachers. They were asked to describe critical incidents in their daily work. The results revealed that teachers were often put in situations of varying ethical difficulty and were left without guidance of explicit norms in finding solutions to the dilemmas.

Barge and Musambira (1992) carried out a study on 86 faculty members at a south-western U.S. university on the type of communicative events that influence faculty-chairperson relationships. The questions focused on characteristics of relationships, turning points, relational perceptions and conversational topics. Seven types of turning points were identified. These relate to performance evaluation including promotion and tenure, recognition, that is, receptivity of faculty ideas, support, that is, managing conflicts, trustworthiness including deceit and promise, job interference, interaction outside the work and interpersonal discussion. The study emphasized on the importance of chairpersons' clarification of goals and reasons for particular actions.

Freyberg et al. (1993) studied the re-socialisation of 19 graduate student teaching assistants at a large Mid-Western U.S. Research University. A comparison of attitudes of pre-candidate and candidate teaching assistants shows differences in self-esteem and attitudes towards under-graduate students and professors. These differences show that the graduate program encourages a shift in self-identity among teaching assistants away from that of teacher and towards that of researcher.

In addition to the above, the studies given below indicate the influence of research, teaching commitments, environment etc.

on the publication productivity of teachers and also highlight the same on gender basis.

Fox (1992) carried out a survey during 1986-87 on a national sample of social sciences faculty in U.S.A. to examine the influence of research and teaching interests, time commitments, orientation of faculty and their perceived environments on publication productivity. The findings point out a strain between research and teaching. Those having high publication productivity have strong investments in research but not in teaching. This indicates that research and teaching do not represent aspects of a single dimension of academic investments. In fact, these are two different conflicting dimensions.

Noordenbos (1992) examined the career tracks, publication rates and time management of 72 female and 40 male Professors of Belgian University in the same working environment. It was revealed by the study that males published no more than females. Again, it was found that females who worked in departments were offered fewer opportunities for publications and generally occupied lower positions than males.

Further, the studies mentioned below highlight the use of pictures and television in the classroom for imparting education to students.

Pettersson (1991) carried out a study on the use of various media and different kinds of pictures used in the classroom activities by the Swedish teachers. Responses from teachers and students and calculations of media utilization index values, showed that media utilization was low or extremely low in social sciences. Even the index of picture type utilization was found to be low. Blackboards and textbooks were the most common media form utilized in the classrooms.

Saeedi (1998) carried out a sociological study on education through television among 208 students and 50 teachers of Malayear University in Iran. The study revealed that the B.S. (graduate) students showed favourable results towards the positive influence of ETV (Education Television). The experimental groups taught by T.V. have shown superior mean achievement score in Geology but not in Geography and English language. Thus, the degree of ETV's impact in education depends on the nature of subject and its course content. Again, it was pointed out by the study that there has to be a mutual complementary role of television and the other tools of instruction. In other words, television as a teaching tool has to be integrated and balanced with other instruments of teaching (teacher) for augmenting education.

Again, the studies stated below focus on the effect of father's education on the educational aspirations of college girls, evaluation of teachers by students, influence of teacher's race, gender and ethnicity on the learning of students and decrease in the enrollment of women students due to economic cuts.

Baali (1967) carried out a study among college girls in Iraq to find out the relationship between their educational aspirations and fathers' education, socio-economic status and authority pattern in the family. It was found that the educational attainment of the father was positively associated with educational aspirations of his daughter(s). Further, it was found that the college girls whose fathers have had high educational attainments tended to be more desirous of education than the girls whose fathers have had low educational attainments.

Feldman, (1992) carried out a study among the college students to ascertain their views about male and female college teachers in the United States of America. The findings of the study revealed that in a minority of cases, male teachers received higher overall evaluations by students than the female teachers. This finding is not supported globally. Further, perceptions and ratings of male and female teachers by students on specific instructional dimensions either showed no differences or inconsistent differences across various courses pursued by students. It was also observed that, no same gender or cross-gender bias existed.

Ehrenberg et al. (1995) examined the influence of the teacher's race, gender and ethnicity on the learning of students in the United States of America. The analysis of data revealed that the match between teacher/student's race, gender and ethnicity had little association with the extent of learning of students. However, in several instances, these factors were found to be significantly determining the teachers' subjective evaluations of their students.

Assie-Lumumba (2000) while analyzing the crisis in higher education due to economic cuts and inadequate state financing support, resulting into curtailment of women students, referred to an earlier study, (1996) and that of Saint (1992). These revealed the impact of financial cut-backs on women's enrollment in higher education in Africa. The lag in their enrollment was even visible before the crisis of higher education in this region. Further, these studies indicated that this gender gap in enrollment was mainly due to the changed investment priorities.

Studies Done in India—An attempt is made here to present the review of studies, by and large, according to the year of their publications. The first review and trend report on the Sociology of Education of India was brought out by Indian Council of Social Science Research (ICSSR) in 1974 (Chitnis, 1974). The second review and trend report in this field was again done by Chitnis in 1980 for ICSSR (Chitnis, 1980). The first trend report had focused on six basic themes. The most prominent among them was the social background, attitudes and values of college students and teachers. Some of these studies have been done by Desai (1953), Ahmed (1968), Shah (1967), Chitra (1970) and Gore et al. (1970). The second theme was related to the socialization functions of education to understand its influence on the modernization of students (Shah, 1963, Sharma, 1968, Cormarck, 1961). The third theme for research in this area had been in relation to expansion and growth of education in Indian society whereas the issues of education, equality, mobility and social straitification had been mentioned as the fourth area in this field (D'souza, 1961; Thirtha, 1967; Joshi, 1967). The organization and structure of education constituted the fifth area of research while roles in education specially that of the teacher and the student had been referred to as the sixth theme of research. However, in the second review and trend report, Chitnis (1980) brought out a systematic analysis of education in the country. Studies conducted in India range from the school, the college and the university to the educational organization of an entire state. But in the context of the present review, we will concentrate on studies related to higher education only.

Brar's (1972) analysis of the role preference of faculty members in a university showed that the faculty members were more teaching than research oriented. Further, it was observed that lecturers and readers were more research oriented than professors who gave preference to the character building role than to research.

Kapoor (1974) in her study has pointed out that in Indian universities and colleges, the women teachers are generally drawn from a relatively higher socio-economic background as compared to male-teachers. Employment for many of them is not a source of livelihood but a status symbol. Many of them are wives of well-placed white collar workers.

Chitnis (1973) studied the role of teachers in the college system and also examined the social background and role performance of college teachers at the University of Bombay (1974). Similar issues have also been looked into by Jayaram (1976) and Ramanamma (1979) in their respective research work. Chitnis (1979) also analyzed the level of the professionalisation of college and university teachers in India and discussed their role as agents of development and change.

Heredia (1979) presents a socio-demographic profile of college teachers at Bombay University and analyses the structure of their situation in the academic organization.

Bhoite (1978) has focused on the degree of commitment of college teachers and also whether they have acquired modernization in certain aspects of life, that is, involvement in religion and religious practices, belief in occult powers etc. Apparently, the teachers are placed in some kind of a dilemma in between what they want through education, what they profess in their class-rooms and what they are required to practice in their daily life situations.

Lal and Nahar (1978) carried out a study on the scheduled caste and the scheduled tribe students in five districts (Jaipur, Ajmer, Jhunjhunu, Jodhpur and Kota) in the state of Rajasthan. The sample constituted 233 scheduled caste and 209 scheduled tribe students. They were drawn respectively from 15 colleges for SCs and 11 colleges for STs in the selected districts. The main finding of the study is that nearly two-thirds of the SCs college students and 90 per cent of the STs college students have not experienced any sort of ill treatment from the upper caste Hindus. Further, a large number of them are satisfied with the reservation policy of government for education and employment. However, they are also equally desirous of extension of this policy for employment in the private sector along with the government sector. The higher education of these students, has shown favourable results for them in seeking employment as well as a change in the attitudes of upper caste students towards them.

Khanna (1979) in her study reports that those who opted for the teaching profession were those inspired mainly by their teachers with whom they remained in contact throughout their educational career. Besides, fascination for professional status in society, desire for higher social prestige, better prospects and chance for self-expression, motivated them to choose teaching as their career.

Singh (1979) in his study gave evidence of academic achievements of teachers in their research pursuits. He suggested a positive relationship between the rank of the teacher and his academic accomplishments. He pointed out that teachers of social sciences had better understanding of the values related to objectivity and rationality. On the other hand, the science teacher had imbibed the mechanistic aspects of science without grasping its basic elements like suscepticism and inquiry. Further, in his analysis he has suggested four-fold typology of teacher value orientations such as pure traditional, traditional-transitional, modern-transitional, and pure modern. He observed that the role structures of teachers were more transitional than pure traditional or pure modern. Those who were pure modern in their outlook constituted a small minority and showed higher commitment, higher proper aspirations and a demand for autonomy in the pursuit of their profession. Similarly, the pure traditional who showed lower aspirations, lower commitment and submission to the decision of others, were also in a minority.

Sharma (1979) analyzed the role of university education in student modernity as well as on the role preference of university teachers. Basing his study on the interviews of 770 students and 241 teachers of the Panjab University Campus, he indicated that there was a trend of negative association between the level of education and modernity. As regards the role preference of university teachers, he reported that the majority of teachers rated the teaching role as most important, the research role (the creator of knowledge) as of considerable importance, character-building role as relatively less important and perspective shaping role (socio-political outlook moulding) as the least important.

Preet Manav (1987) in her study of college teachers examined their professional orientation and role preferences. It was revealed that male teachers were more professionally oriented than their female counterparts. Further, male teachers preferred roles such as teaching and research whereas female teachers emphasized on the character building role and that of teaching.

Singh (1987) in his study of changing status and role of university teachers reported that a large number of them laid emphasis on the career making of the students. Besides, a majority of them considered their role as generators of knowledge. However, most of them did not show much interest in the fact that they could play a role in the development of society.

Ranade (1987) in her study of college going Muslim girls in Bombay, examined issues such as wearing of the veil, knowledge of the "Quran and Shariyat" and need for any change in the latter, the position of women in Islamic countries and awareness of and attitudes towards the feminist movement in India. The respondents belonged to middle and upper middle class backgrounds. The college girls knew very little about the situation of women in Muslim countries except something about Pakistan and about dowry deaths in India. They had picked up this information from film magazines and Urdu newspapers only. They were probed further to find out as to why they did not use the library facilities in the college for seeking information on these issues. The majority of them responded that they were not allowed to sit for long in the library by their family members as they expected them to reach home early.

Talesra (1989) carried out a study on higher education among women in the district of Udaipur in the state of Rajasthan, covering all the institutions of higher learning either financed or administered by the government or voluntary agencies including technical or professional colleges. The sample included 500 women students. The main finding of the study is that most of the benefits of higher education for women have gone in favour of upper segments of the society whereas the disadvantaged groups especially the scheduled tribes (who have an overwhelming majority in the seven of the 18 tehsils of the district) are deprived of these benefits.

Sharma (1989) conducted a study on political awareness among students in the Panjab University. It was found that the socio-economic background of students particularly their gender status, type of schooling done, rural/urban background, education and occupation of parents determined their level of awareness both in terms of political information and its evaluation.

Prasad et al. (1990) studied the motivational pattern of school and college teachers in Bihar. In the case of college teachers, 50 male teachers from a constituent college and 50 from affiliated colleges in the age group of 32 to 36 years, were chosen from a town in South Bihar. The motivational factors for the teachers of constituent college were ranked in the following order in terms of their importance; advancement, security, hours of work, supervisor and pay. Essentially, they were concerned with security of job and advancement of their career. The hours of work, the nature of supervision were not that important factors for them. On the other hand, the affiliated college teachers ranked security, supervisor, pay, hours of work and advancement in that order. In their case, the security of job depended upon the recommendations of the Principal or that of the Secretary of the college. The workload was heavy and there was a feeling of stagnation. As such the question of advancement in their career did not arise. There were different incentive preferences among teachers in both the colleges. Further, the teachers of the constituent college showed more satisfaction with the college climate as compared to the teachers of the affiliated colleges.

Kalra et al. (1994) examined the perception and feelings of teachers about their community and institution. The sample consisted of 176 university and college teachers and the data were collected by using the projective methodology. A significantly large number of teachers were having a negative perception of their community and systems. Only 22.7 per cent teachers wanted to become teachers. Further, a large proportion of them expressed their frustration, anguish and helplessness towards their community and systems. The major pointer of the study is that teachers with a high degree of negative perceptions and feelings along with their low motivation, are less likely to accept the goals and values of their institutions than others. As such, they are not willing to exert a considerable effort for their institutions. It is suggested that the culture of our educational institutions can be improved upon through selection of right type of teachers having holistic personality development.

Kapoor et al. (1997) carried out a study on the future plan of 10+2 male students of scheduled castes belonging to rural areas of district Hisar in Haryana during 1995-96. A sample of 150 students from a cluster of 10 villages was taken. The majority of students (66 per cent) were willing to go in for higher studies whereas 34 per cent of them decided to take up jobs after the completion of their course. It was further revealed that the students aspiring to join higher studies belonged to "Chamar", "Dhanak" and "Balmiki" castes, had nuclear families and urban background and were from higher income groups. Most of them were holders of first and second division and their parents were educated and engaged in service. On the other hand, those students who wanted to take up a job in future were from "Odd", "Doom" and "Khatik" castes, had joint families and rural background. Further, their parents were illiterate and belonged to lower income groups. Besides, most of the students had obtained third divisions. An interesting finding was that with the rise of per capita annual income of the families, the proportion of students willing to go in for higher education also increased. The majority of students planning to join service were drawn from lowest per capita income group.

A synoptic review of studies outlined above throws up some factors influencing the role-analysis of teachers in higher education. While some of these studies indicate the relevance of gender, status or rank of the teachers, stream of courses pursued by teachers (Science, Social Science, Professional), academic attainment of teachers and fascination for professional status in society, in understanding the role of the teacher, others highlight the significance of desire for higher social prestige, better prospects and chance for self-expression, inspiration drawn from their teachers and role preferences of teachers etc. as factors having bearing on their role-analysis. In the context of the present study, some of the factors identified above have been taken into account for analysis purposes.

A look at the literature on the sociology of education in India indicated that it is mainly restricted in coverage. This may be due to the fact that a very small number of sociologists are engaged in research on education. Besides, the consumption of sociological research on education is very limited. There are hardly any quality probes in this area of research. The heterogeneity and plurality of

Indian society further makes it very expensive to cover all the relevant parameters related to education in various studies (Chitnis, 1982).

Also, even in the few studies focusing the role of university and college teachers, the analysis takes into account only the teachers without taking into consideration the perception of students towards their role in education. In the context of the present study, an attempt has been made to examine the expectations of students from the teachers along with that of Chairpersons of the teaching departments and the Principals of the colleges, towards the role performance of teachers.

4. Objectives of the Study

Keeping in view the problem of the study, the following objectives have been laid down for carrying out the study.

1. To examine the socio-cultural and economic characteristics of the selected respondents. (Selected teachers, Chairpersons and students of the University Departments and selected teachers, Principals and students of Colleges).
2. To delineate the role perception and performance of the teachers both at the university and college levels and to relate these to some of their socio-cultural characteristics.
3. To analyse the expectations of selected students as well as Principals of colleges and Chairpersons of the departments in the university towards the role performance of the teachers.
4. To study the nature of role conflicts of teachers and their views on crisis in higher education along with suggestions to make their role more effective.

(II)

1. Theoretical Framework

In order to analyse the role of teachers in a university system, it may be worthwhile to examine certain perspectives on education, role and profession.

I. Education—Basically we could conceive of three major perspectives in the field of sociology of education, namely structural-functional, conflict and interactional.

The structural-functional perspective on education system examines the relationship between the structure of society and the function of education in maintaining, legitimizing and internalizing the collective conscience as a sub-system of the society. This view given mainly by Durkheim, considers moral values as pattern maintaining forces. He treats them largely as social, maintaining that these are responsible for the solidarity of society and for the integration of individuals into the society. This perspective holds that if education has to play its function to transmit these values, then it must work towards solidarity and integration rather than towards differentiation and pluralism. Parsons, refining some of the basic ideas postulated by Durkheim, said that the social order in the society is achieved through operation of an integrating system shared by all members of the society. According to him, there is a link between the reproduction of society and the production of individual personalities through the process of socialization. For Parsons (1959), the system of education is an agency through which individuals are trained to be motivationally and technically adequate in order to perform the adult roles. In this respect, the part played by schooling in allocating men or women to special roles and in teaching them their contributions is tremendous.

The main difficulty with this perspective is that it presents society as an all pervasive entity, that is, overarching men in terms of constraining, moulding and regulating without taking into account the problems of disorganization or of conflicting interests over the balance of power. Moreover, this perspective provides an oversocialized conception of Man wherein he has been depicted as one receiving dominant influences rather than being a creator of things. Further, any failure within the system is mainly attributed to poor organizational factors, lack of fit between the role and personality and to the inadequate adaptation to the emerging social systems (Meighan, 1981).

The second perspective on education is the conflict view, which focuses on the power dimensions of human behaviour. The Marxian analysis has emphasized economic development of social organization including education through the capitalist mode of production. It is mainly in line with what Apple (1979-80) has called the deep structure of education. The focus here is to delineate the ways in which the day to day organization and routine activities of life in class-room are explained in terms of distribution of power in society. In this perspective, schooling is seen not as a process of socialization of new members of society into a collectively established moral order or as a result of creative interaction of local groups but as a phenomenon of distribution of resources and opportunities in societies. It is argued that educational affairs are influenced by the ideologies and direct intervention of socially and politically dominant groups. In other words, the socialization of students is done in an environment which is based on relationships of dominance and sub-ordination. Ivan Illich (1972) has added another dimension to this view. According to him, education should be a liberating experience and should help individuals to freely develop their faculties and acquire skills. He believes that the schooling system is not effective in the above regard. Thus, he suggests the de-schooling of the society.

The main limitation of this perspective is that human behaviour cannot be visualized in terms of a simple response to the structural arrangements of society and upon the settings in which cultural forms are created as a consequence of mode of production, but as something arising out of the dynamic association of these set of factors. As such, it is difficult to establish a simple correspondence between the capitalist mode of production and the school system that serves to produce and reproduce the kind of social relations necessary for its maintenance and development.

The third perspective of interactionist approach considers Man as autonomous, capable of utilizing his full potential to create a truly human social order as and when he is freed from external constraints. The emphasis here is on Men's ability to recognize and influence the world around and the part they play within it. This perspective is basic in analyzing both the objective and subjective social reality. Blumer (1962), however, mentions that structural features such as culture, social systems, social stratification may set conditions for directions but these in no way determine the actions. Douglas (1971) argues that any scientific understanding of human actions must be initiated and built upon an appreciation of the every day life of the members performing these actions. This fact has given impetus to the rise of sociology of education during 1970's in Britain.

In this perspective, the thrust is to examine how teachers and pupils act and interact in schools to construct and understand the definitional categories on which they base their activities. This is with a view to bring the system of education into more direct control of its creators and users. If we want to understand the interaction between the teacher and a student, as sociologists, we may have to comprehend the various definitions of the situations by both these participants in the interaction and also the ways in which these different definitions impinge upon each other. This will, of course, involve a series of negotiations of the acceptable role definitions for these individuals in order to have a totality of interactional setting. Many of the situations may present conflict of interest among the interacting actors and there may be efforts to arrive at a working consensus while in other settings, many individuals may find it difficult to sustain a relationship due to lack of harmony. A continued involvement in it may prove more costly than profitable. In such a situation an individual may try to withdraw completely from the relationship.

The difficulty with the interactionest perspective is that it does not explain the 'concept of power' in terms of dominant positions of some over others as a consequence of unequal interpersonal relationships. Within this perspective, individuals are seen as having the freedom to define reality and to act upon their own definitions. This may result into the most powerful partners in the interacting situations to impose their definitions on others, thus hampering the interactional process.

In the field of Sociology of Education, both the structural-functional as well as conflict perspective are significant. However, in the past couple of decades, the interactionist perspective has gained a great deal of popularity in this field in view of its relevance to the day to day activities and situational contingencies. It is also important because it takes into account the roles of different actors in the interacting situations.

II. Role— In order to analyse the role of the teacher in providing education to the students, it may be worthwhile to examine the conceptualization of role performance. Invariably the concept of role has been implied to denote prescriptions, descriptions, evaluation and action. Primarily, role has been defined from two points of view. Under the structural-functionalist perspective, a role has been defined by Linton (1945) as a set of social norms which are part of the culture transmitted to the interactants in any given situation. It is further elaborated that role is the dynamic aspect of status and the content of role is the totality of cultural patterns associated with a particular status. However, while Linton overlooked the fact that a particular status may involve a whole range of associated roles, this refinement was brought about by Merton (1957) through the concepts of role set and status set. According to him, a role set is considered a complement of role relationships which a person may have by virtue of occupying a particular status. Similarly, a complement of social statuses occupied by an individual is his or her status set. As a part of the dynamic aspect of functional analysis, he also brought in the concept of status sequence which implies successive statuses that an actor may occupy during the course of time provided for the succession to be patterned. In the same manner, the role sequence refers to the succession of role performance of an actor with a specific status. It is also observed that the various role obligations displayed by an actor may result in contradictory performances. This may lead to an individual facing a number of conflicting arrays of role obligations.

Talcott Parsons (1951) defines role as an organized sector of an actor's orientation which constitutes and defines his or her participation in an interactive process. In other words, it may involve a set of complementary expectations concerning one's own actions and those of others with whom one interacts.

Nadel (1957) appears to differ from Linton and Parsons in the sense that he does not treat status as static or positional and role as dynamic or processual. In fact, he considers role as a kind of class concept. According to him, it is the existence of names describing a class of people which make us think of roles. His argument is that any sociologically relevant behaviour is always purposeful. He also considers status as quasi-role which means, "set of rights and obligations in a piece of knowledge", as relevant to a position in a "social structure".

Banton (1965) also defined role as a set of rights and obligations in terms of an abstraction to which the behaviour of people will conform in varying degrees. He considers role in terms of pattern of expected behaviour reinforced by a structure of rewards and penalties that may induce an individual to conform to the pattern. This view takes a static stand and an individual is expected to fit into the position provided to him without making any efforts to alter his activities.

Newcomb (1950) brought the concept of role from social anthropology to social psychology. It is conceived as an expected or appropriate behaviour. To him, a social role is different from its actual performance enacted in a social position. He suggests that an individual's status involves a wide variety of role relations. Consequently, the individual may find himself or herself as holding positions having incompatible role requirements.

Sarbin (1954) conceives role as a patterned sequence of learned actions performed by a person in an interacting situation. He has highlighted the non-normative stimuli and responses as a part of interaction. In this, the action of one actor provides stimulus to another whose response in turn, may become the stimulus for the first actor. In this way, the sequence of interaction continues.

Role has also been examined from the perspective of symbolic interaction. In this perspective, an individual is considered as a creative thinking organism, capable of choosing his or her behaviour and the role orientation or the conception of the part, he or she plays in the social settings. Mead (1934) in his concept of role-taking describes how an individual while taking on the role of others foresees the situation on an objective basis, that is, from the point of view of the "generalised other". He gives a fundamental theory of human sociality where the role has been considered as a situationally specific normative expectation towards the position holders. Further, in this concept of role-taking, he explains how an individual reacts to his or her own gestures and anticipates the behaviour of others as one's own.

Goffman (1967) elaborated his ideas further and highlighted his theory in terms of role performance and role distance. Role performance has been considered as an activity of a particular participant on a particular occasion influencing the performance of other participants, while role distance implies a kind of separateness between an individual and his or her role. Further, role distance seems to fall between the role-obligation and the actual role performance. This concept may be useful while explaining the behaviour of teachers towards students or vice-versa. In certain situations, one incumbent despite resentment or bitterness towards the other may avoid role conflict by conforming to obligations, though with diffidence, and thereby create a wedge between himself or herself and the actual role performance.

The common element in all the above concepts of role is that they are guided by "expected patterns of behaviour". It is argued that the behaviour of people is often influenced by their own expectations and those of others in the group and that of society in which they are participants. As such, it may be desirable to conceive the concept of role in terms of *perception, expectation* and *performance* of incumbents in positions in different settings within the social system.

Roles are also influenced to a large extent by the rewards and sanctions that go in between actors and others. Homans (1961) and Blau (1964) also argue that once a person finds it rewarding to behave in a certain way, he is likely to repeat that form of behaviour in that situation. Thus a teacher while performing his or her role is also likely to be influenced by the set of rewards and facilities available to him or her.

Within the various role perspectives outlined above, the *role perception* is viewed as that set of behaviour, the occupant of the particular position believes he or she should enact. The perception of individuals may vary according to their mental and personality make-up, needs, motives and previous experiences. Invariably, the perceived role may not correspond to the expected role. On the other hand, the *role expectations* are comprised of rights and privileges as well as the duties and obligations that any person in his or her social position may hold in relation to others within a social structure. Role-expectation may often be constrained by certain societal sanctions and measures, as society expects different persons to conform with it description of the same. Therefore, the role enactment or the *role performance* by an individual is carried out within socially defined patterns having many variations at different times and places. Again, although all individuals take part in different role relationships having various obligations, the role of the individual is also influenced by the performance of other individuals. Certain acts that exceed the limits of acceptable behaviour may result in evaluation of invalid and unacceptable role enactments. If there is an agreement between the role expectation and the role performance of an individual, it may provide social stability within the social system.

But if there is an element of disagreement between the two, it may indicate the presence of some conflict leading to a possibility and likely direction of change in the social structure.

In short, an attempt has been made in the present study to analyse the role perception, expectation and performance of university and college teachers taking into account some of the theoretical formulations given above.

III. Profession—There are three major approaches that have been highlighted in the study of professions. Evert C. Huges (1958) of Chicago school, considered occupation as "role performance". However, there is a need to re-examine this approach in view of changing aspects of social interaction. Interactionists among sociologists treat profession as a set of role relationships between an expert and a client. The expert provides skill and knowledge as a part of his or her expertise to the client and he or she in return gives him or her an equitable amount of fee. The second school of thought on profession is vouched by structuralists or occupational sociology group (Lvy League School). They consider professions as essentially stable institutions that reflect values and goals of the community. In other words, the professions are treated as functioning units that perform certain required tasks for the society. The structuralists have mostly approached the study of profession by constructing the continuum of degree of professionalisation. The third approach, that is the social class approach perspective (Marxist) in the study of professions bases its belief on the fact that the contradictions or material dialectics will result into class formation of certain occupations as a result of change in the capitalist mode of production.

Professionals have a tendency to profess of what they know. In other words, occupational competence is an important attribute of a profession. Many attempts have been made to conceptulise and define a profession. However, we do not have any broad acceptance of an authoritative definition (Cogan 1953). Over a period of time, a number of other attributes have become significant in the conception of a profession. Flexner (1915), for example, considered professions as morally superior to other occupations. According to him, a profession would invariably involve intellectual activities based on the processes of learning for tackling problems. These activities can be taught or learnt and a profession gets organized internally. Some of the other attributes associated with profession are professional autonomy, long period of training, service orientation, body of theoretical knowledge and monopoly of judgement (Greenwood, 1957). Besides competence in job demonstrated by passing in test, integrity reflected by adherence to code of conduct and the organisation of profession through establishment of a professional body are other significant attributes (Millerson, 1964).

In fact, there are two main perspectives to analyse the sociology of profession. The first one is mentioned as functional perspective. This provides the understanding of professions as relatively monolithic and homogeneous social groupings and focuses on attributes, which distinguish a profession from other occupations. Professions have certain attributes through which the core needs of the society are served (Barber, 1963, Parsons, 1968). The second perspective on professions is viewed as conflict or processual approach. Johnson considers it in terms of power relations within a society. This view recognizes society as a collectivity having different interest groups participating in the process of negotiation to acquire professionalisation (Johnson, 1972). According to Sharma (1980), the thrust in this perspective is on analyzing intra-professional conflicts, colleagueal relationships and congruities. However, these perspectives are complementary rather than competitive in their approach. They have certain common elements of professions such as specialized knowledge, work autonomy and the selection of a professional body.

Teachers, especially at the university level, have to evolve themselves into a homogeneous social group and make efforts to acquire certain attributes whereby they could share their identities, values, definitions of role and interests. At the same time, they have to make progression towards accomplishments of attributes through resolution of inter-conflicting identities, values and interests within the profession. Some of the aspects related to profession as outlined above will be useful in analyzing the role of the teacher.

2. Hypotheses of the Study

A succint presentation on Sociology of Education, Role and Profession in the preceding pages brings out some significant observations.

Professionals are knowledgeable and they have service-orientation. The system of education trains individuals and motivates them to perform the various roles adequately for the integration of the society. It is also observed that the educational system is not to be seen only as a process of socialization of new members of society into a collective order but as a phenomenon of distribution of resources within the dimensions of power. We also need to understand the interaction between a teacher and a student with a view to comprehend the various definitions of the situations, that both these participants bring upon in different interactional settings. Further, we can discuss four main perspectives on Role; structural functional, stressing upon "expected patterns of behaviour"; social-psychological, emphasizing on an individual's perception in an interactional setting; symbolic interactionism focusing on the interplay of self and other actor's orientation of the part he or she is to play; and exchange theory, signifying the importance of rewards and incentives in a given relationship. All these aspects have a close bearing on the role-analysis of incumbents holding various positions within a social system. An attempt will be made to operationalize some of these concepts in the university system where the role of the teacher permeates as well as mediates.

A university system is a sub-system of the larger societal system. As such, apart from its internal dynamism, it is subjected to the external influences such as political, economic and social. Within its functioning, it has many inter-related and inter-dependent parts which integrate with each other to accomplish the desired academic goals. A university system is basically a representation of professional bureaucratic organization, more autonomous in its functioning than others, with a Vice-Chancellor as its head. By virtue of the power entrusted on him by the decision making or governing bodies (Senate and Syndicate), he manages the academic and non-academic affairs of the university as well as that of its affiliated colleges. He is supported in his task by a team of Financial Manager, Controller of Examination and an Establishment Administrator besides various other bodies and committees, for the smooth functioning of the academic work. There is an Academic Council comprising of Senior Faculty which provides consensus on the pedagogical aspects of education. In addition to the above, there are Departmental Committees such as Board of Control, Board of Studies, Administrative, Academic and Technical Committees which take care of the day to day functioning of various university teaching departments. There are also unions of teachers as well as that of students to safe-guard their respective interests and resolve conflicting issues both through negotiations and confrontational agitations with the university and college administration. In the case of affiliated colleges, although for academic purposes, they have to follow the dictates of the university, yet for administrative purposes, the head of the college (Principal) has to follow the instruction and advice of the Government in respect of Government colleges while the Managing Committee of the Privately-aided colleges is the sole controlling authority for them.

Within this university system, the key actor is a teacher who as a professional, is a specialist in his or her subject and transmits knowledge to the students for their overall development. Teaching, as a profession, is ranked next to Medicine, Engineering and Executive Management. As a result, not many persons are attracted to join it. Some persons by aptitude and temperament may be well-motivated to take up this profession while for others, there may not be any other option except to join it. There are no standards as yet evolved to induct well-motivated and competent persons into this profession despite the introduction of UGC-NET or State Level Entrance Tests. This makes the recruitment process of teachers in the university system inappropriate. However, as teachers move on into this profession and over the years, get higher status (that is, they are promoted to the rank or position of Reader and Professor), their academic levels may also undergo a change. Some may show better academic proficiencies than others.

Further, with the spurt of female education, a large proportion of them have gone in for higher education. As a consequence of that, a substantive number of them have entered into this profession. It is also possible that now males are joining more competitive jobs than teaching. It is also believed that a teaching job for females provides the least familial conflicts and is more suitable to be taken up as a career. However, due to different socialization practices prevailing in our society, their attitudes and value orientations on certain issues may vary from that of their male counterparts.

Like other professionals, teachers also desire that their services are recognized in the society. As stated earlier, some of them may excel others in academic pursuits and acquire a higher level of academic attainment. This factor may also influence the thinking of teachers towards the recognition of their services in the society. It is probable that those having a higher academic level may feel so more positively towards it than others with a lower academic level.

A university system provides a set of prescriptive roles to the teachers and they are expected to perform them adequately for transmitting knowledge to students through effective communication and for creating knowledge through research. Notwithstanding these prescriptive roles, the teachers' perception of their duties and responsibilities may cut across the various groups. As such, it may be worthwhile to examine the relevance of gender, status (rank or position) and academic levels of teachers to their perceived duties, expectations and performance. Again, it may be mentioned that a teacher's performance is often influenced by the type of reward system (incentives and facilities) available to him or her.

A teacher as a role model stimulates students through his or her projective image and innovative ideas while expecting them to respond positively towards making a living and facing the challenges of life. However, in an interactional setting between the teacher and the students, many conflicting situations may arise. These need to be resolved by arriving at some consensus to sustain the relationship and avoid disharmony. The best way to tackle such situations is through negotiated understanding of the different interests of both the interactants.

Over the years, due to the widespread of education, more opportunities have come in the way of girls to pursue higher studies. Besides, there is openness observed in the minds of parents especially those living in urban centers, to encourage girls to compete equally with boys for higher education. In fact, girls are outshining boys in academic pursuits. However, girls due to various gender-bias socialization practices, may feel differently about certain issues than boys. Even their expectations regarding academic activities from teachers may differ from each other.

In the interactional situations, most of the students are fascinated by certain attributes or characteristics of teachers. Besides, they may have reasons to believe that the teachers have played a significant role in their growth and development. Many of them may react positively or negatively towards the various issues involved in higher education. All these aspects may be in variance with their gender status. It is also observed that the students are drawn from the different socio-economic strata. Many of them belonging to lower socio-economic status may confront more difficulties in the pursuit of higher education than those having higher status.

In the light of above discussion some of the general hypotheses of the study are as follows:

1. The academic levels of the teachers may determine the extent of recognition of their services in the society.
2. The gender (sex), status (rank or position held) and the academic levels (high or low index) of teachers may influence their perceived duties, expectations from students and performance. Even the expectations of students from teachers may be related to their gender (sex of the students).
3. The gender of the students may influence their views on (a) issues related to higher education (b) the attributes of teachers that influenced them most and (c) the significant role of teachers in their growth and development.
4. The gender of the students and their family social status standings may be related to their views on difficulties faced by them in going in for higher education.

It may be pointed out here that variations may also be observed on the above aspects in between the university and college teachers and also in between teachers belonging to different streams of courses (science, social science and professional) at the university level and in between the teachers of a government and a privately managed college. These are also examined in view of above stated hypotheses for an explicit comparative analysis of data.

3. Methods of Data Collection

(1) Locale and the Universe of the Study—The study has been carried out in the Panjab University and two of its affiliated degree colleges in Chandigarh. The Panjab University (previously named University of the Panjab) was founded in 1882 at Lahore as the fourth teaching and affiliating university in the Indian sub-continent under the British rule. After the partition of the country, the university got shifted to Chandigarh in1956 and its red stone campus designed by French architects came up within a few years.

During the year 1998, an estimate of over 18,000 students were enrolled in the university teaching departments, out of which 13,000 alone were in the department of correspondence studies. Besides, 69,000 students were enrolled in the 104 affiliated colleges.

In all there are 53 teaching departments in the university having more than 700 teachers. These include four chairs which are mainly managed by a single teaching faculty. Besides, it has seven smaller departments that of foreign languages and south Indian languages which have not more than two faculty members. As such, in effect, there are 42 teaching departments. Thus, for the purpose of this study, we considered the same for drawing the sample (Source: Panjab University diary, 1999 Chandigarh).

(2) Sampling Frame—The following procedures were followed in drawing the sample of the study:

I. Keeping in view the manageability of the study and taking into consideration the problem of research, it was thought best to choose 10 departments from the list of 42 departments identified in the university. A list of all these departments was prepared in an alphabetic manner and 10 departments (nearly 25 per cent of all the departments) were chosen randomly with the help of random number tables. Through this procedure, the departments selected in the University were Bio-Chemistry, Economics, Education, Geography, Laws, Mathematics, Micro-biology, Pharmaceutical Sciences, Political Science and Public Administration in that order. These have been re-grouped as departments of Sciences (Bio-Chemistry, Mathematics, Micro-biology and Pharmaceutical Sciences), Social Sciences (Economics, Education, Geography, Political Science and Public Administration) and Professional (Laws). In view of some departments not having a large number of teachers, it was thought best to include all the teachers in these departments instead of drawing a sample of them for making their number a sizeable one for the purposes of analysis. A list of teachers was prepared for each department. In all, 156 teachers were identified in the 10 selected departments, out of which 14 teachers were on long leave, either had gone abroad or were on maternity leave (in the case of female teachers). Of the remaining 142 teachers in these departments, the non-response to the questionnaire was only 10. In all 132 teachers, 58 in the Science departments, 56 in the Social Science departments and 18 in the Professional (Laws) department, were contacted for interview purposes. The male-female breakdown for the Science departments has been 39 males and 19 females, while in the case of the Social Science departments, it has been 31 males and 25 females. In the case of teachers belonging to the Professional department (Laws) the number of males is 11 while that of females is 7. It involved several visits to each of these departments and constant persuasion of some teachers to keep down the rate of mortality of questionnaire to 7.04 per cent (This excludes 14 teachers who were on long leave).

II. There are in all 10 affiliated colleges functioning in Chandigarh, out of which, 4 are managed by the Government while 6 of them are Privately aided. The selection of two colleges was done on purposive basis, because of the large number of students of both the sexes in the university. The main criterion was to choose colleges having co-educational facilities where both boys and girls could be chosen. Most of the colleges in Chandigarh are exclusive either for boys or girls, barring a couple of them which have co-education either at the post-graduate level or in professional courses like commerce etc. Another criterion to select the colleges was to have one Government college and one Private college for comparative analysis. Accordingly, Government College, Sector 46 and Sri Guru Gobind Singh College, Sector 26, having co-educational facilities at the graduate level were selected. The Government College in Sector 46 was visited and a list of various departments was obtained after contacting the Principal of the college. In all, there were 18 departments listed. These were arranged in alphabetical order and five departments were chosen with the help of random number tables. These were Commerce, Economics, English,

Mathematics and Political Science. All the teachers including the guest faculty in these departments were taken up for interview purposes. In all 23 teachers, 10 males and 13 females were contacted for study purposes. This excluded one teacher who was on leave and another one who did not respond.

The Principal of the SGGS College, Sector 26, was also contacted and a list of teachers was obtained. In all, there were 16 departments. To have a comparative analysis with the Government College, Sector 46, it was considered suitable to choose the same departments as those included in the Government College (Commerce, Economics, English, Mathematics and Political Science). The total number of teachers contacted for the study were 22, 8 males and 14 females. This excluded 2 teachers who were on leave during the period of study and 3 teachers who did not return the questionnaires. In all there were 52 teachers in the 10 departments of both the colleges out of which 4 teachers were in the non-response category (7.69 per cent) and 3 were on long leave.

The total number of teachers in the 18 departments at the Government College, Sector 46 Chandigarh were more than 50 while at the SGGS College, Sector 26 Chandigarh, their number was around 80. This difference in the number of teachers in between the two colleges was because of science departments (Chemistry, Physics, Botany and Zoology) at SGGS college while these were not existing in the other college.*

III. A sample of students was also taken from the final year classes at the post-graduate level in the university and at the graduate level in the two colleges, from the selected departments. In view of large variations observed in the student population ranging from 5 to 150 in some of the selected departments, a difficulty was faced in taking a sample of

---

* It is reported that the foundation stone of the S.G.G.S college was laid down by Sardar Partap Singh Kairon, the former Chief Minister of Panjab on August 29, 1960 while the inauguration of Government college was done by Shri S.S.Ray, former Governor of Panjab on November 17, 1989.

students in proportion to their numbers. Further, there was also a variation observed in regard to the proportion of boys and girls in each of the selected departments both at the university and college levels. In order to overcome this difficulty, it was decided to have an equal proportion of boys and girls in the selected departments to constitute the sample of students. Accordingly, keeping in view the constraints of time and to have a substantial number of students at the same time, it was thought best to have 4 boys and 4 girls from the final year class of the selected departments. However, an exception was made in the case of department of Micro-biology in the university and Mathematics in both the colleges where the number of students was less than eight. In their case, all the students of the final year attending these departments, irrespective of their gender were included in the study. The students were chosen from the final year class mainly because they had longer interaction with the teachers than others. In case of sampling of students, again a purposive approach was followed, the main criterion being the willingness of boys and girls to fill in the questionnaire. In this respect, the help of the teachers, in charge of the regular class in the final year, was taken. They identified the students and helped the researcher in getting their interviews done in those cases who preferred to be interviewed than filling in the questionnaires. In this way, we could get information from 77 students in the university. In one of the science departments in the final year M.Sc class, there were only 4 females and one male. All the five students were taken for the study purposes. This reduced the total sample of students from 80 to 77.

As regards sampling of students in the colleges, a similar procedure was followed in respect of the selected departments. In the case of Government College, we had a total of 35 students (19 males and 16 females). In the final year of one of the departments, that is, Mathematics, there were only 3 male students. This resulted in having one male and 4 females less in the sample. The number of students in SGGS College from the selected departments was 37 (21 males and 16 females). Again in the Mathematics department in the final year class, all the five male students were taken into the sample since there were no female students. This increased the number of male students by one in the sample. In all 72 students from both the colleges (40 males and 32 females) were contacted for interview purposes. The criterion of getting the questionnaire filled in from the students on voluntary basis helped the researcher in getting cent per cent return of the same.

IV. All the Chairpersons of the selected departments in the university and Principals of both the colleges were also included for the study purposes. Out of 10 Chairpersons, seven of them willingly granted interview. However, in one case, the Chairperson frankly told that he did not believe in this kind of research while in another case, the Chairperson diplomatically put the researcher off. In the third case, the Chairperson of a department showed arrogance and refused to hand over the schedule containing guideline questions. These encounters enriched the experiences of the researcher in the field. The Principals of both the colleges because of their busy schedule preferred to fill in the schedule and were kind enough to return the same. In the case of certain Chairpersons of selected departments in the university a number of visits were made on them to persuade them to grant the interview as they had a very hectic schedule. Since the Chairpersons of the department and Principals of colleges were interviewed with the help of guideline questions, they were excluded from the sampling frame of teachers.

3. Instruments of Data Collection

Two set of questionnaires were designed. The first one was designed for eliciting information from all the teachers in different selected departments in the university and colleges. The questions framed were to elicit information regarding age, sex, marital status, caste, religion, educational level, rural-urban background, family background including education, occupation and income of father/mother/spouse, age of entry into this profession, educational achievements, visits abroad etc. Further, questions were framed to know the reason for having joined this profession, regrets if any for having joined this profession, perception of duties and responsibilities in this profession, actual performance of duties as perceived by teachers, gaps in perception and performance, perceived role of teachers in society, factors that raise the status of teachers, performance of role of teachers towards colleagues/ supervisors/students etc.

II. The second one was designed for the students chosen from the selected university departments and two colleges to assess their perception on the role performance of teachers. Questions were framed to know the expectation of students from teachers in respect of classroom teaching, research guidance, social guidance and counselling, gaps in expectation and performance of teachers as perceived by students, problems of students and suggestions thereof to overcome these.

III. The Chairpersons of the 10 departments in the university and the Principals of the two colleges were interviewed with the help of guideline questions. Unlike the first two set of questionnaires, these were mainly kept open-ended so that they could respond to the questions in the manner in which they would like to express themselves. An attempt has been made to develop caselets about these persons on the basis of that.

IV. The questionnaires designed for the study were pre-tested with a few persons other than the chosen. Necessary modifications were instituted before their actual administration to the selected respondents.

4. Analysis of Data

I. After the collection of data, a thorough examination of the questionnaires was done and the entire information was transferred on the sheets with the help of code design.

II. The data were nominal in nature. By and large, these were analysed by making simple and cross tables through ratios and proportions. However, for rating and ranking of various factors influencing the role-analysis of teachers and views of students a simple statistical technique such as the mean score value was employed. The combined mean score value in the case of male and female respondents and the overall mean score values for the various factors (pooled mean score value) for different groups of respondents were worked out to show the relative importance of these factors in the role analysis of teachers, by using the following formula:

$$\bar{X}_C = \frac{N_1\bar{X}_1 + N_2\bar{X}_2 + \ldots\ldots}{N_1 + N_2 + \ldots\ldots}$$

III. In view of a substantial number of female teachers as well as nearly an equal proportion of female students to their male counterparts in the selected departments at the university and college levels, a sex-wise analysis of the data was presented in most of the tables.

IV. At the university level, in regard to analysis of data on teachers, apart from sex-wise interpretation, the same were also analysed according to the stream of courses to which they belong (Science, Social Science and Professional) to have a comparative point of view.

V. Apart from comparing the findings of university teachers with the college teachers, an attempt was also made to analyse the comparative views of teachers belonging to the Government and the Privately managed college.

VI. The fieldwork was started in October, 2000 and the collection of data from the colleges and the university was completed by February, 2001.

4. Limitations of the Study

Some of the main limitations in carrying out this study are as follows

I. This study has been confined to one university (Panjab University) and its affiliated colleges in Chandigarh. Therefore, it may be necessary to test the validity of the present findings in respect of other universities and their affiliated colleges before we could generalise about the role analysis of teachers.

II. As stated earlier, there are 42 main departments in the university and 10 affiliated colleges in Chandigarh. However, since this study has been done by a lone student on this subject, only 10 departments in the university and two affiliated colleges were chosen due to shortage of time and resources. It is assumed that the data generated with respect to teachers and students will reflect the role-analysis of all the teachers in the university system.

III. The data were collected through a subjective reporting method. All the intrinsic limitations associated with this method will, therefore, be valid for this study as well (Selltiz, 1976 and Festinger, 1965)

IV. In the construction of the Family Social Status Index for teachers and students, the variables like education, occupation and income are taken into account. It is assumed that each one of these contributes equally towards the socio-economic status, though this may not be true. However, it is only an attempt to group the families into different socio-economic strata having a bearing on certain views of teachers and students.

V. Again, in the preparation of the Academic Level Index of teachers and the Participation Level Index of teachers in the university bodies and association, it has also been assumed that various dimensions associated with them contribute equally towards their categorization into high or low levels. However, this may also not be true and it is only a methodological exercise to classify them into high or low groups. These may have some relevance to the role-analysis of teachers.

VI. The selection of two affiliated colleges and that of students in the university and colleges has been done through purposive sampling method, for the reasons already explained earlier.

2

Demographic, Socio-Cultural and Economic Profile of Respondents

An individual contributes significantly towards the formation of a group structure. In order to understand the personality structure of individuals, it may become imperative to analyse the demographic, socio-cultural and economic characteristics of the respondents. These factors play an important role at the early socialization stages of individuals and even during the adulthood and maturity period. These affect and shape the opinions, attitudes, value-orientations and values so as to stabilize the personality structure of individuals to a certain extent. Therefore, it may be necessary that while carrying out an empirical study in sociology, one should examine the above factors to analyse their influence on the perception and outlook of individuals towards certain issues. Moreover, the socio-economic characteristics are significant for establishing social relationships between various groups within a society. In other words, these may become facilitators or barriers in the formation of social relationships among the people.

The socio-economic background from which the respondents are drawn may certainly influence the way they relate themselves to each other in the university system. They may uphold certain attitudes and values as they grow in a particular socio-cultural milieu.

Again, it is largely the personal attributes and the characteristics of the family background that influence the internalization of certain values. Therefore, it is essential to examine the personal, socio-cultural and economic characteristics of respondents having bearing on their views related to teaching and in regard to their role in the teaching profession as well as towards higher education. As such, an attempt has been made in this chapter to analyse the same.

This chapter will be divided into two parts. The first part will highlight the characteristics of teachers while the second part will focus on the characteristics of the students.

Characteristics of University and College Teachers

1. Sex

Recently, quite a large number of females have entered into the teaching profession. As such, it may be worthwhile to analyse the sex-wise distribution of teachers.

An examination of Table 2.1, reveals that in our sample, there is a higher proportion of male, 81(61.36 per cent) than female teachers, 51(38.64 per cent) at the university level. However, in the case of college teachers, we find a higher proportion of female 27(60.00 per cent), than male teachers 18(40.00 per cent), in both the colleges. In the case of Private college, the proportion of females is slightly higher than that in the Government college while vice-versa is the case in respect of male teachers. The above analysis is indicative of the fact that an increasing number of females are entering into the teaching profession, though most of them seem to be joining the undergraduate colleges. It may also be due to the fact that males are now entering into more competitive jobs than teaching.

Table 2.1

Sex-wise Distribution of University and College Teachers

S.No	*Sex of the Teachers*	*University Teachers*	*College Teachers*		*Combined Total of Colleges*
			Government	*Private*	
1.	Male	81 (61.36)	10 (43.48)	8 (36.37)	18 (40.00)
2.	Female	51 (38.64)	13 (56.52)	14 (63.63)	27 (60.00)
	Total	132 (100.00)	23 (100.00)	22 (100.00)	45 (100.00)

Note: Figures within brackets represent percentages.

2. Age Composition

Age is an important demographic characteristic of an individual as it denotes both the physical and the intellectual growth. It may also be an indicator of one's occupation.

Table 2.2

Age-wise Distribution of University and College Teachers

S. No.	Age-group (in years)	University Teacher			College Teacher						Combined Total of Colleges
					Government			Private			
		Male	Female	Total	Male	Female	Total	Male	Female	Total	
1.	≤25	0 (0.00)	0 (0.00)	0 (0.00)	0 (0.00)	3 (23.08)	3 (13.04)	0 (0.00)	1 (7.14)	1 (4.54)	4 (8.89)
2.	26-35	10 (12.35)	19 (37.25)	29 (21.97)	0 (0.00)	0 (0.00)	0 (0.00)	2 (25.00)	5 (35.72)	7 (31.82)	7 (15 .55)
3.	36-45	21 (25.92)	20 (39.21)	41 (31.06)	7 (70.00)	4 (30.77)	11 (47.83)	0 (0.00)	7 (50.00)	7 (31.82)	18 (40.00)
4.	46-55	27 (33.33)	6 (11.77)	33 (25.00)	3 (30.00)	6 (46.15)	9 (39.13)	3 37.50)	1 (7.14)	4 (18.18)	13 (28.90)
5.	56-65	23 (38.40)	6 (11.77)	29 (21.97)	0 (0.00)	0 (0.00)	0 (0.00)	3 (37.50)	0 (0.00)	3 (13.64)	3 (6.66)
Total		81 (100.00)	51 (100.00)	132 (100.00)	10 (100.00)	13 (100.00)	23 (100.00)	8 (100.00)	14 (100.00)	22 (100.00)	45 (100.00)

Note— Figures within brackets represent percentages

A cursory look at Table 2.2 indicates that a larger proportion of the teachers, 41 (31.06 per cent) in the university belong to the age group of 36 to 45 years. It is observed that none of the teachers here are below the category of 25 years. However, we have nearly one fifth of the teachers in the age-group of 26 to 35 years. Interestingly, there is a higher proportion of female than male teachers in this age-group. On the other hand, nearly one fourth of the teachers are in the age-group beyond 46 years, out of which a large proportion of them are males while females are in a small number. This is indicative of the fact that now, more females than males are entering this profession as against earlier times when this profession was dominated by males.

Even in the case of college teachers, a higher proportion of teachers belong to the age group of 36 to 45 years followed by the age group of 46 to 55 years. Further, it was observed that there were three females in the case of Government college and one female in the case of Private college who were below the age of 25 years. Even in the age group of 26 to 35 years, we have a higher number of females (5) than males (2). In the case of Government college, there were more number of females (6) than males (3) in age group of 46 to 55 years as against one female to three males in the Private college in the same age group. This may be due to some of the females having joined government service at a younger age.

3. Marital Status

The marital status of individuals may affect their views towards certain issues and also their working patterns. An attempt has been made to analyse the sex-wise marital status of university and college teachers.

It is observed that the majority of university teachers, 118 (80.39 per cent) are married while only 12 (9.09 per cent) are single. Besides, two (1.51 per cent) are widow/er (One male and one female). A higher number of females 9(17.65 per cent) than males 3 (3.70 per cent) belong to single category. On the other hand, a higher proportion of male (95.06 per cent) than female teachers (80.39 per cent) in the university are married.

Again in the case of college teachers, we find a higher proportion of them, 37 (82.23 per cent) are married whereas only 6 (13.33 per cent) are single. Besides, one each is divorced and widowed. The number of unmarried female teachers in the university and colleges is more than that of males. This may be due to the fact that they have joined this profession at a younger age than males. One significant observation is that the sanctity of marriage appears to be highly valued in our society.

4. Religion

Religion is an important aspect of one's life. It integrates the members of the society and influences the behaviour patterns of people.

A cursory look at Table 2.3 highlights that the majority of teachers in the university, 104(78.79 per cent) belong to the Hindu religion. It is followed by those who believe in the Sikh religion, 26(19.69 per cent). One each belongs to the Muslim and the Christian religion. However, in the case of colleges, the majority of teachers, 24(53.33 per cent) belong to the Sikh religion. The next in order, 20(44.44 per cent) believe in the Hindu religion whereas there is only one teacher who follows Christianity. Further, it is interesting to observe that in the Government college, there are more number of teachers 15(65.22 per cent) who follow Hindu religion than those in the Private college 5(22.73 per cent). On the other hand in the case of Private college, there are more number of teachers 17(77.27 per cent) who are followers of the Sikh religion than those in the Government college 7(30.43 per cent). The preponderance of the teachers adhering to the Hindu and the Sikh religious groups, may be due to their higher representation in the population of this region.

Table 2.3

Religion-wise Distribution of University and College Teachers

S.No.	*Religious Groups*	*University Teachers*	*College Teachers*		*Combined Total of Colleges*
			Government	*Private*	
1.	Hindu	104 (78.79)	15 (65.22)	5 (22.73)	20 (44.44)
2.	Muslim	1 (0.76)	0 (0.00)	0 (0.00)	0 (0.00)
3.	Sikh	26 (19.69)	7 (30.43)	17 (77.27)	24 (53.33)
4.	Christian	1 (0.76)	1 (4.35)	0 (0.00)	1 (2.23)
	Total	132 (100.00)	23 (100.00)	22 (100.00)	45 (100.00)

Note— Figures within brackets represent percentages

5. Caste

Caste-stratification is central to the understanding of Indian social structure. An examination of Table 2.4 brings out caste-wise distribution of university and college teachers. It is interesting to observe that the majority of teachers in the university sample, 44(33.33 per cent) belong to Khatri/Arora caste groups whereas another 40(30.30 per cent) are of Brahmin origin. This is followed by Bania/Jain/Kayastha (14.40 per cent), Jat (12.88 per cent), Rajput (6.06 per cent) whereas 3.03 per cent belong to other backward castes including Muslims and Christians. Interestingly, there is no teacher who belongs to the scheduled caste/scheduled tribe.

In the case of colleges, a large number of teachers (17) belong to Khatri/Arora caste followed by Jat (16) and Bania/Jain/Kayastha (7). However, there is only one Brahmin teacher that too, in the Government college. Besides, there are four teachers, two each belonging to SC/ST and BC (Backward Castes) categories respectively. Overall, a higher proportion of persons belonging to upper castes in the teaching profession appears to be in relevance with our prevailing social structure.

Table 2.4

Caste-wise Distribution of University and College Teachers

S.No.	*Caste Groups*	*University Teachers*	*College Teachers*		*Combined Total of Colleges*
			Government	Private	
1.	Brahmin	40 (30.30)	1 (4.35)	0 (0.00)	1 (2.23)
2.	Khatri/Arora	44 (33.33)	7 (30.43)	10 (45.45)	17 (37.78)
3.	Bania/Jain/ Kayastha	19 (14.40)	6 (26.09)	1 (4.55)	7 (15.56)
4.	Rajput	8 (6.06)	0 (0.00)	0 (0.00)	0 (0.00)
5.	Jat	17 (12.88)	7 (30.43)	9 (40.90)	16 (35.55)
6.	SC/ST (scheduled caste/tribe)	0 (0.00)	1 (4.35)	1 (4.55)	2 (4.44)
7.	Any other (Muslim, Saini, Christian, Kushwa, Ahir)	4 (3.03)	1 (4.35)	1 (4.55)	2 (4.44)
	Total	132 (100.00)	23 (100.00)	22 (100.00)	45 (100.00)

Note—Figures within brackets represent percentages

6. Education

For those in the teaching profession, educational attainment is obviously a very important factor. Out of 132 teachers in the university sample, as many as 11 4(86.36 per cent) were holding a Ph.D. degree whereas an equal proportion of them, 9(6.82 per cent) were either post-graduates in their respective subjects or were holding M.Phil/L.L.M. degree. The sex-wise distribution of teachers did not show much difference in terms of educational attainments. However, in the case of colleges, we find very few teachers, three each in the Government and the Private college respectively, holding a Ph.D. degree. Nearly half of them in both the colleges are having a post-graduate degree in their respective subjects while the remaining are having a M.Phil degree. Invariably, all the teachers at the university level either acquire a Ph.D. degree during their job or enter into it, after obtaining the same but this is not the case at the college level.

7. Academic Level Index of Teachers

Academic proficiency of teachers during their professional career may indicate their attainment in the respective fields of their pursuits. An attempt has been made to prepare an Academic Level Index of teachers by assigning scores to the various dimensions such as educational level of the teachers, publications done, research dissertations supervised, research projects guided by them etc. which are associated with their profession. These have been worked out separately for the university and college teachers into high and low groups (For details, kindly refer to Appendix II).

An examination of Table 2.5, indicates that out of 132 teachers in the university sample, as many as 50(37.88 per cent) are having a high academic level index whereas 82(62.12 per cent) belong to low academic level index. As regards distribution of teachers faculty-wise into high and low academic level index, there appears not much difference in the case of science and social science teachers. However, in the case of professional course, more number of teachers (13) are having low academic level index while only 5 belong to high academic level index. This may be due to less inputs of research in the case of Law teachers. On the other hand, in the case of colleges, out of 45 teachers in both the

Table 2.5

Academic level Index of University and College Teachers

S. No	Academic Level Index	University Teachers				S. No	Academic level Index	College Teachers		Combined Total of Colleges
		Science	*Social Science*	*Profess-ional*	*Combined Total*			*Govern-ment*	*Private*	
1.	High (23 and above score)	22 (37.93)	23 (40.07)	5 (27.77)	50 (37.88)	1.	High (8 and above score)	5 (21.73)	12 (54.55)	17 (37.78)
2.	Low (22 and below score)	36 (62.07)	33 (58.93)	13 (72.33)	82 (62.12)	2.	Low (7 and above score)	18 (78.27)	10 (45.45)	28 (62.22)
	Total	58 (100.00)	56 (100.00)	18 (100.00)	132 (100.00)		Total	23 (100.00)	22 (100.00)	45 (100.00)

Note :

1. Figures within brackets represent percentages.
2. For details on the preparation of Academic Level Index, please refer to Appendix-II

colleges, only 17(37.78 per cent) are having a high academic level index while the remaining belong to low academic level index. In between the Government and the Private college, we observe that in the Government college, only a small number of them (5) are having a high level whereas in the case of the Private college, more than half of them belong to this category. This may be because in the government service, many of them tend to become complacent due to security of job.

The preparation of academic level index in respect of university and college teachers in a way may also reflect their role attainment or performance as professionals. However, it is mentioned here as one of the characteristics of teachers having some bearing on their views related to various aspects of their role.

8. Rural-Urban Schooling Background

In order to ascertain the rural-urban background of teachers, they were asked to indicate the place of their schooling. A majority of university teachers, 74(56.06 per cent) had their schooling in the city while another 38(28.79 per cent) studied in a town. Only 20(15.15 per cent) had their schooling in a village. Interestingly, it is observed that a higher proportion of female (80.39 per cent) than male (40.74 per cent) university teachers had their schooling in a city. On the other hand, twice the proportion of females (17.65 per cent), the male teachers (35.80 per cent) studied in a town.

Again, in the case of college teachers, we have an overwhelming majority of them (64.45 per cent), having studied in a city while another 20.00 per cent have studied in a town. The proportion of teachers who have studied in a village school (15.55 per cent) is nearly the same as that of university teachers in the same category (15.15 per cent). However, more number of female than male teachers in both the colleges have studied in a city. This may be because most of them might have been born and brought up in the city itself.

9. Status Designation or Rank of Teachers

Out of 132 university teachers in our sample, a large proportion of them, 49(37.12 per cent) are holding the rank of a Lecturer while 43 of them (32.58 per cent) are having a status of a Reader. Another 40 of them (30.30 per cent) are holding the position of a

Professor. It is observed that a fairly large proportion of females (60.78 per cent) are in the category of Lecturers while their representation in the group of Professors is marginal (9.80 per cent). This may be due to the fact that many of the young women have gone in for higher education during the last decade or so. As such, they appear to have entered into this profession in a big way. The proportion of male and female teachers in the category of Readers does not show much of variation. However, a large proportion of male teachers (43.21 per cent) are in the category of Professors.

In the case of college teachers, we have three classifications of the rank of a teacher, that is, Guest Faculty, Lecturer, Senior Lecturer. The guest faculty is hired on a lecture basis while the lecturer/senior lecturer constitutes the regular faculty. The senior lecturers are in the selection grade. More than half of the college teachers are holding the position of a lecturer whereas fairly a good number of them (17) are also in the category of senior lecturers. Only 4 of them are guest faculty, all these are females, three in the Government college and one in the Private college.

10. Income of the Teachers

In view of teachers holding different rank or position in the university system, they will be found in different income brackets. An investigation of Table 2.6, indicates that out of 132 university teachers, a higher proportion of them 42(31.82 per cent) are in the income group of Rs. 10,001-15,000 per month, whereas another 33(25.00 per cent) are in the income group of Rs. 15,001-20,000. Again, it is observed that nearly one fourth of them are in the income group of Rs. 20,001-25,000 whereas those above Rs. 30,001 per month and in between Rs. 5001-10,000 are marginally represented. A larger proportion of university teachers in the income group of Rs. 10,001-15,000 may be due to a higher proportion of lecturers who might have joined university during the last few years.

In the case of the college teachers, we observe that nearly half of them (22) are in the income group of Rs. 15,001-20,000 per month whereas 9 of them are in the income group of Rs. 10,001-15,000. Only 10 of them are in the higher income group above Rs. 20,000. There are 4 teachers who are drawing less than Rs. 5000 per month. They are all guest faculty. In between the colleges, we observe that a larger number of teachers (14) of the Government college than that of Private college (8) are in the income group of Rs. 15,001-20,000.

Table 2.6
Income-wise Distribution of University and College Teachers

S.No.	*Income Groups (in Rs. per month)*	*University Teachers*	*College Teachers*		*Combined Total of Colleges*
			Govern-ment	*Private*	
1.	Upto 5000	0 (0.00)	3 (13.04)	1 (4.55)	4 (8.89)
2.	5,001-10,000	2 (1.51)	0 (0.00)	0 (0.00)	0 (0.00)
3.	10,001-15,000	42 (31.82)	2 (8.70)	7 (31.82)	9 (20.00)
4.	15,001-20,000	33 (25.00)	14 (60.86)	8 (36.36)	22 (48.89)
5.	20,001-25,000	34 (25.76)	2 (8.70)	5 (22.72)	7 (15.55)
6.	25,001-30,000	20 (15.15)	2 (8.70)	1 (4.55)	3 (6.67)
7.	30,001& Above	1 (0.76)	0 (0.00)	0 (0.00)	0 (0.00)
	Total	132 (100.00)	23 (100.00)	22 (100.00)	45 (100.00)

Note—Figures within brackets represent percentages

11. Family Social Status Index (F.S.S.I.) of Teachers

The social status of the families of teachers provides an indication of their relative positions in the society. As such, an attempt has been made to prepare a Family Social Status Index of teachers by taking into account the education, occupation and income level of their fathers and education and occupation of their mothers (For details, please refer to Appendix I). This index has been worked out separately for university and college teachers keeping in view the range of score values. The families of the teachers have been classified as High, Medium and Low in terms of their Family Social Status Index.

An examination of Table 2.7 shows that out of 132 university teachers, only 30 of them (22.73 per cent) are in the high category while 73(55.30 per cent) of them belong to the medium status. Nearly one-fifth of them are having low F.S.S.I. On the other hand, in the case of college teachers, we do not observe any difference in between teachers belonging to the Government and the Private college as almost an equal number of them (four each) are in the high category. Even in the medium category, the distribution of teachers in the Government and the Private college is 13 and 12 respectively. Besides, 6 each in both the colleges belong to low group. It is apparent from the above analysis that the majority of the teachers are having medium or low family social status index. This may be because their parents had limited opportunities to go in for higher education and to enter into higher income occupations.

Table 2.7

Familiy Social Status Index of University and College Teachers

S.No.	*Family Social Status Index*	*University Teachers*	*S No*	*Family Social Status Index*	*College Teachers*	
					Govern-ment	Private
1.	High (17-23 score)	30 (22.73)	1.	High (18-24 score)	4 (17.39)	4 (18.18)
2.	Medium (10-16 score)	73 (55.30)	2.	Medium (11-17 score)	13 (56.52)	12 (54.55)
3.	Low (3-9 score)	29 (21.97)	3.	Low (4-10 score)	6 (26.09)	6 (27.27)
	Total	132 (100.00)		Total	23 (100.00)	22 (100.00)

Note: 1. Figures within brackets represent percentages.
2. For details on the preparation of index, please refer to Appendix I.

12. Educational Level of the Spouses of the Teachers

Out of 132 university teachers in the sample, as many as 12 were unmarried. Of the remaining 120, including 118 married and 2 widow/er, the educational level of the teachers' spouses was analysed. A large number of teachers' spouses 38(31.67 per cent) were educated upto M.Phil/Ph.D level whereas 31(25.83 per cent) were holding professional degrees. Another 31(25.83 per cent) were educated upto post-graduate level. The remaining 17 were educated upto graduate level while 3 had studied up to Matric and 10+2 level. It is observed that a higher proportion of male than female teachers had their spouses educated upto M.Phil/Ph.D level. On the other hand, a large proportion of female (61.90 per cent) than male teachers (6.41 per cent) had their spouses having professional degrees. Again, we find a large proportion of male than female teachers having their spouses educated up to post-graduate and graduate level.

In the case of college teachers, more number of them (17) have their spouses educated up to post-graduate level whereas 9 of them, all females (4 in the Government and 5 in the Private college) have their spouses having a professional degree. As many as 8 of them have their spouses educated up to M.Phil/Ph.D level and only 5 of them up to graduate level. In the Government college, there are more number of male (7) than female teachers who have their spouses educated up to post-graduate level.

13. Occupation of the Spouse of theTeacher

The occupational status of the spouse of the teachers gives an idea about their family social status. Both among the university and college teachers, a higher proportion of them (32.50 per cent in the university and 30.77 per cent in the colleges) are having their spouses in college/university teaching jobs, yet quite a proportion of them are also house-wives. It is interesting to observe that many of the female teachers (14) in the university as well as in the colleges (5) are having their spouses in the professional jobs such as engineering, management, accountancy and legal field. Again, more number of female (6) than male teachers (1) in the university and two female teachers in the Private college are having their spouses in medical profession.This shows that those in the professional jobs prefer to have their wives in the teaching profession as it is generally thought that they can do full justice to both professional and familial roles. However, it is also observed that more number of male (26) than female teachers (13) in the university and more number of male (7) than female (5) teachers in the colleges are having their spouses in the teaching profession at the university/college level. The spouses of teachers are marginally represented in other occupations.

The above analysis suggests that the engagement of spouses of teachers in prestigious occupations may contribute to their higher socio-economic status. When compared to their parental families, there appears an inter-generational mobility.

14. Income Level of the Spouse of the Teacher

The Income level of the spouse of the teachers is also indicative of their family status. Out of 83 university teachers (This excludes 37 house-wives), slightly more than half of the teachers' spouses are having income above Rs.15,000 per month. It is observed that more number of female (15) than male teachers (7) have their spouses in the income group of Rs.15,000-20,000. Again, we have more number of female (9) than male (4) teachers who are having their spouses in the income group of Rs.20,001-25,000 per month. However, we have 7 female teachers and 3 female teachers having their spouses in the income groups of Rs.25,001-30,000 and above Rs.30,000 respectively.

In the case of college teachers, we have a high number of teachers having their spouses in the income group of Rs. 15,001-20,000. It is also observed that like university teachers, it is more female than male teachers who have their spouses in the higher income groups in both the colleges. However, in the income groups below Rs. 10,000 per month, we have more number of spouses of male than those of female teachers having their representation in this group both in the university as well as the colleges. The same holds good for the income group of Rs. 10,001-15,000 per month in the case of university teachers. It is apparent from the above analysis that due to more representation of female teachers' spouses in the higher income brackets, they have acquired a better socio-economic status of their families in comparison to their parental families.

15. Age of Teachers at which they entered into this Profession

The age at which the teacher enters into the profession may indicate the span of his or her academic life. A large proportion of teachers (32.58 per cent) in our sample, have entered into this profession between the age group of 24-26 years at the university level. However, the proportion of female teachers (39.21 per cent) is higher than that of males (28.40 per cent) in the same age group. We have nearly one-fourth of the teachers having joined this profession in the age-group of 27-29 years. Besides, an equal number of them entered into this profession above the age of 30 years. The proportion of males in both the above age groups (25.92 per cent) is almost equal to that of females (25.49 per cent). We have a relatively smaller proportion of teachers (15.90 per cent) who joined this profession in the age group of 21-23 years. Again, there is a pre-ponderence of male over female teachers in this age group. On the other hand, in the case of college teachers, more than half of them (24) have joined this profession when they were in the age group of 21-23 years. Of these, 12 are in the Government college while an equal number is in the Private college. In both the colleges, the number of female teachers is 8 and that of male teachers is 4. Besides, as many as 16 teachers have joined this profession in the age group of 24-26 years. In the case of the Private college, there are more number of females than males in this age group who have joined this profession, however this is vice-versa in the case of the Government college. All those who joined this profession in the age group of 27-29 years and above 30 years (5) belong to the Government college. As compared to university, more female teachers in both the colleges have entered into this profession in the younger age group of 21-23 years.

16. Length of Teaching Experience of Teachers

The length of teaching experience of teachers is an indicator of their academic maturity and proficiency. An examination of Table 2.8, clearly brings out that nearly half of the teachers at the university level have more than 15 years of teaching experience. There is a greater proportion of male than female teachers having teaching experience in the categories of 16-20 years, 21-25 years, 26-30 years and more than 30 years. However, there is a larger proportion of female (53.94 per cent) than male teachers (19.74 per cent) having teaching experience upto 5 years and between 6-10 years when combined together. This may reflect that in the last few years, more number of females have gone in for higher education and entered into this profession at the university level.

At the college level, nearly 60 per cent of the teachers have more than 15 years of teaching experience. However, in the category

Table 2.8

Distribution of Universtity and College Teachers according to length of Teaching Experience

S. No.	Length of teaching experience (In Years)	University Teachers			Colleges Teachers						Combined Total of College
					Government			Private			
		Male	Female	Total	Male	Female	Total	Male	Female	Total	
1.	Upto 5	6 (7.40)	14 (27.45)	20 (15.15)	0 (0.00)	3 (23.08)	3 (13.04)	0 (0.00)	2 (14.29)	2 (9.09)	5 (11.12)
2.	6-10	10 (12.34)	13 (25.49)	23 (17.42)	0 (0.00)	1 (7.69)	1 (4.35)	2 (25.00)	3 (21.43)	5 (22.72)	6 (13.34)
3.	11-15	10 (12.34)	11 (21.57)	21 (15.91)	3 (30.00)	0 (0.00)	3 (13.04)	0 (0.00)	4 (28.58)	4 (18.18)	7 (15.55)
4.	16-20	9 (11.11)	3 (5.88)	12 (9.09)	2 (20.00)	4 (30.77)	6 (26.09)	0 (0.00)	3 (21.42)	3 (13.64)	9 (20.00)
5.	21-25	13 (16.06)	4 (7.84)	17 (12.88)	3 (30.00)	3 (23.08)	6 (26.09)	0 (0.00)	1 (7.14)	1 (4.55)	7 (15.55)
6.	26-30	16 (19.76)	1 (1.96)	17 (12.88)	2 (20.00)	1 (7.69)	3 (13.04)	3 (37.50)	1 (7.14)	4 (18.18)	7 (15.55)
7.	More than 30	17 (20.99)	5 (9.81)	22 (16.67)	0 (0.00)	1 (7.69)	1 (4.35)	3 (37.50)	0 (0.00)	3 (13.64)	4 (8.89)
	Total	81 (100.00)	51 (100.00)	132 (100.00)	10 (100.00)	13 (100.00)	23 (100.00)	8 (100.00)	14 (100.00)	22 (100.00)	45 (100.00)

Note : Figures withing bracket represent percentage

of 16-20 years of teaching experience, we have more number of female than male teachers in both the colleges. But in the categories of 26-30 years, we have more number of males than females. Again, in the category of upto 5 years and in between 6-10 years, we have more number of female than male teachers. This again, is indicative of females also entering into the teaching profession alongwith males.

17. Length of Service of Teachers in their Present Institutions

The length of service of teachers in their present institutions may provide an idea about the joining of new entrants in the university and colleges. In the university sample, a larger number of teachers, 36(27.27 per cent) have their length of service less than five years. Even the sex-wise distribution in this category shows that there is a higher proportion of female (35.29 per cent) than male teachers (22.22 per cent). Again, it is observed that also in the category of 6-10 years and 11-15 years, the proportion of female teachers is more than that of males. A similar pattern is being observed in the case of college teachers. This is indicative of the fact that in the recent past, more number of females than males have entered into teaching profession. On the other hand, in the case of university teachers, there is a higher proportion of male than female teachers having longer length of service beyond 16 years in this institution. A higher proportion of male than female teachers in the university belonging to the beyond 16 years categories may be explained in terms of females not encouraged to go in for higher education in the early stages of expansion of education. This provided the males an edge over the females to join the university service. However, in the case of colleges, an almost equal number of male and female teachers are in the above category (beyond 16 years).

18. Participation Index (PI) of Teachers in the University/College Bodies and Associations

Over the years, teachers are being actively involved in the decision making bodies of university. There is also democratization of administration through rotation of headship of the departments as well as through the functioning of various committees at the department level. Even some teachers from the colleges are also represented in the Senate/Syndicate in the university. Further, it is also observed that teachers' associations in the university as well as in the colleges are contributing directly or indirectly to the decisions taken for their functioning. As such, the teacher Unions have also become a part of the university decision making system. An attempt has been made to prepare a participation index of teachers in university/college bodies and associations. A point-score has been given to various dimensions in which teachers take active part. The Participation Index (PI) has been classified as high and low on the basis of score values (For details, please refer to Appendix III). Those teachers who did not participate in any of the above activities were given a score of 0. The participation index has been worked out separately for the university and college teachers because of different score values.

As revealed in Table 2.9, among the university teachers, nearly one-fourth of them have a high participation index whereas 68.18 per cent are having a low participation index. The remaining 6.07 per cent had no participation in the above activities. It is interesting to observe that among those who have a high PI, there is a higher proportion of teachers belonging to Social Sciences and Professional stream of courses. On the other hand, in the category of low PI, we have a higher proportion of teachers belonging to Science stream of courses. It may be that Science teachers have relatively less interest than other categories of teachers in these activities due to paucity of time.

In the case of college teachers, more than half of them (25) showed no participation in these activities. Out of remaining 20, 7 of them were having a high PI whereas 13 had a low PI in these activities. However, in between the two colleges, we observe a higher proportion of teachers having a high PI in the Private than in the Government college. Again, in the Government college, the non participation of teachers was fairly high than that of the Private college. It may be that those in the Government college because of strict rules and regulations are reluctant or show indifference to participate in such activities.

Table 2.9

Participation Index of University and Coolege Teachers in the Universtity/College Bodies and Associations

S. No.	Participation Index	University Teachers				S. No.	Participation Index	College Teachers		Combined Total of Colleges
		Science	Social Science	Professional	Combined Total			Government	Private	
1.	High (6 to 10 score)	12 (20.69)	17 (30.36)	5 (27.78)	34 (25.75)	1	High (5 to 8 score)	2 (8.70)	5 (22.73	7 (15.55)
2.	Low (1 to 5 score)	42 (72.41)	36 (64.28)	12 (66.67)	90 (68.18)	2.	Low (1 to 4 score)	3 (13.04)	10 (45.45)	13 (28.89)
3.	No Participation (0 score)	4 (6.90)	3 (5.36)	1 (5.55)	8 (6.07)	3.	No Participation (0 score)	18 (78.26)	7 (31.82)	25 (55.56)
	Total	58 (100.00)	56 (100.00)	18 (100.00)	132 (100.00)		Total	23 (100.00)	22 (100.00)	45 (100.00)

Note :

1. Figures within brackets represent percentage.
2. For details of Particiaption Index, please refer to Appendix III

Characteristics of University and College Students

The various characteristics of university and college students in our sampleare as given below.

1. Sex—Out of 77 students in our sample in the university, over half, that is, 40(51.95 per cent) are females while the remaining 37(48.05 per cent) are males. Further, out of 35 students in the Government college, 19(54.29 per cent) are males while the remaining 16(45.71 per cent) are females. However, in the case of the Private college, out of 37 students, as many as 21(56.76 per cent) are males while 16(43.24 per cent) are females. Overall, there is a higher proportion of female students in the university than in the colleges.

2. Age—Out of 77 students in the university sample, a majority of them, that is, 43(55.84 per cent) are in the age-group of 21-22 years whereas another 25(32.47 per cent) are in the age category of 23-24 years. A very small proportion (6.49 per cent) of them are in the lower age-group of 19-20 years while 5.20 per cent are in the higher age group of 24-25 years. Incidentally, there is a higher proportion of female students in the age group of 21-22 years. On the other hand, out of 72 students in the two colleges, the majority of them, that is, 51 (70.83 per cent) are in the younger age group of 19-20 years whereas 20 of them (20.79 per cent) are in the age group of 21-22 years. Only one student that too, male in the Private college is in the age group of 23-24 years. Again, we have a higher proportion of female than male students in both the colleges in the age group of 19-20 years.

3. Religion—Out of 77 students in the sample, as many as 57(74.02 per cent) in the university belong to the Hindu religion whereas another 18 (23.38 per cent) are of Sikh religion. Only 2 of them (2.60 per cent) follow Muslim religion. Nearly an equal proportion of male and female students follow the Hindu religion while a higher proportion of female than male students are in the Sikh religion. Interestingly, the only 2 Muslim students in the sample are males. On the other hand, out of 72 students in the two colleges, again the majority of them 47(65.28 per cent) belong to the Hindu religion whereas 24 of them (33.33 per cent) have adherence to the Sikh religion. One student, that too male in the Government college, belongs to the Muslim religion. The college-wise analysis suggests that there is a higher proportion of students (40.54 per cent) belonging to Sikh religion in the Private college than in the Government college (25.71 per cent). The high representation of students belonging to the Hindu and Sikh religious groups in both the colleges may be due to their numerical pre-ponderence in this region.

4. Caste—Out of 77 students in the university sample, the largest proportion of them, that is, 28(36.36 per cent) belong to Khatri/Arora caste group whereas an equal proportion of them 11 (14.28 per cent each) belong to the Brahmin and Jat caste groups respectively. As many as 9 (11.69 per cent) belong to Scheduled caste/Scheduled tribe category whereas another 8 of them are in the any other category including Saini, Yadavs, Kamboj and Muslims. Six of them (7.79 per cent) belong to the Rajput caste group whereas 4(5.20 per cent) are of Bania/Jain/Kayastha caste group. Again, in the colleges out of 72 students, the major proportion of them 24(33.33 per cent) belong to Khatri/Arora Caste groups. Besides, 17(23.61 per cent) belong to the Brahmin caste group, followed by Jat (12), Bania/Jain/Kayastha (8), Scheduled Caste/ Scheduled Tribe (6), Rajput (3) and any others including Saini, Yadav etc (2). In the Private college, there are more number of students(8) belonging to the Jat caste group than in the Government college. A higher proportion of students belonging to Khatri/Arora and Brahmin Caste both in the university as well as in the colleges may be due to their greater representation in this region.

5. Family Strucure—Out of 77 students in the university sample, the majority of them 64(83.12 per cent) have a nuclear family structure whereas the remaining 13(16.88 per cent) belong to the joint family. We have a higher proportion of female than male students belonging to the nuclear family while it is vice versa in the case of the joint family. Again, out of 72 students in the two colleges, a majority of them 60(83.33 per cent) belong to the nuclear family whereas only 12(16.67 per cent) are having joint family structure. The college-wise analysis also nearly conforms to the same distribution of pattern of students belonging to the nuclear and joint family structure. A higher proportion of nuclear families of students is indicative of the urban structure of the city in which the university and colleges are located.

6. Family Size—Out of 77 students in the university sample, a majority of them 62(80.52 per cent) have a family size of 4-6 members, whereas 8 of them are having 7-9 members. There are only 5 students whose family size is upto 3 members whereas only 2 of the students in the sample have a family size of 10 members and above.

Again, in respect of two colleges, out of 72 students in the study, the majority of them 63(87.50 per cent) are having a family size of 4-6 members whereas 6 (8.33 per cent) are having family size of 7-9 members. There are only 2 students (one male each in Government and the Private college) who have a family size of upto 3 members and one male in the Private college who has a family size of 10 members and above. By and large, the family size appears to be in correspondence with the nuclear family structure of the students.

7. Mean Number of Earners—The mean number of earners in the family among the university students is 1.50 whereas in the case of college students in the combined form, it is 1.39. However, the sex-wise analysis of students in the university shows that the mean number of earners for the male students is 1.58 with range varying from 1-7 members while in the case of female students, it is 1.43 with range varying from 1-3 members.

In respect of the Government college, the mean number of earners in the family is 1.29. However, for male students in this college it is 1.21 with range varying from 1-2 members. But in the case of female students, it is 1.37 with range varying from 1-3 members. However, in the case of the Private college, the mean number of earners in the family for the students in the combined form is 1.49. But for male students, it is 1.62 with range varying from 1-4 members while for female students it is 1.37 with range varying from 1-2 members. The above analysis shows that the mean number of earners are more for male than female students in the university as well as in the Private college. But in the case of Government college, it is vice-versa.

8. Type of Schooling—Out of 77 students in the university sample, a large proportion of them, that is, 33(42.85 per cent) had their schooling done in Convent/Public schools, whereas 26 (33.77 per cent) had their education in the Government schools. However, 18(23.38 per cent) studied in the Private schools. Interestingly, a higher proportion of female (60 per cent) than male students (24.32 per cent) had their schooling in Convent/Public schools. On the other hand, a higher proportion of male than female students had studied in the Government as well as in the Private schools. In the case of college students, out of 72 in both the colleges a little over half of them, 37(51.39 per cent) had their schooling done in Government schools whereas another 21(29.17 per cent) studied in a Convent/Public school. Only 14(19.44 per cent) studied in the Private schools. The college-wise analysis suggests that out of 35 students in the Government college, nearly three-fourth of them (26) had studied in the Government school, while 7 of them had their schooling done in a Convent/Public school. Only 2 of them studied in a Private school. The sex-wise distribution of students in this college is not very marked except that more male than female students had studied in a Government school. However, in respect of the Private college, out of 37 students, 14 had attended a Convent/Public school while 12 of them studied at a Private school. Another 11 of them had gone to a Government school. Further, there were more number of male than female students who had attended Convent/Public schools. It appears that, by and large, students having studied at a Government school have opted to go in for a Government college.

9. Rural/Urban Background—Out of 77 students in the university sample, nearly three-fourth of them (75.32 per cent) had an urban background while the remaining one-fourth (24.68 per cent) belonged to the rural areas. Further, it is observed that a higher proportion of female (85.00 per cent) than male students (64.86 per cent) came from an urban background. On the other hand, correspondingly a higher proportion of male (35.14 per cent) than female students (15.00 per cent) had a rural background. Again, in the case of 72 students in the two colleges, a majority of them, that is, 60(83.33 per cent) had an urban background while only 13(16.67 per cent) came from the rural areas. In the case of Government college, out of 35 students, 30 of them had an urban background (17 males and 13 females) while only 5 came from rural areas (2males and 3 females). However, in the case of the Private college, out of 37 students, 30 of them (16 males and 14 females) had an urban background whereas only 7 students (5 males and 2 females) came from rural areas.

10. Family Social Status Index (F.S.S.I)—An attempt was made to construct the Family Social Status Index of the university and college students separately by taking into account the occupational and educational status of their parents as well as their family monthly income (for details please refer to Appendix IV). The family social status index of students has been categorized into high, medium and low on the basis of cut off values of mean score worked out in respect of families of all the students on the identified factors.

Out of 77 students in the university , as many as 39(50.65 per cent) belong to medium family social status index whereas nearly one-fourth of them (25.97 per cent) have a high F.S.S.I. Only 18(23.38 per cent) students showed a low F.S.S.I. On the other hand, in the case of two colleges, out of 72 students, a majority of them 41 (56.94 per cent) belong to medium F.S.S.I, whereas another 15(20.83 per cent) are having high F.S.S.I Only 16 of them (22.23 per cent) have a low F.S.S.I. The college-wise break down of F.S.S.I of students, however, shows that in the case of Government college, only 4 students belong to high F.S.S.I, 19 to medium and 12 to low F.S.S.I. But in the case of the Private college, a higher number of them (11) are in the high category whereas only 4 are in low category. The remaining 22 students have a medium F.S.S.I. It is apparent from above that more number of students in the Private than in the Government college are having high F.S.S.I whereas it is vice versa in the case of low category.

3

Role Socialization and Views of Teachers Towards the Profession

In order to orient themselves into teaching role, teachers have to go through a process of socialization. Socialization refers to learning of social roles. It has been defined as a process by which persons selectively acquire the values and attitudes, the interests, skills and knowledge, in short, the cultural content of the groups to which they belong or may become members of (Merton, 1957). However, professional socialization is seen as the process of shaping the individual to fulfill the needs of the profession as well as that of the society. In analyzing it, one has to consider reciprocity between an individual's aspirations and occupational and institutional structures (Goode, 1960). Further, in order to socialize oneself into an occupation, the primary group assumes significance. It is suggested that the conception of oneself is the reflection of one's behaviour in response to that of one's primary group (Cooley, 1956).

Parsons (1975) is of the opinion that the difference between the professional and the business role is only that of profit motive. This difference is mainly influenced by the core values prevailing in the two settings, that is, the profession and the business. In this connection he provides a theoretically more consistent distinction between the particularistic and the universalistic societies. According to him, rationality, functional specificity and universalism are the salient features of the professional as well that of the business role. These are derived mainly from the fundamental character of modern or universalistic against traditional or particularistic societies, emphasizing on particularism and functional diffuseness. These affect the roles of the individuals in the two different settings. In this theoretical schema, Parsons also includes acquiring scientific and systematic body of knowledge as a part of the professional socialization.

Professional role socialization is largely experienced within an institutional setting, be it a university, college or a specialized academy. In the recent past, especially during the twentieth century, the spread of liberal education and the progression of university system has opened many opportunities for persons to enter into professions such as Law, Medicine, Engineering etc. and gain academic legitimation. In this regard, Parsons (1968) contends that universities have opened faculties to impart training in these areas and to systematize cognitive basis of professional socialization. However, teaching as a profession is not attractive to many as it cannot provide an elite status to them. It is observed that with the spread of education, it has lost its esoteric knowledge base. Further, with the growth of diversified occupational structure in specialized fields, teachers have also lost their relative income levels. It is suggested that the outstanding characteristics of teachers as an occupational group are, its large size, its high proportion of female members, its low social class composition, its small measure of autonomy as a group and its segmentation (Leggatt, 1970).

In the context of the present study, an attempt has been made to analyse certain aspects of role socialization of teachers and their views towards the profession.

Professional Role Socialization of Teachers

It is often observed that people are not very keen to join the teaching profession. Given an opportunity they would prefer to join some other occupation. However, quite a few of them may be inspired to join it because they have some family members in it while others may do so because they enjoy working in this profession. Besides, there may be different set of factors which may motivate individuals to join it. Some of them may also express regret for having joined this profession and show reservations about its role in fulfilling their expectations. Quite a few of them, may feel that their services have not been recognized in the society while others may contend that they as teachers, can play an important role in the society. Further, some teachers may feel that their status can be raised in the society through adopting certain ways and means. The above aspects have been analysed to understand the views of teachers as a part of professional role socialization.

1. Family Members in the Teaching Profession—Family as a primary group assumes importance in influencing the behaviour of its members. An attempt was made to find out whether the teachers had any member of the family in the profession. Among the 132 university teachers, half of them had family members in the teaching profession. A slightly larger proportion of female (52.94 per cent) than male (48.15 per cent) teachers were having family members in it. In the case of college teachers, out of 45, only 20 teachers (44.45 per cent) were having family members in this profession. A higher proportion of teachers in the university than in the colleges having family members in this profession, may be due to a more conducive environment prevailing at home, necessary for pursuing an academic career. In between the Government and the Private college, more number of teachers in the Private (12) than in the Government college (8) had family members in the teaching jobs. However, the sex-wise distribution shows that more male (6) than female (2) teachers in the Government college and more female (8) than male (4) teachers in the Private college had family members in it. The above analysis suggests that a fairly good proportion of teachers might have been inspired to join this profession because of the influence of their family members.

2. Kin Relations of Teachers in this Profession—Those teachers who expressed that they had some members of their family in this profession, were further asked to specify their relationship with them.

As revealed Table 3.1, among the university teachers, a large proportion of them (43.93 per cent) referred to wife/husband working in the teaching job. This was followed by sister/brother relationships in it (37.87 per cent). A higher proportion of male (51.28 per cent) than female (33.33 per cent) teachers mentioned that they had wife/husband in this profession. However, in the case of sister/brother category, there is a higher proportion of female than male teachers. The other close relations mentioned in this profession were father (10), in Laws (8), aunt/uncle (6), daughter/son (4) and mother (2). However, there was not any marked difference in terms of responses of teachers on the sex-basis.

Table 3.1

Kin Relations of Teachers in this Profession

S. No.	Kin Relations	University Teachers			College Teacher						Combined Total of Colleges
					Government			Private			
		Male N=39	Female N=27	Total N=66	Male N=6	Female N=2	Total N=8	Male N=4	Female N=8	Total N=12	N=20
1.	Wife/ Husband	20 (51.28)	9 (33.33)	29 (43.93)	5 (83.33)	1 (50.00)	6 (75.00)	3 (75.00)	3 (37.50)	6 (50.00)	12. (60.00)
2.	Sister/ Brother	12 (30.76)	13 (48.14)	25 (37.87)	1 (16.64)	0 (0.00)	1 (12.50)	0 (0.00)	2 (25.00)	2 (16.60)	3 (15.00)
3.	Father	5 (12.82)	5 (18.51)	10 (15.15)	0 (0.00)	0 (0.00)	0 (0.00)	0 (0.00)	1 (12.50)	1 (8.33)	1 (5.00)
4.	In-Law	3 (7.69)	5 (18.51)	8 (12.12)	0 (0.00)	0 (0.00)	0 (0.00)	0 (0.00)	3 (37.50)	3 (25.00)	3 (15.00)
5.	Uncle/ Aunt	4 (10.25)	2 ((7.40)	6 (9.09)	0 (0.00)	0 (0.00)	0 (0.00)	0 (0.00)	0 (0.00)	0 (0.00)	0 (0.00)
6.	Daughter/ Son	4 (10.25)	0 (0.00)	4 (6.06)	0 (0.00)	0 (0.00)	0 (0.00)	1 (25.00)	0 (00.0)	1 (8.33)	1 (5.00)
7.	Mother	1 (2.56)	1 (3.70)	2 (3.03)	0 (0.00)	1 (50.0)	1 (12.50)	0 (0.00)	1 (12.50)	1 (8.33)	2 (10.00)

Note :

1. Figures within brackets represent percentages
2. Multiple Reponses

On the other hand, in the colleges, again, out of 20 teachers who mentioned that they had some relation in this profession, as many as 12 had indicated that they had wife/husband in it. There appears no difference in this category in between the two colleges. However, more male than female teachers in the Government college have referred to it whereas in the case of Private college, there is an equal proportion of male and female teachers, having stated as such. Further, three teachers each, have mentioned sister/brother and in-laws respectively in this profession while two have mentioned mother, in it. Again, one each has mentioned either father/daughter/son in this profession, whereas none has mentioned about uncle/aunt category. Interestingly, in the case of Private college, all the 3 female teachers had mentioned about their in-laws being in the teaching jobs. This may be because their in-laws may have preferred to have a daughter-in-law in the same profession.

3. Teachers Interested in taking up other Occupations Initially—The teachers were asked to specify whether they were interested in taking up other occupations initially. Out of 132 teachers in the university sample, only 34(25.75 per cent) were interested in following other occupations initially while 98(74.25 per cent) were not interested in other occupations. There does not appear any marked difference between the male (27.16 per cent) and female (23.50 per cent) teachers in terms of responding positively to this question. However, in the case of colleges, out of 45 teachers, 17(37.78 per cent) responded that they were interested in taking up other occupations initially. A higher proportion of teachers in the university than in the colleges not interested initially in following occupations other than teaching, may be due to their greater interest and motivation to go in for this profession. In between the Government and the Private college, there was not any difference observed as only 8 teachers in the Government and 9 teachers in the Private college, gave a positive response to this question. But more male (6) than female (2) teachers in the Government college and more female (6) than male (3) teachers in the Private college mentioned about their taking up other occupations initially. The above analysis indicates that, by and large, teachers were not interested in taking up other occupations initially. This may show that most of them were already fairly pre-disposed towards taking up the teaching profession.

Table 3.2

Occupations other than teaching in which Teachers were interested intially

S. No.	Occupations	University Teachers			College Teachers						Combined Total of Colleges
					Government			Private			
		Male	Female	Total	Male	Female	Total	Male	Female	Total	
1.	Professional jobs (Law, Medicine, Engineering, M.B.A.)	3 (13.64)	4 (33.33)	7 (20.59)	2 (33.33)	0 (0.00)	2 (25.00)	0 (0.00)	2 (33.33)	2 (22.22)	4 (23.53)
2.	Pharmaceutical/ Drug Industries	4 (18.18)	3 (25.00)	7 (20.59)	0 (0.00)	0 (0.00)	0 (0.00)	0 (0.00)	0 (0.00)	0 (0.00)	0 (0.00)
3.	Research Institutes Scientists	4 (18.18)	3 (25.00)	7 (20.59)	0 (0.00)	0 (0.00)	0 (0.00)	0 (0.00)	0 (0.00)	0 (0.00)	0 (0.00)
4.	IAS/ Allied Services (Civil Services)	4 (18.18)	2 (16.67)	6 (17.65)	1 (16.67)	2 (100.00)	3 (37.50)	0 (0.00)	4 (66.67)	4 (44.45)	7 (41.17)
5.	Defense Services	5 (22.72)	0 (0.00)	5 (14.70)	2 (33.33)	0 (0.00)	2 (25.00)	2 (75.00)	0 (0.00)	2 (22.22)	4 (23.53)
6.	Judicial Services	1 (4.55)	0 (0.00)	1 (2.94)	1 (16.67)	0 (0.00)	1 (12.50)	1 (25.00)	0 (0.00)	1 (11.11)	2 (11.77)
7	Private Sector (Banking and Financial Organizations)	1 (4.55)	0 (0.00)	1 (2.94)	0 (0.00)	0 (0.00)	0 (0.00)	0 (0.00)	0 (0.00)	0 (0.00)	0 (0.00)
		22 (100.00)	12 (100.00)	34 (100.00)	6 (100.00)	2 (100.00)	8 (100.00)	3 (100.00)	6 (100.00)	9 (100.00)	17 (100.00)

Note : Figures within brackets represent percentages.

Those respondents who replied that they were initially interested to take up other occupations than teaching, were further asked to specify the type of occupations they were interested in.

As revealed in Table 3.2, out of 34 university teachers, 7 each stated that they would have preferred to join professional jobs (law, medicine, engineering, MBA etc), pharmaceutical/drug industries and research institutes respectively. Another 6 of them mentioned that they would have liked to join civil services while 5 would have opted for defense services (all males). One each would have preferred to take up judicial service and a job in the private sector respectively. A higher proportion of female than male teachers appear to have opted for the professional jobs mentioned above.

On the other hand, in the case of colleges, out of 17 persons who responded positively to their taking up occupations other than teaching initially, as many as 7 of them would have opted for civil services. Another 4 each would have preferred to join professional jobs and defense services respectively, while 2 of them would have opted to join judicial services. There appears not much difference in between the two colleges so far as responses to various categories of jobs are concerned except that more female than male teachers in the Government college and all female teachers in the Private college would have preferred to join civil services.

3. (a) Reasons given by Teachers for not having joined these Occupations—A variety of reasons were provided by the respondents to explain why they had not joined the profession of their choice. The reasons given by teachers have been classified sex-wise, separately for the university and college teachers. These are multiple responses and the figure within a bracket represents number of respondents. In view of small number of responses, these have been clubbed together for teachers belonging to different courses in the university and teachers in both the colleges.

1. Reasons given by University Teachers

(a) Males

I. Could not clear defence entrance examination/resistance shown by mother to join the armed forces/could not join army due to health reasons (5).

II. Non-availability of opportunity and personal circumstances such as mother's ill-health not permitting to move out of Chandigarh (4).

III. Due to poor family background and financial constraints, could not join professional courses like medicine/engineering/ agriculture (3).

IV. Got teaching job immediately after post-graduation/Ph.D, so could not appear for I.A.S/Judicial service (3).

V. Could not qualify the civil services examination (2).

VI. Not many research institute in life-sciences available in the country (2).

(b) Females

I. Could not join medical college because of non-admission/ not able to do dissections/fell seriously ill and parents did not allow to join medical profession (4).

II. Could not get selected as a research scientist in an institute/ never got an opportunity to join a research institute (2).

III. Could not appear for I.A.S as parents convinced that teaching was best suited for girls and one could encounter difficulties in family adjustments after joining the above service (2).

IV. Got married locally, as such could not join the industry. Besides, there is a hectic schedule in industries and there are no big industries around (2).

V. Was not aware of advertising schools, as such took up science stream (1).

2. Reasons given by College Teachers

(a) Males

I. Could not join defense services on medical grounds/was not in a position to qualify the interview for getting into army (4).

II. Could not clear the competitive examination for civil/judicial services (3).

III. Wanted to stay with parents despite clearing and getting a class-II post in civil services (1).

IV. Did not get a good job in the private sector (1)

(b) Females

I. Could not clear the competitive examinations for civil services (3).

II. Chartered Accountancy was a time-consuming profession, so preferred to join teaching (1).

III. Father interested in teaching profession rather than encouraging to join I.P.S. (Indian Police Service) (1).

The above analysis brings out that most of the teachers both in the university and colleges, have failed to take up the desired occupations mainly because of their personal and familial circumstances. In the case of female teachers, they were mainly guided by their parents to take up teaching jobs as their argument was that this would also help them to perform their family roles adequately.

4. Enjoy Working in the Teaching Profession or not

In order to be productive in one's profession, one needs to enjoy working in it. This is also indicative of one's involvement in and satisfaction with the profession. The respondents were asked whether they enjoyed working in the teaching profession or not. All the teachers in the university and colleges except one male in the science stream in the university, have stated that they enjoy working in this profession. This shows that they are fairly well pre-disposed and motivated to take it up. However, they may have different motives to pursue their interest in this profession.

5. Factors Motivating Teachers to Join this Profession

Motivations are certain kinds of drives that influence the behaviour patterns of people. An attempt has been made to analyse the factors motivating teachers to join this profession. A set of eight factors was provided to the respondents and they were asked to rank these in order of their preferences. A factor ranked first, was given a score of one while that ranked second was assigned a score of two. In the same way, the other factors were ranked and the scores were assigned according to their ranking positions till the last factor, which was assigned a score of eight. A mean score value was worked out for each of these factors separately

Table 3.3

Factors Motivating Teachers to Join this Profession

S. No.	Motivating Factors	Overal l Mean Score Value	Rank	University Teachers								
				Science (Mean Score Value)			Social Science (Mean Score Value)			Professional (Mean Score Value)		
				Male	Female	Combined Mean	Male	Female	Combined Mean	Male	Female	Combined Mean
1.	Inspired by teachers in contact during educational career	2.98	1	3.07	3.00	3.04	2.74	3.00	2.85	3.18	3.28	3.22
2.	Desire to serve humanity	3.54	2	3.02	4.42	3.49	3.03	4.08	3.64	3.72	3.85	3.38
3.	Chance for self-expression	3.56	3	4.07	3.42	3.85	3.83	2.73	3.33	3.18	3.71	3.38
4.	Plain liking for the job	3.86	4	3.86	4.63	4.11	4.03	2.84	3.49	4.72	3.57	4.27
5.	Fascination for professional status	3.98	5	4.15	3.57	3.96	3.87	4.12	3.98	4.36	3.70	4.05
6.	Desire for recognition in the society	4.50	6	4.55	3.68	4.26	4.77	4.92	4.83	4.27	4.28	4.27
7.	Better prospects to go abroad	6.26	7	5.81	6.15	5.92	6.22	6.80	6.48	6.45	7.00	6.66
8.	No other option in terms of a carrier	7.20	8	6.94	7.00	6.96	7.80	7.40	7.62	6.09	7.71	6.72

(Contd.)

(Contd. Table 3.4)

S. No.	Motivating Factors	Overall Mean Score Value	Rank	College Teachers					
				Government (Mean Score Value)			Private (Mean Score Value)		
				Male	Female	Combined Mean	Male	Female	Combined Mean
1.	Desire to serve humanity	2.98	1	3.10	2.46	2.73'	2.37	3.78	3.26
2.	Inspired by teachers in contact during educational carrer	3.21	2	3.90	3.15	3.47	3.87	2.42	2.94
3.	Fascination for professional status	3.25	3	2.30	3.84	3.17	3.25	3.42	3.35
4.	Desire for recognition in the society	4.27	4	4.20	4.69	4.47	4.75	3.71	4.08
5.	Chance for self-expression	4.34	5	4.20	4.38	4.30	5.00	4.07	4.40
6.	Plain liking for the job	4.41	6	4.30	4.30	4.30	4.12	4.78	4.54
7.	Better prospects to go abroad	6.39	7	6.50	5.84	6.12	6.75	6.64	6.68
8.	No other option in terms of a career	6.71	8	6.40	7.30	6.90	5.87	6.92	6.53

sex wise as well as in the combined form for all the university and college teachers. Further, an overall mean score value for these factors was also worked out separately for university and college teachers to analyse the relative preferences of factors motivating them to join this profession. The lower the mean score value, the higher was the rank assigned to that factor by the teachers.

An examination of Table 3.3, reveals that in the overall analysis, the teachers in the university have ranked "inspired by teachers in contact during educational career" as a factor motivating them on the top (2.98). This is followed by "desire to serve humanity" (3.54) and "chance for self-expression" (3.56) in that order. In the Parsonian framework, these three top ranking factors reflect rationalistic and universalistic orientation of teachers. The 'inspiration got from teachers' show role-commitment and dedication as well as 'chance for self-expression' as a part of personality development, also indicates a rationalistic orientation whereas 'desire to serve humanity' reflects a universalistic outlook of teachers. 'Plain liking for the job' has been assigned the fourth rank. This shows an affective orientation of teachers. This is followed by 'fascination for professional status in the society' and 'desire for recognition in the society' as fifth and sixth factors motivating them to join this profession. To a certain extent, these are indicative of achievement and individualistic orientations. The next factor ranked in order is, 'better prospects to go abroad'. However 'no other option in terms of a career'(7.20) is the lowest ranked factor motivating teachers to join this profession.

In between teachers belonging to different streams of courses in the university, it is observed that science teachers have placed the factor of 'fascination for professional status in the society' higher than 'plain liking for the job'. However, in between male and female teachers in this group, male teachers, have assigned first rank to the factor 'desire to serve humanity'(3.02). Again 'plain liking for the job'(3.86) has been ranked higher than the 'chance for self expression'(4.07). On the other hand, the female teachers have placed 'fascination for professional status in the society' and 'desire for recognition in the society' as factors above the 'desire to serve humanity'. They seem to be more achievement and individualistic oriented.

Among the social science teachers, it is observed that they have assigned 'plain liking for the job' (3.49) a rank higher than 'desire to serve humanity'(3.64). Even the factor of 'chance for self-expression'(3.33) has been placed next to the top ranked factor, 'inspired by teachers in contact during educational carrier'(2.85). The rest of the factors follow the overall pattern of ranking. But in between the male and the female teachers in this group, there are some variations observed. While male teachers tend to place the factor, 'desire to serve humanity,' higher than 'chance for self-expression,' female teachers have assigned first and second ranks to factors such as 'chance for self-expression'(2.73) and 'plain liking for the job'(2.84) respectively. In their case, the outlook appears to be a mix of rational and affective orientations. This is likely to happen in the society which is in transition from traditional to a modern one.

In the case of professional teachers, the ranking pattern of factors motivating them to join this profession is same as indicated by the overall mean score values. Among them, in the case of males, the factor 'desire for recognition in the society'(4.27) has been ranked next to 'chance for self-expression'(3.18). However, in the case of female teachers 'plain liking for the job'(3.57) has been ranked higher than 'chance for self-expression'(3.71). Even 'fascination for professional status in the society' has been placed next to 'plain liking for the job' and before 'chance for self-expression'. In fact, they have assigned second rank to 'plain liking for the job'. It again shows that female teachers are more affective than rationalistic in their orientation.

In respect of college teachers, we observe a slightly different pattern of ranking of factors motivating them to go in for the teaching profession than that given by the university teachers. In their overall ranking pattern, they have given first rank to 'desire to serve humanity'(2.98) followed by 'inspired by teachers in contact during educational career'(3.21) and 'fascination for professional status in the society' as a third ranking factor. 'Desire for recognition in the society' and 'chance for self-expression' have been assigned fourth and fifth rank respectively whereas 'plain liking for the job' has been given the sixth rank. 'Better prospects to go abroad' and 'no other option in terms of a career' have been assigned the same ranking positions as given by the university teachers, that is, the seventh and the eighth rank respectively. However, in the case of the Government College teachers, they have given a higher ranking to 'chance for self-expression' and 'plain liking for the job,' than 'desire for recognition in the society'. A sex-wise analysis of teachers in this college shows that male teachers have assigned first rank to 'fascination for professional status in the society'(2.30) whereas female teachers have placed 'plain liking for the job' and 'chance for self-expression'(4.38) higher than 'desire for recognition in the society'(4.69). It shows that females appear to be more affective than male teachers, though most of them have rationalistic orientations towards these factors.

In the case of Private college, we observe that teachers have assigned the first rank to 'inspired by teachers in contact during educational career'(2.94) while 'better prospects to go abroad'(6.68) has been ranked last and 'no other option in terms of a career' has been assigned the seventh rank. The sex-wise response of teachers in this college shows that 'plain liking for the job' has been assigned a higher rank than 'desire for recognition in the society' by the male teachers. Even 'no other option in terms of a career' has been placed higher than' better prospects to go abroad'. On the other hand, the female teachers have assigned first rank to 'inspired by teachers in contact during educational career' while 'fascination for professional status in the society' gets second position and 'desire for recognition in the society' has been assigned a third rank. Interestingly, 'desire to serve humanity' has been placed at fourth position. The factor 'inspired by teachers in contact during educational career' apart from having rationalistic orientation in terms of following the dedication and role-commitment of teacher, has also an element of affectivity as one tends to empathize with him/her to imbibe such a value.

In short, the above analysis suggests that teachers, by and large, being educated are rationalistic and universalistic in giving ranks to various motivating factors, though they, especially females, have some element of affectivity in their orientations. Another observation is that there are varied responses given by teachers on sex-basis to factors motivating them to take up this profession in the different faculties in the university as well as in the two colleges.

6. Regrets by Teachers for having joined this Profession

The respondents were asked to specify whether they had any regret for having joined this profession or not. The majority of teachers in the university (54.54 per cent) stated that they rarely experienced regrets for having joined the teaching profession. Further, as many as, 34.09 per cent of them mentioned that they had never felt any regrets for taking up this profession. Only 15(11.37 per cent) teachers stated that they sometimes felt so, while none of them responded to the 'often' category. Teachers belonging to science, social science and professional courses have responded more or less in the same proportion as all the teachers in the combined form except in the case of professional teachers who have responded to a higher proportion in the 'never' category. Even in this group, there is a higher proportion of male than female teachers for the 'never' category and vice-versa is the case in the 'rarely' category. Again, among the social science teachers, there is a higher proportion of female than male teachers in the 'never' category. But in the case of science teachers, though we have a higher proportion of male teachers in the 'never' and 'sometimes' categories, yet we have a large proportion of female teachers in the response category of 'rarely'.

In the colleges, also, we have got similar responses. A higher number of teachers (28) were opting for the response category of 'rarely' whereas 9 mentioned that they had 'never' regretted their choice while 8 impressed that they regretted 'sometimes' for having joined this profession. More female than male teachers in the Government college have responded to the category of 'rarely'. However, all female but none of the male teachers in the Private college, stated that they 'sometimes' felt regretful for having joined this profession. It appears that more female than male teachers seem to have some element of regret for having taken up this profession.

Views of Teachers on Various aspects of the Profession

The teachers were asked to specify their views on various aspects of the profession such as not being upto one's expectations, not providing high social status etc. An examination of Table 3.4, reveals that out of 132 teachers in the university sample, as many as 56 (42.42 per cent) did not respond to this question. Twenty nine (21.96 per cent) stated that this profession was not upto their expectations, 26 (19.69 per cent) felt that it did

Table 3.4

Views of Teachers on various aspects of the Profession

S. No.	Aspects of Profession	University Teachers			College Teachers						Combined Total of Colleges
					Government			Private			
		Male (N=81)	Female (N=51)	Total (N=132)	Male (N=10)	Female (N=13)	Total (N=23)	Male (N=8)	Female (N=14)	Total (N=22)	(N=45)*
1.	No Response	34 (41.97)	22 (43.13)	56 (42.42)	0 (0.00)	0 (00.0)	0 (00.0)	0 (00.0)	0 (00.0)	0 (00.0)	0 (00.0)
2.	This profession is not upto one's expectation	21 (25.92)	8 (15.68)	29 (21.96)	4 (40.0)	8 (61.53)	12 (52.17)	2 (25.0)	0 (00.0)	2 (9.09)	14 (31.11)
3.	Does not provide high social status	16 (19.75)	10 (19.60)	26 (19.69)	5 (50.0)	1 (7.69)	6 (26.08)	4 (50.00)	7 (50.0)	11 (50.0)	17 (37.77)
4.	Is not well paid	9 (11.11)	12 (23.52)	21 (15.90)	1 (10.0)	1 (7.69)	2 (8.69)	2 (25.0)	3 (21.42)	5 (22.72)	7 (15.55)
5.	Interferes in meeting family obligations	3 (3.70)	4 (7.84)	7 (5.30)	0 (00.0)	3 (23.07)	3 (13.04)	0 (00.0)	1 (7.14)	1 (4.54)	4 (8.88)
6.	Any other (Specified as below)	9 (11.11)	9 (17.64)	18 (13.63)	1 (10.0)	1 (7.69)	2 (8.69)	0 (00.0)	4 (28.57)	4 (18.18)	6 (13.30)

(Contd.)

(Contd. Table 3.4)

University Male Teachers 1) Fully satisfied and contented with the profession. 2) Does not provide any power and special cadre in the administrative set-up. 3) Status of university teacher is being diluted because of college teacher being clubbed with them in the UGC Grade. 4) The profession has not been adopted by the majority by choice. **University Female Teachers** 1) Gives one self-respect, dignity and satisfaction. 2) Politics by senior faculty members blocks opportunity for growth of the younger faculty members. 3) Lacks honesty of purpose and has not evolved a professional work ethic. 4) Profession should be more creative, innovative and practical. 5) it is being assessed in terms of monetary values.	**College Male Teachers** 1) The Profession provides fully satisfaction **College Female Teachers.** 1) Best profession for women as it is a noble profession. 2) Educational system requires drastic streamlining as it is ignored by the administrative setup. 3) This profession lacks opportunity for personal advancement, is not challenging, lacks creativity and is monotonous.

Note :

1. These responses are from only those respondents who have responded to this question.

2. * Multiple responses.

3. Figures within brackets represeent percentages

not provide high social status, 21 (15.90 per cent) responded that it was not a well paid profession, while 7 stated that it interfered in meeting family obligations. As many as 18 of them specified other reasons given in the table (In view of small number of responses, these have been grouped together in respect of male and female teachers. Moreover, these are multiple responses).

The sex-wise analysis of teachers in the university shows that a higher proportion of female (23.52 per cent) than male (11.10 per cent) teachers expressed that it was not a well-paid profession. Again, a higher proportion of female than male teachers felt that it interfered in meeting their family obligations.

In the case of college teachers, more number of them (17) expressed that it did not provide high social status. Further, as many as 14 of them mentioned that this profession was not upto their expectations. Besides, 7 of them mentioned that it was not a well-paid profession while 4 expressed that it interfered in meeting family obligations. Most of the teachers responding to this category were females. Responses of teachers to "any other category" as given in the table are self-explanatory. The underlying emphasis is in making this profession more creative, innovative and practical.

1. Recognition of services rendered by Teachers

The teachers were asked to specify whether the services rendered by them were being recognized in the society or not. The responses of teachers were classified in terms of i) very definitely, ii) In most respects, iii) In some respects and iv) not at all. Those who responded to the last category were also asked to give reasons for their reply.

As revealed in Table 3.5, out of 132 university teachers in our study, a larger proportion of them 53(40.15 per cent) felt that their services were being recognized 'in some respects' while another 51(38.64 per cent) expressed that these were being recognized 'in most respects'. Another 24(18.18 per cent) thought that these were being recognized 'very definitely'. Only 4 mentioned that their services were not being recognized "at all". In respect of science teachers in the university, a higher proportion of female than male teachers have expressed that their services are recognized 'in some respects'. Again, a higher proportion of female than male teachers in the social science group have expressed

Table 3.5
Outlook of Teachers towards Recognition of Services Rendered by them

S.No. Recognition of services of teachers	University Teachers										College Teachers						Comb-ined Total of Colleges
	Science			Social Science			Professional			Com-bined	Government			Private			
	Male	Female		Male	Female	Total	Male	Female	Total	Total	Male	Female	Total	Male	Female	Total	
1. Very	5	2	7	9	3	12	4	1	5	24	1	2	3	4	1	5	8
definitely	(12.82)	(10.53)	(12.07)	(29.03)	(12.00)	(21.43)	(36.36)	(14.28)	(27.78)	(18.18)	(10.00)	(15.38)	(13.04)	(50.00)	(7.14)	(22.73)	(17.78)
2. In most	16	7	23	9	10	19	6	3	9	51	5	7	12	1	5.	6	18
respects	(41.03)	(36.84)	(39.65)	(29.03)	(40.00)	(33.93)	(54.54)	(42.86)	(50.00)	(38.64)	(50.0)	(53.85)	(52.17)	(12.50)	(35.71)	(27.27)	(40.00)
3. In some	16	10	26	12	11	23	1	3	4	53	3	4	7	2	6	8	15
respects	(41.03)	(52.63)	(44.83)	(38.71)	(44.00)	(41.07)	(9.10)	(42.86)	(22.22)	(40.15)	(30.00)	(30.77)	(30.44)	(25.00)	(42.86)	(36.36)	(33.33)
4. Not at all	2	0	2	1	1	2	0	0	0	4	1	0	1	1	2	3	4
	(5.12)	(00.0)	(3.45)	(3.23)	(4.00)	(3.57)	(00.0)	(00.0)	(00.0)	(3.03)	(10.0)	(00.0)	(4.35)	(12.50)	(14.29)	(13.64)	(8.89)
TOTAL	39	19	58	31	25	56	11	7	18	132	10	13	23	8	14	22	45
	(100.0)	(100.0)	(100.0)	(100.0)	(100.0)	(100.0)	(100.0)	(100.0)	(100.0)	(100.0)	(100.0)	(100.0)	(100.0)	(100.0)	(100.0)	(100.0)	(100.0)

If Not at all

Reasons:

Male Teachers:

(i) Teachers are not dedicated to the cause of teaching

(ii) Universities are dens of politics.

(iii) Materialism has overtaken ethics of morality as teaching is not now a public services like any other service.

(iv) Poor conduct of teachers and poor student teacher/society interaction.

Female Teacher.

(i) Bureaucratic procedures for academic activities hamper growth of teachers.

Male and Female Teachers:

(i) Output is not result-oriented and there is devaluation of education in general.

(ii) There is bureaucratization of education and there are different syllabi for entrance tests.

(iii) Teacher is not taken into confidence for educational policy and is treated just as an employee.

(iv) Students expect too much from the teachers.

that their services are being recognized 'in some respects' (44.00 per cent) as well as 'in most respects' (40.00 per cent). However, a higher proportion of male (29.03 per cent) than female (12.00 per cent) teachers have stated that their services are being recognized 'very definitely'. In the case of professional group, more male than female teachers have stated that their services are being recognized 'in most respects' and 'very definitely' whereas more female than male teachers feel that these are being recognized 'in some respects'.

As far as college teachers are concerned, a larger proportion of them (18) have opted for 'in most respects' whereas 15 have mentioned that these are being recognized 'in some respects'. As many as 8 of them feel that these are being recognized 'very definitely', while 4 of them think that these are 'not at all' being recognized. In between the two colleges, the teachers in Government college, in majority (12) have stated that these are being recognized 'in most respects' whereas in the Private college only 6 have opted for it. Again, more female than male teachers in both the colleges have given this option. But, in the overall analysis, a fair number of teachers in the university and colleges are not very much satisfied with the recognition given to them for their services. As regards those who responded to the 'not at all' category, by and large, they feel that teachers are not dedicated to the cause of teaching and universities have become dens of politics. Besides, there is bureaucratization of education and students expect too much from the teachers especially at the college level.

2. Relationship between the Academic Level Index and the Recognition of Their Services

An attempt was made to relate the academic level index of teachers and the extent of recognition of their services in the society. A score of 3 was assigned to those who responded to the category of 'very definitely' whereas a score of 2 and 1, were given to those who responded to the category of 'in most respects' and 'in some respects' respectively. Those who responded that their services were not being recognized at all were given a score of 0. A mean score value was worked out for the teachers in the high and low academic level index both for the university (faculty-wise) and the two colleges.

Table 3.6

Relationship between the Acadmic Level Index of Teachers and the extent of recognition of their services

S. No.	Academic Level Index	University Teachers				S. No.	Academic Level Index	College Teachers		
		Science (Mean Score Value)	Social Science (Mean Score Value)	Professional (Mean Score Value)	Combined Mean			Government (Mean Score Value)	Private (Mean Score Value)	Combined Mean
1.	High (23 and above score)	1.81	1.78	2.20	1.83	1.	High (8 and above score)	2.20	1.50	1.70
2.	Low (22 and below score)	1.44	1.60	1.92	1.58	2.	Low (7 and below score)	1.61	1.80	1.67

As revealed in Table 3.6, among the university teachers, there appears some positive relationship between the academic level index of teachers and the recognition of their services in the society. The teachers with a high academic level index have a higher mean score value (1.83) indicating a larger extent of recognition of their services than those with a low academic level index, the mean score value being 1.58. Even the faculty-wise analysis shows that teachers in the science, social sciences and professional streams with a high academic level index (mean score values of 1.81, 1.78 and 2.20 respectively) express that their services as teachers are recognized more than those with low academic level index (mean score values of 1.44, 1.60, 1.92 respectively for science, social science and professional groups). Even in the case of college teachers, it is observed that teachers with a high academic level index feel that their services are being recognized more (mean score value 1.70) than those with the low academic level index (mean score value 1.67). However, if we take into account the mean score values for the Government and the Private college teachers separately, there appears some relationship between the academic level index of teachers and the extent of recognition of their services in the society for the teachers in the Government college, whereas in the case of the Private college, it is not so.

However, on the basis of the overall analysis for the university and college teachers, there is some relationship shown by the academic level index of teachers and the extent of recognition of their services in the society. In other words, those with a high academic level index than those with a low academic level index show more association with it. This lends support to our hypothesis that the academic level index of teachers influences the recognition of services rendered by them in the society.

3. Relationship between the Family Social Status Index (F.S.S.I.) of Teachers and the recognition of their Services

An attempt was also made to show whether the Family Social Status Index of teachers had any influence on the recognition of their services in the society. A score of 3 was assigned to those who responded to the category 'very definitely', a score of 2 for those who stated 'in most respects'. A score of 1 to those who mentioned 'in some respects' and a score of 0 to 'not at all' category.

Table 3.7

Relationship between Family Social Index of Teachers and the extent of recognition of their services.

S. No.	Family Social Status Index	University Teachers: Science (Mean Score Value)	University Teachers: Social Science (Mean Score Value)	University Teachers: Professional (Mean Score Value)	University Teachers: Combined Mean	S. No.	Family Social Status Index	College Teachers: Government (Mean Score Value)	College Teachers: Private (Mean Score Value)	College Teachers: Combined Mean
1.	High (17-23 score)	1.33	1.40	1.66	1.39	1.	High (18-24 score)	2.25	1.50	1.87
2.	Medium (10-16 score)	1.75	1.85	2.00	1.82	2.	Medium (11-17 score)	1.61	1.75	1.67
3.	Low (3-9 score)	1.69	1.61	2.66	1.75	3.	Low (4-10 score)	1.66	1.33	1.49

The extent of recognition of their services was worked out by finding out the mean score values, for each of these responses, in respect of both the university (faculty-wise) and the college teachers having High, Medium and Low Family Social Status Index.

As indicated in Table 3.7, in the case of university teachers, there is no clear cut relationship between the Family Social Status Index of teachers and the extent of recognition of their services in the society. In fact, teachers with the Medium F.S.S.I (mean score value of 1.82) have shown more positive relationship than those with a low F.S.S.I (1.75). However, those teachers with a high F.S.S.I show least relationship (1.39) in this regard. Even, the faculty wise analysis shows that there is no clear indication of any direct relationship between the above two variables. Infact, teachers in the professional group exhibit an inverse relationship between the level of F.S.S.I and the extent of recognition of their services in the society.

However, in the case of college teachers taken together, there is some association between the level of F.S.S.I and the recognition of their services in the society. In other words, those with a High F.S.S.I show more direct relationship about this than those in the Medium and Low F.S.S.I groups. In between the two colleges, there appears no clear cut relationship between the level of F.S.S.I of teachers and the extent of their services being recognized. It may be that teachers in the university with a Medium or Low F.S.S.I than those with a High F.S.S.I, have experienced an upward social mobility, as such they may show more relationship between their status and the recognition of their services in the society. In the case of college teachers, it is just possible that they may have lower expectation level than the university teachers. As such, they may tend to show more direct relationship between the above two factors.

3. Can Teachers Play an Important Role in the Society?

Can teachers play an important role in the society? This question was asked from the teachers in the university and colleges. As revealed in Table 3.8, all teachers in the university except 3 males in the science and 4 males in social sciences stream of courses as well as all teachers in the colleges, expressed that they could play an important role in the society.

Table 3.8

Ways in which the work of the Teachers can be useful to the society

S. No.	Ways in which teachers can be useful	University Teachers										College Teachers						Combined Total of Colleges (N=45)*
		Science			Social Science			Professional			Combined Total* (N=125)	Government			Private			
		Male (N=36)	Female (N=19)	Total (N=55)	Male (N=27)	Female (N=25)	Total (N=52)	Male (N=11)	Female (N=7)	Total (N=18)		Male (N=10)	Female (N=12)	Total (N=23)	Male (N=8)	Female (N=14)	Total (N=22)	
1.	By upholding human values	20 (55.55)	8 (42.10)	28 (50.90)	19 (70.37)	18 (72.00)	37 (71.15)	5 (45.45)	6 (85.71)	11 (61.11)	76 (60.80)	6 (60.00)	8 (61.53)	14 (60.86)	5 (62.50)	10 (71.42)	15 (68.18)	29 (64.44)
2.	By providing a role-model of conformity for others	17 (47.22)	10 (52.63)	27 (49.09)	16 (59.25)	12 (48.00)	28 (53.84)	5 (45.45)	3 (42.85)	8 (44.44)	63 (50.40)	5 (50.00)	6 (46.15)	11 (47.82)	4 (50.0)	9 (64.28)	13 (59.09)	24 (53.33)
3.	Being innovative and creative in tackling societal problems.	11 (30.55)	11 (57.89)	22 (40.00)	14 (51.85)	16 (64.00)	30 (57.69)	6 (54.54)	3 (42.85)	9 (50.00)	61 (48.80)	4 (40.00)	7 (53.84)	11 (47.82)	1 (12.50)	6 (42.85)	7 (31.81)	18 (40.00)

(Contd.)

(Contd. Table 3.8)

S. No.	Ways in which teachers can be useful	University Teachers										College Teachers						Combined Total of Colleges (N=45)*
		Science			Social Science			Professional			Combined Total* (N=125)	Government			Private			
		Male (N=36)	Female (N=19)	Total (N=55)	Male (N=27)	Female (N=25)	Total (N=52)	Male (N=11)	Female (N=7)	Total (N=18)		Male (N=10)	Female (N=12)	Total (N=23)	Male (N=8)	Female (N=14)	Total (N=22)	
4.	By providing direction and leadership to society	11 (30.55)	9 (47.36)	20 (36.36)	12 (44.44)	11 (44.0)	23 (44.23)	5 (45.45)	2 (28.57)	7 (38.88)	50 (40.00)	9 (90.00)	7 (53.84)	16 69.56)	5 (62.50)	5 (35.71)	10 (45.45)	26 (57.77)
5.	Any other (as specified below)	4 (11.11)	2 (10.50)	6 (10.90)	3 (11.11)	1 (4.00)	4 (7.69)	0 (00.0)	0 (00.0)	0 (00.0)	10 (8.00)	1 (10.00)	0 (00.0)	1 (4.34)	1 (12.50)	2 (14.28)	3 (13.63)	4 (8.88)

Males

(i) Nations building.

(ii) By inculcating rational thinking among students.

(iii) By transmitting knowledge and guidance to students to prepare them to become engineers and doctors.

Female

(i) Career building of students and nation building

Males and Females

(i) By acting as a change agents.

(ii) Guidance to the students.

(iii) Setting examples for others to follow.

Note :

1. Figures in brackets represent percentages.
2. * Multiple responses.

All those who responded positively to the above question were further asked to specify the ways in which the work of the teachers could be useful to the society.

An examination of Table 3.8, reveals that the majority of teachers in the university (60.80 per cent) state that teachers can be useful to the society by upholding human values. A higher proportion of teachers with social science and professional background than those with science background, have opted for this response. Although there is not much difference in the proportion of responses between male and female teachers in the social science category, yet we observe a higher proportion of male than female teachers in science and more female than male teachers in the professional category, expressing the same. Besides, as many as 50.40 per cent of teachers have suggested that they can be useful to the society by providing a role model of conformity for others. There appears not much difference in the responses faculty-wise as well as sex-wise within each faculty, except that a higher proportion of male than female teachers in the social science category, have given this reply. Further, it is observed by 48.80 per cent teachers that they can be useful to the society by being innovative and creative in tackling societal problems. A higher proportion of teachers with social science and professional background than those with science background have given this response. Again, a higher proportion of female than male teachers in social science and science backgrounds than those in the professional group have answered so. Another 40.00 per cent of teachers feel that they can be useful to the society by providing direction and leadership A higher proportion of teachers in social science (44.23 per cent) than those with professional (38.88 per cent) and science (36.36 per cent) backgrounds feel so. The sex-wise analysis within each faculty shows that a higher proportion of female (47.36 per cent) than male teachers (30.55 per cent) in the science group and more male (5) than female (2) teachers in the professional group are for this response whereas in the case of social science teachers, there is no difference on sex basis. Besides, they have also suggested that teachers can help in nation building and in the career making of students.

On the other hand, in the case of college teachers, we observe that a large majority of them (64.44 per cent) feel that they can be useful to the society by upholding human values. This is followed by teachers (57.77 per cent) who believe that they can be useful to the society by providing direction and leadership to the society, while the next factor highlighted by them is 'by providing a role model of conformity for others'(53.33 per cent). The rest of the responses are same in the order as that given by the university teachers. In between the two colleges, the teachers in the Government college as compared to those in the Private college have mentioned in greater number, factors such as 'providing direction and leadership to society' and 'being innovative and creative in tackling societal problems' through which they can be useful to the society. Sex-wise in both the colleges, more female than male teachers have opted for 'being innovative and creative in tackling societal problems'. It is further suggested by teachers that they can act as a change agent to the society and set examples for others to follow. As compared to university, college teachers are more positive about their role in providing direction and leadership to the society.

4. Factors that raise the Status of Teachers in the Society

As professionals, teachers have to acquire a status in the society. A set of eight factors was provided to university and college teachers and they were asked to rank these in order of their preferences, for raising their status in the society. A score of one was assigned to a factor ranked first while a score of two was given to a factor ranked second. In the same way, the factors ranked from third to eighth positions were assigned a score accordingly. A mean score value was worked out for each of these factors faculty and sex-wise for the university teachers as well as sex-wise for the college teachers. An overall mean score value for these factors was worked out for the university and college teachers. In the case of university teachers, a combined score value was also worked out for both the male and the female teachers, in the science, social science and professional groups while in the case of colleges, a combined mean score for teachers of both the sexes was worked out in respect of the Government and the Private college. The score values were arranged in an ascending order, the lower the mean score value, the higher was the rank assigned to that factor.

An examination of Table 3.9, reveals that in the overall analysis, the university teachers have assigned first rank to 'teaching

Table 3.9
Factors that raise the status of Teachers in the Society

S. No.	Factors raising the status of Teachers	Overall Mean Score Value	Rank	University Teachers								
				Science (Mean Score Value)			Social Science (Mean Score Value)			Professional (Mean Score Value)		
				Male	Female	Combined Mean	Male	Female	Combined Mean	Male	Female	Combined Mean
1.	Teaching competence	1.77	1	1.79	2.15	1.90	1.83	1.60	1.72	1.54	1.57	1.55
2.	Setting personal standards of excellence.	2.12	2	2.10	3.00	2.39	1.77	2.00	1.87	1.90	2.42	2.10
3.	Research competence	2.61	3	2.53	2.36	2.47	2.58	2.80	2.67	3.00	2.71	2.88
4.	Academic achievements (Publications, Foreign assignments etc.)	3.90	4	3.89	3.68	3.82	3.93	4.24	4.06	3.81	3.57	3.71
5.	Popularity with students as a good academician	4.86	5	5.05	4.31	4.80	5.22	4.40	4.85	5.09	5.14	5.10
6.	Active participation in Teachers' association	6.18	6	6.25	5.94	6.14	6.35	6.24	6.30	6.00	6.00	6.00
7.	Raising income through various sources	7.14	7	7.12	7.31	7.24	6.90	7.28	7.06	7.00	7.28	7.10
8.	Active involvement in politics.	7.24	8	7.15	7.21	7.16	7.32	7.24	7.28	7.45	7.42	7.43

(Contd.)

(Contd. Table 3.9)

S.No.	Factors raising the status of Teachers	Overall mean Score Value	Rank	College Teachers					
				Government (Mean Score Value)			Private (Mean Score Value)		
				Male	Female	Combined Means	Male	Female	Combined Means
1.	Setting personal standards of Excellence	1.72	1	1.20	2.00	1.65	1.87	1.78	1.81
2.	Teaching competence	1.92	2	2.30	1.76	1.99	1.75	1.92	1.85
3.	Academic achievements (Publications, Foreign assignments etc.)	3.83	3	4.50	3.61	3.99	4.12	3.42	3.67
4.	Popularity with students as a good academician.	3.88	4	4.40	4.30	4.34	3.50	3.35	3.40
5.	Research competence	4.10	5	3.70	3.38	3.51	4.50	4.85	4.72
6.	Active participation in Teacher's association	6.05	6	5.90	6.00	5.95	6.12	6.21	6.17
7.	Active involvement in politics	7.01	7	6.90	7.00	6.95	6.62	7.35	7.08
8.	Raising Income through various sources	7.47	8	7.00	7.84	7.47	7.62	6.50	6.90

competence' (1.77) followed by 'setting personal standards of excellence' (2.12), 'research competence' (2.61), 'academic achievements' (3.90), 'popularity with students as a good academician' (4.86), 'active participation in teachers' association' (6.18), 'raising income through various sources' (7.14) and 'active involvement in politics' (7.24), in that order. The faculty-wise analysis suggests that social science and professional teachers have given the same rank order as outlined in the overall analysis. But in the case of science faculty, we observe teachers placing 'active involvement in politics' above 'raising income through various sources'. However, there are differences observed in the ranking of these factors sex-wise in between science and social science teachers.

In the case of science teachers, it is observed that female teachers have placed 'research competence' (2.36) above 'setting personal standards of excellence' (3.00) as a factor contributing towards raising their status in the society. Again, they have given higher rank position to 'active involvement in politics' (7.21) than 'raising income through various sources' (7.31). In the case of social science teachers, male teachers have given a higher rank to 'setting personal standards of excellence'(1.77) than 'teaching competence'(1.83) whereas female teachers have placed 'active involvement in politics'(7.24) above 'raising income through various sources'(7.28). By and large, teachers in the university have shown a rationalistic and individualistic orientation for raising their status in the society. Some of the other teachers especially females, are also for collective mobilization through teachers' associations and involvement in politics.

On the other hand, in the overall analysis, college teachers have given a different pattern of ranking of these factors for raising their status in the society than that given by the university teachers. They have assigned first rank to 'setting personal standards of excellence'(1.72). This is followed by 'teaching competence'(1.92), 'academic achievements'(3.83), 'popularity with students as a good academician' (3.88), 'research competence'(4.12), 'active participation in teachers' association'(6.05), 'active involvement in politics'(7.01), and 'raising income through various sources'(7.47), in that order. The college-wise analysis suggests that in the case of Government college, teachers have placed 'research competence'(3.51) above 'academic achievements'(3.99) However, in the case of Private college, the factor of 'raising income through various sources'(6.90) has been given a higher rank to 'active involvement in politics'(7.08). The sex-wise analysis of teachers in the Government college shows that male teachers have given a higher rank to 'research competence'(3.70) than 'popularity with students as a good academician' (4.40) and 'academic achievements' (4.50). On the other hand, female teachers have placed' teaching competence' (1.76) above 'setting personal standards of excellence' (2.00). They have also ranked 'research competence' (3.38) above 'academic achievements' and 'popularity with students as a good academician'. In the case of Private college, again, the 'teaching competence'(1.75) has been ranked above 'setting personal standards of excellence'(1.87) by the male teachers whereas female teachers have given a higher rank to 'raising income through various sources'(6.50) than 'active involvement in politics'(7.35). In view of less or practically no input of research in colleges, the factor of 'research competence' has been given a lower rank order than popularity with students.

There is a need to imbibe some of the values such as teaching competence, setting personal standards of excellence, research competence, academic achievements and popularity with students as a good academician by the university and college teachers as a part of their professional role socialization. The acquiring of some of these attributes by the teachers may equip them to have more specialized knowledge, work autonomy and service orientation. These may provide a full fledged professional status to the occupation of teaching in the long run.

4

Role Perception and Expectation of Teachers

An attempt has been made in this chapter to delineate the role perception and expectation of teachers in the university system. Before analysing these, a brief account is given on the role structure in general, and that of the role of a teacher in particular, in higher education.

Role is a central concept in the sociological analysis of the social system. Role theorists often try to understand the relationships between different spheres of social activity by analysing behavioural regularities resulting from certain specific social contexts such as families, organizations and communities. Their main assumption is that a large proportion of all behaviour is brought about through socialization within specific contexts. However, some part of behaviour is routine and is established through learning the traditional modes of adaptations and dealing with specific tasks. As such, the positions which persons occupy in organizations and the community account for much of their behaviour. Further, their argument is that knowledge of one's identity or social position is a good indicator of the expectations a person is likely to face in social situations. It is suggested that since behaviour is highly correlated with expectation, there is a strong possibility of its prediction. Role theorists have focused on the study of behaviour within organizations through useful role concepts in explaining recruitment, socialization, interaction, personality and the formal structures of organizations. In short, the concept of role provides an effective linkage between social structure, social process and social character (Mechanic, 1978).

Parsons and Shils define a social system as having collective goals, shared goals and as a single system of interaction with boundaries defined by incumbents in the roles. (Parsons and Shils,

1951). The involvement of plurality of actors in a social interaction for the accomplishment of desired goals, gets bounded by the expected role behaviour of the actors who are responsible for the continuity and stability of the system. In role analysis, the social behaviour is often influenced by certain rules of conduct guided by cultural values, norms, traditions and customs of the individuals involved in interaction.

Further, it is observed that the social behaviour is not only oriented to and influenced by normative order but it is also perceived by it. Besides, role reciprocity and role complementarity in social situations also affect social behaviour (Rushing, 1964).

According to role theory, social behaviour is not to be considered random and meaningless, rather it gets patterned and becomes predictable and consequential for the participants. However, this should not be taken as a static view of social behaviour. Instead, it should be viewed in a dynamic perspective which allows a considerable range of variability among individuals enacting the same role (Sarbin and Allen, 1968; Turner, 1962). The main thing to be analysed in role theory is how the 'socializee' learns the gestalt, that is, the organized whole. In other words, one has to analyse how the idea of a whole is incorporated into the individual and to know how an individual becomes capable of recognizing certain innovative behaviours as expressions of the role and to rule out others which are not expressions of the role (Joas, 1985). In this regard, Turner (1985) also points out that the role incumbent through his/her learning process can decide that some of the accepted standard features of the role, may not be really part of the role. In this way, the role-relationship between various actors in different settings and situations may help us in understanding the entire process of professionalization.

In short, we can say that the social behaviour of individuals is influenced to some extent by their own expectations, and those of others in the group and that of society in which they participate. In other words, individuals in social locations behave with reference to expectations (Gross et al, 1958). As such, if the concept of role has to be employed as an evaluative yardstick, then it must be understood in terms of perception, expectation and performance of incumbents holding different positions within the social system.

A university social system may also constitute a network of inter-personal relationships having a varying degree of complexity within a hierarchical order. The role differentiation processes of various actors may get structured within the prescribed norms to form some definite and distinctive patterns. The social interaction of teachers with the students and that with the university administrators and other colleagues may get structured into a network of inter-personal relationships within the university social system. However, it must be borne in mind that the social behaviour in various interacting situations in the university may also be influenced to a greater extent by many situational factors because the individuals remaining the same, their behaviour would appear different in different situations.

Dutta (1998) makes a reference to the National Commission of Teachers (1983-85) which clearly states that without under-playing the importance of economic factors, teachers through their professional excellence and character have to demonstrate that they deserve the trust placed in them. Further, it is observed that teachers cannot raise the status if they are negligent in their work and are not involved fully in their profession even when they are given an increase in their salary structure and other benefits. In fact, the teacher should be the one to introspect and scrutinise his or her own value system so as to raise it to the highest moral standard.

Rani (1998) points out that teachers ought to be vigilant and should make an effort to provide models of sobriety and "Cool observation and thinking" They have to develop professional idealism, morality, conscious standards of behaviour and spirit. In line with the changed socio-political conditions of the country and what the Education Commission (1964-65) suggested, she highlights the essential roles of teachers in our universities and colleges. These are:

i. To seek and cultivate new knowledge, to engage vigorously and fearlessly in the pursuit of truth and to interpret old knowledge and texts in the light of new needs and discoveries.

ii. To provide the right kind of leadership in all walks of life.

iii. To provide society with competent men and women trained in various fields and equipped with the capacity for independent thought.

iv. To strive to promote equality and social justice and to reduce social and cultural differences through diffusion of education.

v. To foster in the students and through them in society, the attitudes and values needed for developing good life in individuals and society.

The present chapter will be divided into two parts. In the first part, perceived roles and responsibilities of the teachers and the extent of satisfaction with the work will be analysed. In the second part, the role expectations as perceived by teachers from their supervisors and students will be examined along with perceived expectation of students and supervisors from them.

(1)
Role Perception

In an organization, there are roles attached to certain positions which become more or less standardized. Yet, there are variations observed in the way these roles are played and that some people may willingly or unwillingly deviate from the prescribed patterns of behaviour (Lindgren, 1974). This variation in adherence to the prescribed roles may also be influenced by the way these are perceived by the individuals. The perception of an individual may vary according to his or her personality structure, previous experiences and the sensory factors, that is, psychological occurrences in the nervous system of the individual due to stimulation. The perceived role may not always correspond exactly to the expected role. However, a person's knowledge of role expectation of others for him or her may facilitate interaction with them, even if his or her own conception of role does not coincide with theirs.

1. Perceived Roles and Responsibilities of Teachers

First, an attempt has been made to analyse the roles and responsibilities of teachers. A set of roles and responsibilities such as teaching, research, career making of students, conducting of examination, preparation of syllabi etc. was provided to the university and college teachers and they were asked to rate these, according to their perception, on a five-point scale of importance. The task rated as most important was assigned a score of 5 whereas the one rated as fairly important was given a score of 4. Further, a role which was rated as important was given a score of 3, the one rated as less important was given a score of 2 while the role rated as the least important was assigned a score of 1. A mean score value was worked out for all these tasks for male and female teachers in different stream of courses in the university as well as in the colleges. The mean score values were arranged in the descending order, the higher the mean value, the greater was the importance attached to the role by the teachers. An overall mean score value was also worked out for these roles in respect of the university and college teachers as well as a combined mean score for both male and female teachers in each of the faculties (science, social science, professional) in the university and the two colleges was also calculated.

An examination of Table 4.1, shows that among the university teachers, the most important role perceived is transmission of knowledge (teaching) (4.76). This is followed by building up of knowledge (research) (4.70), character building of students (4.23), career-making of students (3.79), preparation of syllabi and courses (3.78), guidance and counselling to students (3.77), extension of knowledge for the welfare of society beyond classroom (3.67), evaluation of answer books (3.50), participate actively in the development activities of the society (3.32), shaping socio-political outlook of students (3.20) and conducting of examination (3.18), in that order.

For analysis purposes, we can classify these roles of teachers as professional oriented (transmission of knowledge, building up of knowledge, character building of students, preparation of syllabi and courses and guidance and counselling to students); examination oriented (evaluation of answer books and conducting of examination) and societal oriented (extension of knowledge for the welfare of the society, participate actively in the development activities of the society and shaping socio-political outlook of the students). Although, examination oriented roles are also part of the professional role orientation, yet most of the teachers show disdain towards these and perform them reluctantly. For analysis purposes, these have been categorized separately.

The faculty-wise analysis among university teachers suggests that in the case of science teachers, the task of 'career-making of

Table 4.1

Relationship between the Sex of the Teachers and their perceived Roles and Responsibilites

S. No.	Perceived Roles and Responsibilities	Overall Mean Score Value	Rank	University Teachers								
				Science (Mean Score Value)			Social Science (Mean Score Value)			Professional (Mean Score Value)		
				Male	Female	Combined Mean	Male	Female	Combined Mean	Male	Female	Combined Mean
1.	Transmission of knowledge (Teaching)	4.76	1	4.58	4.94	4.70	4.80	4.80	4.80	4.81	4.85	4.82
2.	Building-up of knowledge (Research)	4.70	2	4.89	4.31	4.70	4.61	4.84	4.72	4.81	4.50	4.69
3.	Character building of students	4.23	3	4.23	4.47	4.30	3.83	4.44	4.10	4.36	4.57	4.44
4.	Career making of students	3.79	4	3.89	4.05	3.94	3.64	3.80	3.71	3.45	3.85	3.60
5.	Preparation of syllabi and courses	3.78	5	3.82	3.68	3.77	3.90	3.92	3.90	3.18	4.00	3.50
6.	Guidance and Counselling to students.	3.77	6	3.74	3.73	3.73	3.83	3.76	3.79	3.63	4.14	3.83
7.	Extension of knowledge for the welfare of society beyond classroom	3.67	7	3.58	3.36	3.50	3.58	4.20	3.85	3.81	3.42	3.66
8.	Evaluation of answer books.	3.50	8	3.43	3.42	3.42	3.22	4.12	3.62	3.27	3.57	3.38
9.	Participate actively in the development activities of society	3.32	9	3.17	3.21	3.18	3.25	3.75	3.47	2.81	3.85	3.21
10.	Shaping socio-political outlook of students	3.20	10	2.79	3.15	2.90	3.16	3.68	3.39	3.63	3.42	3.54
11.	Conducting of examination	3.18	11	3.20	3.36	3.25	3.00	3.08	3.04	3.27	3.71	3.44

(Contd.)

(Contd. Table 4.1)

S. No.	Perceived Roles and Responsibilities	Overall mean Score Value	Rank	College Teachers					
				Government (Mean Score Value)			Private (Mean Score Value)		
				Male	Female	Combined Means	Male	Female	Combined Means
1.	Transmission of the knowledge (Teaching)	4.78	1	5.00	4.84	4.92	4.75	4.57	4.63
2.	Character building of students	4.55	2	4.60	4.53	4.56	4.75	4.42	4.54
3.	Career making of students	4.11	3	4.30	4.07	4.17	4.12	4.00	4.04
4.	Guidance and counselling to students	4.08	4	4.40	3.84	4.08	4.25	4.00	4.09
5.	Building up of knowledge (Research)	4.08	4	3.70	4.46	4.13	4.25	3.92	4.04
6.	Extension of knowledge for the welfare of the society	3.97	6	4.20	4.23	4.21	3.75	3.71	3.72
7.	Shaping socio-political outlook of students	3.89	7	4.00	4.53	4.29	3.62	3.42	3.49
8.	Preparation of syllabi and courses	3.79	8	4.10	3.61	.3.82	3.62	3.85	3.76
9.	Participate actively in the development activities beyond classroom	3.48	9	4.20	3.76	3.95	3.12	2.92	2.99
10.	Evaluation of answer books	3.39	10	3.70	3.00	3.30	4.12	3.14	3.49
11.	Conducting of examination	3.32	11	3.60	3.07	3.30	3.62	3.21	3.35

students' (3.94) has been placed above 'preparation of syllabi and courses' (3.77). Even the 'conducting of examination' (3.25) has been placed above 'participate actively in the development activities of the society' (3.18) and next to 'evaluation of answer books' (3.42). The sex-wise analysis of science teachers shows some variations in their perception of roles. The male teachers have given more importance to research than teaching as it has a higher mean score value (4.89). Even they have placed 'conducting of examination' (3.20) above 'participate actively in the development activities of society' (3.17). On the other hand, female teachers in this group have given more importance to 'character building of students' than 'building up of knowledge' (research) while 'career making of students' has been given a higher importance to 'guidance and counselling to students'. They have also, like their male counterparts, given higher importance to 'conducting of examinations' than 'participate actively in development activities of society'. It appears the female teachers are less research oriented and are more for guidance and counselling to students than male teachers.

In the case of social science teachers, it is observed that they have perceived the professional oriented roles as more important than the examination and the societal oriented tasks. However, in the professional oriented roles, they seem to be giving more importance to 'preparation of syllabi and courses' than 'guidance and counselling to students' and 'career making of students'. But they seem to be also giving more importance to 'extension of knowledge for the welfare of society' as they place this task next to 'preparation of syllabi and courses' and above 'guidance and counselling to students'. This may be due to their exposure to social sciences. Further, the sex-wise analysis in this group shows that male teachers have placed 'preparation of syllabi and courses' above 'character building of students' and 'guidance and counselling to students'. They have also given higher importance to 'participate actively in the development activities of society' to 'evaluation of answer books'. In the case of female teachers, there are many variations observed. The 'extension of knowledge for the welfare of society beyond classroom,' and 'evaluation of answer books' have been rated higher than 'preparation of syllabi and courses' (3.92) which in turn has been rated higher than 'guidance and counselling to students' (3.76). A higher position assigned to 'extension of knowledge for the welfare of society' again may be due to their exposure to social sciences.

In the case of professional group, it is observed that they have given more importance to societal oriented roles such as, 'extension of knowledge for the welfare of society' and 'shaping socio-political outlook of students' than some of the professional and examination oriented tasks. The male teachers in this group have given a higher importance to 'extension of knowledge for the welfare of society' and 'shaping socio-political outlook of students' and 'guidance and counselling to students' than 'career making of students' Besides, 'evaluation of answer books' has been given a higher rating to 'preparation of syllabi and courses'. The female teachers in the professional group have given a higher rating to 'character building of students' than 'building up of knowledge' (research). Even, 'guidance and counselling to students' and 'preparation of syllabi and courses' have been given more importance to 'career-making of students' and 'participate actively in the development activities of the society'. The 'conducting of examination' has been placed higher than 'evaluation of answer books' whereas 'extension of knowledge for the welfare of society' and 'shaping socio-political outlook of students' have been assigned lower importance. The female teachers appear to be giving more importance to professional and examination oriented tasks than societal oriented tasks.

As compared to university teachers, college teachers have rated 'transmission of knowledge' (teaching) (4.78), 'character building of students (4.55) and 'career making of students' (4.11) as the three most important tasks. The 'guidance and counselling of students' and 'building up of knowledge (research) find an equal importance next to the above tasks. A lower importance has been given to 'preparation of syllabi and courses' and least to 'evaluation of answer books' and 'conducting of examination'. The societal oriented tasks have been given more importance than the examination and some professional oriented tasks.

In the case of the Government college, we find a higher importance given to 'shaping socio-political outlook of students' and 'extension of knowledge for the welfare of the society' than 'career making of students . Even, the task 'participate actively in the development activities' has been placed above 'preparation of syllabi and courses'. The sex-wise analysis of teachers in the Government college shows that male teachers have given more importance to 'guidance and counselling to students' than 'career making of students'. 'The extension of knowledge for the welfare of the society' and 'participate actively in the development activities' have been placed higher than 'preparation of syllabi and courses' and 'shaping socio-political outlook of students'. On the other hand, the female teachers are giving more importance to 'character building of students', 'shaping the socio-political outlook of students,' research component and 'extension of knowledge for the welfare of society' than 'career making of students'. 'To participate actively in the development activities' has been placed above 'preparation of syllabi and courses', while 'conducting of examination' is also rated higher than 'evaluation of answer books'.

In the case of the Private college, the task of 'guidance and counselling to students' is given more importance to 'career making of students' while 'preparation of syllabi and courses' has been placed above 'extension of knowledge for the welfare of the society'. Even, "evaluation of answer books' and 'conducting of examination' is placed higher than 'participate actively in the development activities'. Interestingly, the sex-wise analysis of teachers in the Private college shows that male teachers have rated, 'guidance and counselling to students' and 'building up of knowledge' higher than 'career making of students' and 'evaluation of answer books'. The 'conducting of examination' also finds a higher rating than 'participate actively in the development activities'. In the case of female teachers, they have given more importance to 'preparation of syllabi and courses' than 'extension of knowledge for the welfare of society' while 'evaluation of answer books' and 'conducting of examination' are rated higher than 'participate actively in the development activities'.

On the basis of sex-wise analysis of teachers in the university and colleges, we can suggest a relationship between the gender of the teachers and their perceived roles and responsibilities. This is in support of our hypothesis that gender of the teachers influences their perceived roles.

1 (a). Relationship between Status (Designation Held) of Teachers and their Perceived Roles and Responsibilities

An attempt was also made to relate the status (rank or designation held) of teachers with their perceived roles and responsibilities. As revealed in Table 4.2, on the basis of mean score values, in the overall analysis for the university teachers, the roles perceived in order of importance are 'transmission of knowledge' (teaching), 'building up of knowledge' (research), 'character building of students', 'guidance and counselling to students', 'career making of students', 'preparation of syllabi and courses', 'extension of knowledge for the welfare of society', 'participate actively in the development activities', 'evaluation of answer books', 'shaping socio-political outlook of students' and 'conducting of examination'.

The faculty-wise analysis reveals that among the science teachers, 'the career-making of students' and 'preparation of syllabi and courses' have been placed higher than 'guidance and counselling to students' while 'evaluation of answer books' has also been rated higher than 'participate actively in the development activities'. Even,'conducting of examination' has been given a higher rating than 'shaping socio-political outlook of students'. The status-wise analysis of teachers in this group shows that although Professors have rated professional oriented roles higher than other tasks, yet they seem to be giving more importance to examination oriented activities than societal oriented roles. However, Readers in this group apart from giving more importance to the professional oriented roles are also more for societal than examination oriented roles. But in the case of Lecturers, we observe that their pattern of rating is similar to that of Professors in the sense that they are also giving more importance to examination oriented tasks than societal roles.

In case of social science teachers, it is observed that they have also rated the professional roles higher in order of importance to societal and examination oriented tasks except that 'extension of knowledge for the welfare of society' has been placed slightly above 'preparation of syllabi and courses'. The status-wise analysis shows that Professors in this group have given higher importance to the professional oriented roles than others but the 'extension of knowledge for the welfare of society' has been given precedence

Table 4.2

Relationship between Status (Designation Held) of Teachers and their perceived Roles and Responsibilities

S. No.	Perceived Roles and Responsibilities	Overall Mean Score Value	Rank	University Teachers											
				Science (Mean Score Value)				Social Science (Mean Score Value)				Professional (Mean Score Value)			
				P	R	L	Combined Mean	P	R	L	Combined Mean	P	R	L	Combined Mean
1.	Transmission of knowledge (Teaching)	4.84	1	4.87	4.82	4.92	4.87	4.81	4.85	4.70	4.78	4.75	5.00	4.75	4.83
2.	Building up of knowledge (Research)	4.58	2	4.75	4.35	4.28	4.43	4.68	4.70	4.70	4.69	4.75	4.83	4.50	4.72
3.	Character building of students	4.20	3	4.00	4.64	4.28	4.30	3.87	3.90	4.25	4.01	4.50	4.50	4.25	4.44
4.	Guidance and Counselling to students.	3.81	4	3.50	4.11	3.72	3.75	3.81	4.00	3.90	3.90	3.75	3.66	4.00	3.78
5.	Career making of students	3.81	4	3.68	4.00	4.08	3.94	3.31	4.05	3.70	3.71	3.75	3.83	3.50	3.72
6.	Preparation of syllabi and courses	3.78	6	4.00	3.70	3.68	3.77	3.75	3.95	3.95	3.89	3.12	3.66	4.00	3.49
7.	Extension of knowledge for the welfare of society beyond classroom	3.70	7	3.00	4.00	3.56	3.53	3.62	3.80	4.25	3.90	3.76	4.00	3.00	3.67
8.	Participate actively in the development activities of society	3.33	8	3.00	3.41	3.36	3.27	3.06	3.55	3.65	3.44	2.87	3.66	3.25	3.21
9.	Evaluation of answer books.	3.30	9	3.56	3.11	3.60	3.44	2.62	3.25	3.40	3.12	3.12	3.66	3.50	3.38
10.	Shaping socio-political outlook of students	3.20	10	2.68	3.17	2.88	2.91	3.06	3.65	3.45	3..41	4.00	3.16	3.15	3.53
11.	Conducting of examination	3.15	11	3.25	3.00	3.36	3.22	2.68	3.05	3.15	2.98	3.25	3.50	3.75	3.44

Note : P = Professor, R = Reader, L = Lecturer

(Contd.)

(Contd. Table 4.2)

S. No.	Perceived Roles and Responsibilities	Overall Mean Score Value	Rank	College Teachers							
				Government (Mean Score Value)				Private (Mean Score Value)			
				Senior Lecturer	Lecturer	Guest Faculty	Combined mean	Senior Lecturer	Lecturer	Guest Faculty	Combined mean
1.	Transmission of knowledge (Teaching)	4.77	1	4.71	5.00	5.00	4.91	4.60	4.81	3.00	4.63
2.	Building up of knowledge (Research)	4.59	2	4.42	4.84	4.33	4.64	4.50	4.54	5.00	4.54
3.	Character building of students	4.12	3	4.00	4.23	4.66	4.21	4.30	3.90	3.00	4.04
4.	Guidance and Counselling to students.	4.10	4	4.28	3.92	4.66	4.12	4.20	4.18	2.00	4.09
5.	Career making of students	4.03	5	4.14	4.07	3.66	4.03	4.20	3.90	4.00	4.04
6.	Preparation of syllabi and courses	3.99	6	4.00	4.23	4.66	4.21	3.70	3.90	3.00	3.76
7.	Extension of knowledge for the welfare of society beyond classroom	3.83	7	4.00	3.92	3.66	3.91	4.00	3.63	3.00	3.76
8.	Participate actively in the development activities of society	3.68	8	3.57	4.07	3.66	3.86	3.80	3.36	2.00	3.50
9.	Evaluation of answer books.	3.47	9	3.42	4.15	4.00	3.90	3.00	3.09	3.00	3.04
10.	Shaping socio-political outlook of students	3.34	10	3.57	3.30	2.66	3.29	3.90	3.09	2.00	3.40
11.	Conducting of examination	3.33	11	3.57	3.23	3.00	3.30	3.80	3.09	2.00	3.36

over 'career making of students' while the examination oriented duties have been given least importance. This may be due to their exposure to social sciences that they are giving more importance to societal than examination oriented tasks. However, Readers in this group are giving more importance to 'career making of students' 'guidance and counselling to students' and 'preparation of syllabi and courses' than 'character building of students'. Even Lecturers in this group have a similar pattern of rating the various roles, except that they are giving a higher importance to the 'extension of knowledge for the welfare of the society' than 'preparation of syllabi and courses' 'guidance and counselling to students' and 'career making of students'. By and large, teachers in this group are inclined to give more importance to societal oriented roles than examination oriented tasks.

In the professional group, it is observed that, no doubt, teachers have given higher importance to professional oriented roles yet 'extension of knowledge for the welfare of the society' and 'shaping socio-political outlook of students' have been given precedence, over 'preparation of syllabi and courses' while 'conducting of examination' and 'evaluation of answer books' have been given more importance to 'participate actively in the development activities'. The status-wise analysis shows that the Professors' pattern of rating is similar to that given by this group in the combined form but Readers in this category are giving more importance to 'evaluation of answer books' and 'conducting of examination' than 'shaping socio-political outlook of students'. In the case of Lecturers, it is noted that they are giving more importance to examination oriented tasks than societal oriented activities, of course their first preference is for professional oriented roles. The above analysis for university teachers suggests that their status influences their perceived roles and responsibilities to a large extent.

In the case of college teachers, the perceived roles in order of importance are 'transmission of knowledge (teaching), 'character building of students, 'career making of students,' 'building up of knowledge' (research),' guidance and counselling to students,' 'extension of knowledge for the welfare of society,' 'preparation of syllabi and courses,' 'shaping socio-political outlook of students,' 'participate actively in the development activities,' 'evaluation of answer books' and 'conducting of examination'.

In the case of Government college, it was observed that 'extension of knowledge for the welfare of society' (4.21) was placed higher than 'building up of knowledge' (research) (4.12). Even 'preparation of syllabi and courses', (3.91) was given a lower rating. This is understandable as teachers in the college hardly do any research and are not involved in the preparation of syllabi and courses. However, the status-wise analysis in this college shows that Senior Lecturers are assigning a higher rating to research and 'guidance and counselling to students' than 'career making of students'. They seem to be giving least importance to 'participate actively in the development activities of the society' (3.42). Interestingly, Lecturers in this college have given a higher rating to societal oriented roles than some of the professional oriented tasks such as 'guidance and counselling to students', 'research' and 'preparation of syllabi and courses'. The Guest Faculty is emphasizing equally on research, career making of students and extension of knowledge for the welfare of society. 'To participate actively in the development activities' has been placed higher than 'guidance and counselling to students,' 'preparation of syllabi and courses' and 'shaping socio-political outlook of students' while examination oriented tasks have been given least importance. He or she seems to show more inconsistency in his or her rating pattern than the other categories of teachers. This may be due to his or her less exposure to this profession.

In the case of the Private college, it is interesting to observe that teachers seem to be giving importance to research task (4.09) after character building of students (4.54). They have also given a higher rating to 'preparation of syllabi and other courses' alongwith 'extension of knowledge for the welfare of society' above 'shaping socio-political outlook of students'. Even, 'evaluation of answer books' and 'conducting of examination' have been given a higher rating than 'participate actively in the development activities.' The Senior Lecturers in this college are also giving more importance to research than preparation of syllabi and courses. The above two tasks find a higher placing than 'evaluation of answer books,' 'conducting of examination' and 'shaping socio-political outlook of students'. To them, the least important is 'extension of knowledge for the welfare of society'. Lecturers in this college are rating research component of their role (4.18) next to character building of students whereas the examination oriented tasks have been given the least importance. The Guest Faculty, is giving more importance to 'character building of students' and 'guidance and counselling to students' than even 'teaching' whereas 'preparation of syllabi and courses' has been rated higher than research component. This may be because he or she being new to the profession is concerned about guidance and counselling to students along with their character building. The status-wise analysis of teachers in the university as well as in the colleges shows that status or designation held by them influences their perceived roles and responsibilities. This clearly lends support to our hypothesis.

2. Perception of jobs that Teachers do not enjoy as part of their Duties

The teachers in the university as well as in the colleges were asked to specify the jobs that they perceived as not enjoyable. Nearly one-fourth of the teachers in the university as well as in the colleges do not enjoy some kinds of jobs as a part of their duties. Among the university teachers, a higher number of male (25) than female (7) teachers in science, social science and professional courses do not enjoy certain jobs. However, in the case of college teachers there are differences observed between the Government and the Private college. While in the Government college there is a higher number of males (4) than females (3) who do not enjoy some specific jobs, in the case of the Private college it is vice-versa [more number of female teachers (4) than male teachers (1)]. A higher proportion of male than female teachers showing dislike for certain jobs may be due to their inclination to do more professional work than routine activities. All those teachers who did not enjoy certain jobs were asked to specify the same. In view of small number of responses, these have been grouped together and are being given below separately for the university and college teachers.

1. University Teachers

a. Males—Many of them (7) have shown disdain for the administrative work. Quite a few of them (6) did not like the examination duties as well as the evaluation of answer books of students. There is resentment shown by some (5) towards decisions taken in various departmental committees where no one takes responsibility for one's acts and omissions. Besides, they do not like attending too many useless meetings where members have not done their home work. They also do not like participation in Board of Studies meetings where decisions are taken only by the Chairperson and the Senior Faculty members. A few of them (2) also do not like to attend to election duties. Besides, they feel that there is lack of freedom and flexibility in this profession (2). In addition to the above, a few of them do not like taking roll-calls of students, taking classes having thin attendance of students, participating in rural development activities and facing audit objection on bills of research projects.

b. Females—Some of the female teachers are not comfortable with the evaluation of answer books, examination duties, administrative work related to submission of applications for funding of projects.

2. College Teachers

a. Males—Some of the teachers are not happy doing jobs related to co-ordination of financial affairs, disciplinary duties, election duties, examination duties and marking as well as calculating the attendance of students.

b Females—A few of the female teachers do not like the evaluation of answer books of students, besides examination duties. Further, they do not enjoy paper-work like making bills, preparing students for extra-curricular activities, disciplinary duties and teaching out-dated syllabi.

On the basis of observations made by teachers, both in the university and colleges, one can find out diffuseness in their roles. This may bring in some element of role ambiguity and result into intra-role conflict among teachers to a certain extent. This can be resolved only if the teachers change their initial belief and accept these non-professional activities as a part of their duties. It is also observed that individuals occupying various positions may learn appropriate role behaviours through imitation, by responding to the expectation of others. (Lindgren, 1974). In the learning process, there may be inadequate internalization of certain roles and they may rule out certain activities as not a part of their professional orientation as highlighted by Turner (1985).

3. Relationship between the Sex of the Teachers and their Extent of Satisfaction with the Job

The extent of satisfaction with one's job is an important indicator of one's integration within an organization. It is observed that a low level of satisfaction with the job may bring in some element of role conflict. The teachers in the university as well as the colleges were asked to specify their job in terms of most satisfied/fairly satisfied/satisfied/less satisfied and least satisfied. A score of 5 was assigned to those who responded to most satisfied while a score of 1 to least satisfied. A mean score value was worked out, sex-wise within science, social sciences and professional courses in the university and in the two colleges. An overall mean score was also worked out for the university and college teachers.

A cursory look at Table 4.3 shows that on the basis of combined mean score values, the university teachers (4.29) have a better extent of satisfaction than the college teachers (4.17). Among the university teachers, the highest satisfaction with the job is shown by teachers in the social sciences group (4.53) followed by professional teachers (4.21) while science teachers exhibit a lower level of satisfaction with the job (4.10). On the other hand, teachers belonging to the Private college have a higher level of satisfaction with the job (4.31) than those in the Government college (4.04).

An attempt has also been made to relate the level of satisfaction of teachers with their gender status. It is clear from the table that in the university, female teachers have a higher level of satisfaction (4.35) than males (4.26). However, it is vice-versa in the case of college teachers. It is interesting to observe that in the university, among the science teachers, male teachers have a lower satisfaction level (3.95) with the job than females (4.42). But in the case of social science and professional groups, male teachers have a higher level of satisfaction than the females. It may be that male teachers in the science group may have higher expectations and aspirations from the profession than those in social sciences and professional groups. On the other hand, in case of college teachers, we observe that male teachers in both the colleges especially those in the Private college have a high level of satisfaction with the job than females.

Table 4.3
Relationship between the Sex of the Teachers and the extent of their satisfaction with the Job

S. No.	Sex of the Teachers	University Teachers: Extent of Satisfaction (Mean Score Value)			University Teachers: Combined Mean Score Value	College Teachers: Extent of Satisfaction (Mean Score Value)		College Teachers: Combined Mean Score Value
		Science	Social Science	Profes-sional		Gover-nment	Pri-vate	
1.	Male	3.95	4.67	4.27	4.26	4.10	4.75	4.38
2.	Female	4.42	4.36	4.14	4.35	4.00	4.07	4.03
Overall Mean Score Value		4.10	4.53	4.21	4.29	4.04	4.31	4.17

If we examine the mean score values in all categories, it is clearly indicated that the majority of teachers both in the university and colleges are fully satisfied with their jobs. Except for male teachers in the science group, the mean score values fall in between 'most satisfied' and 'fairly satisfied' responses. Even in the case of male teachers in the science group, the mean score value comes close to 'fairly satisfied' response. It may be inferred from the above analysis that teachers in the university and colleges are well-adjusted to their positions and this may be also an indicator of their having least role-conflict with in their respective organizations.

(2)
Role Expectation

Role has been defined as a complementary set of expectations and the actions to be performed in accordance with these expectations. It further involves right to certain type of reactions which the actor is entitled to expect from others and the obligations to perform certain types of action which the actor believes others are entitled to expect from him (Parsons and Shils, 1951). Kahn et al (1964) conceived roles in organisations as occurring in interlocking, inter-related networks or "role sets". It is observed that individuals while performing certain roles respond to the expectations of others involved in their role-set as well as to their own expectations.

Role expectations do have certain limits of range of the tolerated behaviours. A person who is assigned a role in a position, is expected to behave, exercise rights and privileges and fulfill duties and obligations within these limits. Sometimes, it is observed that the expectation of different members of his or her role set within an organization may be such that compliance with one would make compliance with the other difficult. In addition, role expectations held by specific 'others' for a certain position may be uncertain, vague or indefinite. In case, these are unclear and ambiguous, the behaviour of the actors will not be easily predictable and as such it may result in ineffective and dissatisfying relationships. In certain cases, the personal preferences, abilities and personality characteristics of the actors may be quite incompatible with the role expectations. Moreover, the persons in certain situations may find that they cannot complete all the tasks required of them within the stipulated time-period. It is, therefore, suggested that no role demand as such is a spontaneous pleasure that conformity with it is always automatic (Goode, 1960).

It is observed that every social system has certain functional problems which need to be solved if the system has to maintain itself. Actors involved in interaction within the social system are generally required to enact or perform two types of roles. One type of role is directed towards goal attainment of the system while the other focuses on the maintenance of the system or perpetuation of the order. These have been referred to as 'instrumental' and 'expressive' roles respectively. Both these roles have an equal contribution for the functioning of any social system and they hold good even for the university social system.

An attempt will be made in this section to analyse the role expectations of the Chairpersons/Principals and that of students in the university and colleges as perceived by teachers. Besides, role expectations from teachers as perceived by the Chairpersons of university departments/Principals of colleges and by the students in both the settings will be examined.

1. Relationship between Sex of the Teachers and the Expectations of Chairpersons/Principals of the University Departments/Colleges as Perceived by Teachers

A set of roles such as taking classes regularly, conforming to the rules, behaving properly in the meetings, having cordial relationship with the colleagues was provided to the university and the college teachers and they were asked to rate these on a scale of importance. A role that was perceived as most important by the teachers was given a score of 5 while that perceived as least important was assigned a score of 1. The roles perceived as 'fairly important', 'important' and 'less important' were given a score of 4, 3, 2 respectively. A mean score value was worked out for each of these roles separately for male and female teachers in each of the three faculties in the university as well as in the two colleges. A combined mean score value was also worked out for science, social science and professional teachers as well as for the two colleges. An overall mean score value for these roles in the university and colleges provided a rank order for role preferences. The higher the mean score value, the greater was the rank assigned to a given role.

An examination of Table 4.4 reveals, that in the university, the Chairpersons of the departments expect teachers to take classes regularly (4.84), conform to the rules (4.31), behave properly in the meetings (4.08), obey the order and carry out the task assigned (3.93), to have cordial relationship with colleagues (3.91), not to involve students in factional politics (3.84) and participate in discussion during meetings (3.75) in the above order of their importance. Of these roles, 'behave properly in the meeting,' 'cordial relationship with colleagues' and 'not to involve students in factional politics' may be classified as 'expressive' roles while others may be considered as instrumental roles for analysis purposes.

In the case of science teachers, it is observed that they have placed' cordial relationship with colleagues' and 'participation in discussion during meetings' above 'not to involve students in factional politics'. The genderwise analysis of teachers in this group shows that male teachers have assigned a higher rank to 'cordial relationships with colleagues' (4.00) than 'obey the order and carry out the task assigned' (3.94). Even, 'participation in discussion during meetings' (3.74) has been placed higher than 'not to involve students in factional politics' (3.66). On the other hand, the female teachers in this group have given the same preferences to these roles as observed in the overall analysis of teachers.

Table 4.4
Relationship between the Sex of the Teachers and Perceived Expectations of the Chairpersons/ Principals of the Departments/Colleges

S. No.	Expectations of Chairpersons as perceived by Teachers	Overall Mean Score Value	Rank	University Teachers								
				Science (Mean Score Value)			Social Science (Mean Score Value)			Professional (Mean Score Value)		
				Male	Female	Combined Mean	Male	Female	Combined Mean	Male	Female	Combined Mean
1.	Take Classes regularly	4.84	1	4.84	4.84	4.84	4.80	4.80	4.80	5.00	5.00	5.00
2.	Conform to the rules	4.31	2	4.17	4.42	4.25	4.35	4.32	4.33	4.54	4.42	4.49
3.	Behave properly in the meetings	4.08	3	4.07	4.21	4.11	4.06	3.92	3.99	4.27	4.28	4.27
4.	Obey the order and carry out task assigned	3.93	4	3.94	4.21	4.02	3.87	3.84	3.85	3.72	4.28	3.93
5.	Cordial relationship with colleagues	3.91	5	4.00	3.78	3.92	3.80	4.08	3.92	4.09	3.57	3.88
6.	Not to involve students in factional politics	3.84	6	3.66	3.73	3.68	3.87	3.80	3.83	4.63	4.14	4.43
7.	Participation in discussion during meetings	3.75	7	3.74	3.73	3.73	3.54	3.92	3.70	4.27	3.57	3.99

(Contd.)

(Contd. Table 4.4)

S.No.	Expectations of Principals as perceived by Teachers	Overall mean Score Value	Rank	College Teachers					
				Government (Mean Score Value)			Private (Mean Score Value)		
				Male	Female	Combined Mean	Male	Female	Combined Mean
1.	Take Classes regularly	4.68	1	5.00	4.69	4.82	4.37	4.64	4.54
2.	Conform to the rules	4.28	2	4.20	4.61	4.43	3.75	4.35	4.13
3.	Obey the order and carry out task assigned	4.25	3	4.40	4.30	4.34	4.12	4.21	4.17
4.	Behave properly in the meetings	4.08	4	4.30	4.00	4.13	4.25	3.92	4.04
5.	Not to involve students in factional politics	3.73	5	4.10	3.84	3.95	3.50	3.50	3.50
6.	Cordial relationship with colleagues	3.68	6	3.40	3.69	3.56	4.00	3.71	3.81
7.	Participation in discussion during meetings	3.48	7	3.40	3.38	3.39	3.75	3.50	3.59

In the case of social science teachers, it is observed that 'cordial relationships with colleagues' has been rated higher than 'obey the order and carry out the task assigned'. The sex-wise analysis of teachers in this group shows that male teachers have provided the same rating pattern as observed in the overall analysis while female teachers have placed 'cordial relationships with colleagues' (4.08) higher than 'behave properly in the meetings' (3.92) and 'participation in discussion during meetings' (3.92) along with it.

In the professional group, it is observed that teachers have given a higher rating to 'not to involve students in factional politics' (4.43) than 'behave properly in the meetings' (4.27), while 'participation in discussion during meetings 'has been placed below it (3.99). The sex-wise analysis of teachers in this group shows that male teachers have placed 'not to involve students in factional politics' (4.63) above 'conform to the rules' (4.54), while 'participation in discussion during meetings' has been bracketed along with 'behave properly in the meetings and 'cordial relationships with colleagues' has been placed below them. However, in the case of female teachers, they have assigned a higher rating to 'not to involve students in factional politics' (4.14) than 'cordial relationships with colleagues' (3.57).

The above analysis suggests that in the case of science and social science teachers, the expressive role of 'cordial relationship with colleagues' and instrumental role of 'participation in discussion during meetings' have been given more importance while teachers in the professional group have over-emphasized 'not to involve students in factional politics'. There are male and female differences observed in regard to role preferences expected of teachers from their supervisors.

In the case of colleges teachers, it is observed that the most important roles expected of them by their respective Principals are 'take classes regularly', 'conform to the rules,' 'obey the order and carry out the task assigned,' 'behave properly in the meetings,' 'not to involve students in factional politics,' 'cordial relationship with colleagues' and 'participation in discussion during meetings, in that order. The teachers in the Government college have also rated these roles in the same order as expected by their Principals. The sex-wise analysis of teachers in this college brings out that male teachers have given more importance to 'obey the order and carry out the task assigned' (4.40) and 'behave properly in the meetings' (4.30) than 'conform to the rules.' (4.20). However, female teachers are in agreement with the overall rating pattern.

In respect of the Private college teachers, they seem to be giving more importance to 'obey the order and carry out the task assigned' than 'conform to the rules'. Moreover, they have placed 'cordial relationship with colleagues' and 'participation in discussion during meetings' above 'not to involve students in factional politics'. A gender-wise analysis in this college shows that male teachers have given more importance to 'behave properly in the meetings' (4.25) than 'obey the order and carry out the task assigned' (4.12). Even 'cordial relationships with colleagues' (4.00) has been placed above 'conform to the rules' (3.75) while 'participation in discussion during meetings' (3.75) has been bracketed along with it. In the case of female teachers, they have rated 'cordial relationships with colleagues' (3.71) higher than 'not to involve students in factional politics' (3.50).

It is clear from the above analysis that in respect of both the university and college teachers, the instrumental and expressive roles have been emphasized equally except 'participation in discussion during meetings' which in the perception of teachers is the least preferred role expected by their supervisors. This may be due to the fact that teachers are not encouraged to participate in discussions during the meetings and they are expected to act according to the instructions given by their supervisors. The sex-wise analysis do suggests that the gender-status of teachers is related to the role expected of them by their supervisors. This again supports our hypothesis.

2. Relationship between Status (Designation Held) of Teachers and Expectations of Chairpersons of the University Departments/ Principals of the Colleges as Perceived by Teachers

An attempt was made to show relationship between the status or designation of teachers and expectations of their supervisors in the university and colleges. An examination of Table 4.5 reveals that on the basis of the overall mean score values, the teachers in the university perceive that the Chairpersons of their respective departments, expect them to take classes regularly, conform to the rules, behave properly in the meetings, obey the order and carry out the task assigned, have cordial relationship with colleagues, not to involve students in factional politics and have participation in discussions during meetings. The procedure for working out the mean score values is the same as explained earlier in connection with Table 4.4.

In the case of science teachers in the university, the rank order of various roles as expected of them by their supervisors is same as mentioned in the overall analysis. However, the status-wise analysis shows that Professors are assigning 'cordial relationship with colleagues' a second rank (4.18) next to 'take classes regularly' (4.93) Even, Readers in this group have given a higher rating to 'cordial relationship with colleagues'(3.88) and 'participation in discussion during meetings'(3.88) than 'obey the order and carry out the task assigned'(3.64). However, Lecturers in this group have given second position to 'obey the order and carry out the task assigned' next to 'take classes regularly'. Even, 'not to involve students in factional politics' has been rated higher than 'cordial relationship with colleagues'. This may be due to the fact that they being younger in age group, are expected by their supervisors to follow the orders and not to involve students in factional politics. However, senior teachers have perceived that their supervisors expect them to have more of cordial relationship with their colleagues and participation in discussions during the meetings.

In the case of social science teachers, it is observed that in their perception, their supervisors expect them to have more of cordial relationships with the colleagues than obey the order and carry out the task assigned. The status-wise analysis shows that in this group, Professors have given a higher rating to 'not to involve students in factional politics' (4.00) than 'obey the order and carry out the tasks assigned' (3.87). However, Readers in this group have given more importance to 'cordial relationships with colleagues' (4.25) next to 'take classes regularly' (4.85). Even 'not to involve students in factional politics' (3.95) has been placed higher than 'behave properly in the meetings' (3.90). The Lecturers in this group are placing 'participation in discussion during meetings' (3.85) higher than 'not to involve students in factional politics' (3.60). Senior teachers such as Professors and Readers, are

Table 4.5

Relationship between Status (Designation Held) of Teachers and their perceived Expectations of the Chairpersons/Principals of the Departments/Colleges.

S. No.	Expectations of Chairpersons as Perceived By Teachers	Overall Mean Score Value	Rank	University Teachers											
				Science (Mean Score Value)				Social Science (Mean Score Value)				Professional (Mean Score Value)			
				P	*R*	*L*	*Combined Mean*	*P*	*R*	*L*	*Combined Mean*	*P*	*R*	*L*	*Combined Mean*
1.	Takes Classes regularly	4.84	1	4.93	4.64	4.92	4.84	4.56	4.85	4.95	4.80	5.00	5.00	5.00	5.00
2.	Conform to the rules	4.31	2	4.12	4.17	4.40	4.25	4.25	4.20	4.55	4.33	4.62	4.16	4.75	4.49
3.	Behave properly in the meetings	4.08	3	4.12	3.88	4.28	4.11	4.06	3.90	4.05	4.00	4.25	4.00	4.75	4.27
4.	Obey the order and carry out the task assigned	3.98	4	3.87	3.64	4.48	4.06	3.87	3.80	3.90	3.85	4.12	4.16	4.25	4.16
5.	Cordial relationship with colleagues	3.93	5	4.18	3.88	3.84	3.94	3.62	4.25	3.90	3.94	4.25	3.50	3.75	3.88
6.	Not to involve students in factional politics	3.83	6	3.75	3.23	3.96	3.68	4.00	3.95	3.60	3.83	4.37	4.50	4.25	4.38
7.	Participation in discussion during meetings	3.81	7	3.62	3.88	3.68	3.72	3.62	3.70	3.85	3.73	4.62	4.66	3.50	4.38

(Contd.)

Note : P = Professor, R = Reader, L = Lecturer

(Contd. Table 4.5)

S. No.	Expectation of Principals as perceived by Teachers	Overall Mean Score Value	Rank	College Teachers							
				Government (Mean Score Value)				Private (Mean Score Value)			
				Senior Lecturer	Lecturer	Guest Faculty	Combined means	Senior Lecturer	Lecturer	Guest Faculty	Combined means
1.	Take Classes regularly	4.68	1	4.57	4.92	5.00	4.82	4.70	4.45	4.00	4.54
2.	Conform to the rules	4.28	2	4.00	4.69	4.33	4.43	4.00	4.27	4.00	4.13
3.	Obey the order and carry out the task assigned	4.15	3	4.57	3.76	4.66	4.12	4.20	4.09	5.00	4.18
4.	Behave properly in the meetings	4.08	4	4.14	4.15	4.00	4.12	4.00	4.09	4.00	4.04
5.	Not to involve students in factional politics	3.74	5	3.71	4.07	4.00	3.95	3.60	3.63	2.00	3.54
6.	Cordial relationship with colleagues	3.65	6	2.71	3.69	4.66	3.51	3.70	4.00	3.00	3.81
7.	Participation in discussion during meetings	3.50	7	2.71	3.61	4.33	3.43	3.60	3.63	3.00	3.58

emphasizing more on expressive roles than on instrumental roles. This may be due to their exposure to social sciences for a longer duration.

In the case of professional group, the teachers are giving a higher rating to 'not to involve students in factional politics' and 'participation in discussion during meetings' than 'behave properly in the meetings'. The status-wise analysis further shows that Professors have given a higher rank to 'participation in discussion during meeting' (4.62) along with 'conform to the rules' (4.62), and 'not to involve students in factional politics' (4.37) than 'behave properly in the meeting' (4.25) and 'cordial relationship with the colleagues' (4.25). Even, Readers in this group have given a second rank to 'participation in discussion during meetings' (4.66) and the third position to 'not to involve students in factional politics' (4.50). Besides, they have rated 'obey the order and carry out the tasks assigned' (4.16) along with 'conform to the rules' (4.16) above 'behave properly in the meetings' (4.00). Again, Lecturers have given a higher rank to 'not to involve students in factional politics' (4.25) than 'cordial relationship with the colleagues' (3.75). It is probable that students in the law department are more politicized than those in other departments and the supervisors expect the teachers to discourage their involvement in factional politics.

In the case of college teachers, the perceived roles expected of them by their supervisors in order of importance are to 'take classes regularly,' 'conform to the rules' 'obey the order and carry out the task assigned,' 'behave properly in the meetings', 'not to involve students in factional politics' 'cordial relationship with colleagues' and 'participation in discussion during meetings'. For teachers in the Government college, it is observed that they have rated the various roles in the same order as mentioned in the overall analysis. However, in the case of Senior Lecturers, they have placed 'obey the order and carryout the task assigned' (4.57) and 'behave properly in the meetings (4.14) higher than 'conform to the rules' (4.00). In regard to Lecturers, it is observed that 'behave properly in the meetings' (4.15) and 'not to involve students in factional politics' (4.07) have been placed higher than 'obey the order and carry out the task assigned' (3.76). However, the Guest Faculty is giving a higher rank to 'cordial relationship with colleagues' (4.66) along with 'obey the order and carry out the task assigned'

(4.66) than 'participation in discussion during meetings' (4.33) and 'conform to the rules' (4.33). On the other hand, in the case of Private college, the role 'obey the order and carry out the task assigned' has been given a second position and placed above 'conform to the rules' while 'participation in discussion during meetings' has been given a higher rating than 'not to involve students in factional politics.'

The status-wise analysis of teachers in this college shows that Senior Lecturers have given 'obey the order and carry out the task assigned' (4.20) more importance than 'conform to the rules' (4.00) while 'cordial relationship with colleagues' (3.70) has been placed higher than 'not to involve students in factional politics' (3.60). Again, in the case of Leoturers, 'cordial relationship with colleagues' (4.00) has been rated higher than 'not to involve students in factional politics' (3.63). The Guest Faculty has given the highest rank to 'obey the order and carry out the task assigned' (4.00) while he or shehas placed 'cordial relationship with colleagues' and 'participation in discussion during meetings' (3.00) higher than 'not to involve students in factional politics' (2.00). It appears from the above analysis that the teachers in the Government college as compared to those in the Private college, are emphasizing more on expressive than instrumental roles.

The status-wise analysis of teachers in the university as well as in the colleges clearly brings out that there are varied responses to various roles expected of them by their supervisors. In other words, there are effects of status observed on the role expectation of teachers. This, too, reinforces our hypothesis.

3. Expectations of Supervisors (Chairpersons of the University Departments/Principals of Colleges) From the Teachers

In order to understand the role analysis of teachers, the administrative heads in the selected university departments and colleges were interviewed to analyse the various aspects related to expectation, performance and effectiveness of teachers. An attempt has been made to build up caselets of these persons with the help of guideline questions. As mentioned earlier, under the methods of data collection, two Chairpersons in the science and one in the social science department did not grant interviews. On the basis of qualitative data provided by the respondents, seven caselets in respect of university Chairpersons and two for the college Principals are presented to ascertain their views on the management of their departments and colleges respectively.

Case-I

The Chairperson of a department in the Faculty of Science is 55 years old and holds a doctorate degree in science. He started his teaching career in 1977 and has been serving this university since then. He is satisfied with the present organizational setup of his department and approves of the willingness of his colleagues to help each other whenever required in the interest of the students. He does not find any difficulty in exchanging views and information about professional matters with members of his department as well as with the teachers and students of other departments who come to study subsidiary subjects in his department. By and large, he is satisfied with the functioning of his department. However, he feels that there are always some difficulties confronted by him.

His major expectation from a teacher is that he or she should be in the department at least for the time prescribed by the University Grants Commission. Further, he or she should not miss any class and take it on regular basis. In regard to performance of teachers matching with his expectations, he considers the same for some teachers but not for all. In certain cases, the main factor of dissatisfaction is that they do not take the classes regularly and stay on in the department for the prescribed time. He is not sure about the status of teacher in the society and expects that there should be free and frank relationship between the teachers and the students. His major source of annoyance towards the teachers is their absenteeism. In ordinary circumstances, he manages it through verbal communication while in extreme cases, it is taken care of through the issue of a letter to the concerned teacher. In his opinion, students rarely share their problems with him. However, he has no difficulty in communicating either with his colleagues or with the students. The major problem faced by him in managing the department is that both the teachers and students are not very regular in attending their classes. He suggests that in order to make the role of teacher effective, a time schedule like in other offices should also be provided for the university and college teachers and they should be expected to adhere to the time-schedule (working hours). In order that this time-schedule is strictly followed, there should be someone to supervise it.

Case-2

The Chairperson of this department in the Faculty of Science is 59 years old and holds a doctorate degree in science. He started his career as a teacher in 1972 and since then he is serving in this department. He is of the opinion that at least well-established departments in the university should be provided autonomous status in regard to their functioning. He is satisfied with the co-operation of his colleagues in order to serve the needs of the students. He does not find any difficulty in exchanging views and information about professional matters with his colleagues in his department as well as with those in other departments. In his opinion his department is functioning very well.

He expects that teachers should pursue research so as to match the highest international levels. Besides, teaching should be of high standards with a focus on communicating updated knowledge to the students. He is of the opinion that, by and large, the performance of teachers is matching with his expectations. He is not very positive about the status of teachers in the society. However, he feels that the teachers and students do have a very cordial relationship. He reports no reasons which cause annoyance in him towards the teachers. He, however, feels that students share their problems with him especially related to academic, research, career-making, personal and social matters. He hardly finds any difficulty in communicating with his colleagues and students. In regard to problems faced in managing the department, he shows concern both with the financial and the administrative difficulties. There is a need to make funds available for undertaking research. Further, for teaching and research activities, decisions must be taken quickly and positively. In order to make the role of teacher effective, a teacher should be a member of all decision making bodies at National level (UGC, CSIR, ICMR, Department of Science and Technology, All India Council of Technical Education etc) The science and technology teachers should look after their disciplines while the basic science teachers should confine themselves to their own areas of study. Further, he opined that a teacher should not be involved in trade unions and politics should not have any place in universities and colleges. Instead, a teacher must be committed to education and research only. The government must award the highly qualified and committed teachers in the universities and colleges. A suggestion has also been made to get the lectures delivered on contract basis and a minimum of 75 per cent attendance should be laid down both for the teachers and the students to create work culture.

Case-3

The Chairperson of a department in the faculty of Arts is 48 years old and holds a doctorate degree. He started his career as a teacher in 1977 and is continuing with the department since then. He is satisfied with the present organizational setup of the department as well as with the willingness of his colleagues to assist each other in the interest of the students. He does not find any problem in exchanging views and information about professional matters with members of his department as well as with that of other departments. In his opinion, his department is functioning extremely well.

His main expectations from the teachers are that they should be regular in taking classes, should be active researchers and should spend a substantial period of time in the department. He feels that the performance of teachers, more or less, matches with his expectations but he is not happy with the fact that some teachers do not spend enough time in the department. As regards status of teachers in the society, he observes that it should be better than what it is at present but to acquire that, the teachers must contribute more towards the society. The relationship between the teachers and the students in the present educational setup is quite unsatisfactory as most of the students are not sincerely interested in studies. His major causes of annoyance towards the teachers are carelessness, irresponsibility, absenteeism and intellectual dishonesty in some cases. He prefers to talk to teachers on one to one basis, for taking care of these problems. He feels that students do share their problems with him but they do so more essentially on problems related to academic or administrative matters. He does not find any difficulty in communicating with either his colleagues or with the students. As such, he does not feel any difficulty in managing the department but he advocates more number of seminars to be organized for the academic growth. In order to make the role of teachers effective, he suggests a system of punishment and reward to be evolved. He is also in favour of having an assessment made by students on the performance of teachers. He expects that students should be regular in attending classes and they should be required to attend a minimum of 60 to 70 per cent of the classes.

Case-4

The Chairperson of a department in the faculty of Arts is 55 years old, and holds a doctorate degree. He started his career in 1973 and is continuing in the same department since then. He is satisfied with the present organizational structure of the department. Further, he points out that, more or less, he is satisfied with the willingness of his colleagues to help each other in the interests of the students. But the main problem is lack of personal rapport among the teachers. He does not have any problem in exchanging views and information about professional matters with members of his department as well as that of others. In his opinion, the teachers are not very enthusiastic in contributing fully to the functioning of the department. However, by and large, the students are satisfied.

He expects that a teacher should show excellence in teaching and research. Besides, he should participate in academic development of the department as well as in the day to day administration of the department. He should also help the students and promote good research. He expresses that, more or less, his expectations match with the performance of the teachers. The main short comings observed are lack of interest or seriousness on the part of teachers and lack of high commitment among them.

According to him, the status of teacher in the society is not very high. In fact, it is deteriorating despite a raise in the salaries. The facilities at the work place are not adequate for academic growth. As regards relationship between the teacher and the students, he is of the opinion that these have become very formal, only confined to that of teacher/taught aspects whereas non-academic relationship between the two have been marginalized. The teacher is losing respect outside the class. There is also an apathy observed on the part of students as many of them believe that if they study from the reference books, they could score good marks without attending the classes. His major reason for annoyance with the teachers is irresponsibility on their part. There is lack of enthusiastic co-operation among many of them. This often results into disinterestedness and non-sharing of responsibilities towards the development of the department. He prefers to speak to teachers on one to one basis, for some of these problems. In his opinion, students do share their problems off and on with him but they are mainly related to the academic work. He finds no difficulty in communicating either with his colleagues or with his students. The main difficulty in managing the department is related to less responsible behaviour of the non-teaching staff especially that of peons. Even, there is less commitment on the part of some teachers. There is also scarcity of funds for maintaining the department. As such, there is hardly any scope of expanding the academic work in the department. The teachers have been observed to have a luke-warm interest in the activities of the department and they show some apathy towards building its prestige. In order to make the role of teachers effective, he suggests that the size of classes should be reduced so that there could be increased interaction of a teacher with the student on personal basis. Students need to be encouraged to have out of class-room academic discussions as well as non-academic interaction with the teachers. Besides, a continuous evaluation system should be developed or at least a periodic assessment should be made about the performance of the teachers. There is also a need to effect a change in the method of teaching. Though, we have the present system of class-room instruction, tutorials, seminars etc, yet students are not interested to attend them. The quality of teaching gets diluted mainly because there are departments such as correspondence studies/evening college which offer the same subjects as taught by this department.

Case-5

The Chairperson of a department in the faculty of Arts is 40 years old, and she holds a doctorate degree. She started her teaching career in 1983 and is continuing in the same department since then. She is fully satisfied with the organizational structure of the department as well as with the willingness of her colleagues to assist each other whenever it is required in the interest of the students. She faces no difficulty in exchanging views and information with members of her department as well as that of others. According to her, the department is functioning in an excellent manner and is having the special assistance programme of the UGC. It is vibrant with various academic activities throughout the year. She expects that the teacher should be good in communication, have better understanding of the subject and he or she should be well-quipped with latest information and technology. Further, he or she should be aware about latest advancements made in the discipline. He or she should also have an inter-disciplinary approach which he or she can acquire by attending seminars, workshops etc of other cognate disciplines. By and large, she feels that her expectations match with the performance of teachers. She is of the opinion that the status of teachers in the society is deteriorating day by day. In terms of money, no doubt, there is an improvement in status but in terms of respect, it is not what it used to be in the past. In regard to relationship between the teachers and the students, she observes that a large variation exists. At some levels, it is praiseworthy while in other cases, it is not very healthy. The main reasons which cause annoyance in her towards the teachers, are their carelessness, irresponsible behaviour and absenteeism. She tries to tackle these by requesting the individuals concerned in ordinary cases while in the extreme cases, she brings it in the faculty meeting for discussion. Most of the students do share their personal and academic problems with her. She also finds no difficulty in communicating with her colleagues and students. The major problem faced by her in managing the department is availability of funds and authority to spend money for academic purposes. The procedures are very long and cumbersome and the chairpersons must be given more financial powers. In her opinion, the role of a teacher can be made more effective in providing education to the students through increased interaction with them at various forums. Besides, teachers should be given more opportunities to learn through participation in refresher courses, training programmes, workshops etc so that they are well-equipped and are confident to perform their role effectively.

Case-6

The Chairperson of the departmentin the Faculty of Education is 59 years old, and she holds a doctorate degree. She started her teaching career in 1964 and she has been working in this department since 1978. By and large, she is satisfied with the organizational set-up of department except for stringent financial position. Because of that, growth and development is restricted. She expresses satisfaction with the willingness of her colleagues to help each other for meeting the needs of the students. She finds no problem in exchanging views and information related to professional matters with the members of her department as well as that of others. She is in favour of respecting the opinions of others in the department. However, she feels that each individual teacher should take greater responsibility in the functioning of the department. She appreciates and accepts the views of others if these contribute towards proper functioning of the department.

She expects teachers to show a personal code of conduct and be an example to the students. The performance of teachers does not always match with her expectations and it varies from teacher to teacher. There is a feeling among teachers that there are no job risks involved and that affects their role performance. The status of teachers as compared to two to three decades back is much better now in the society. The relationship between the teacher and the students should be such that a teacher should act as their guide and a friend. The main reasons for her annoyance with the teachers are, carelessness, irresponsibility and absenteeism. Some of the teachers have been observed to finish their classes in 20-30 minutes, which is damaging to the interest of the students. She tries to bring it to the notice of teachers directly or indirectly so that they do not steal time of the classes. The students, by and large, share their academic problems with her and even some of them share their personal problems. She has no difficulty in communicating with her colleagues and students. At times, she finds difficulty in making the whole department as a close-knit group, despite her wish to do so, mainly because of different interests of the teachers. Teachers can become more effective if they exhibit an inner code of conduct, that is, they should be motivated from within to uphold moral values. Besides, they should be subjected to external pressures of the employer to perform the roles adequately.

Case-7

The Chairperson of the department in the Professional course is 57 years old and holds a doctorate degree. He started his teaching career in 1968 and is working in this department since then. He is not satisfied with the organizational set up of his department. He feels that the rotation of chairpersonship among members of the faculty and the committee system introduced as a method of democratization of the functioning of the department, has made the administrative work weak. However, he is satisfied with the willingness of his colleagues to help each other in order to serve the interests of the students. There is no difficulty for him to exchange views and information about professional matters with members of his department as well as with others who are associated with the departmental work. In his opinion, the department is functioning reasonably well.

He expects teachers to devote sufficient time for research and have more interaction with the students. In some cases, his expectations match with the performance of teachers while in other cases, it is not so. His main reason for dissatisfaction with the performance of teachers is their inadequate contribution towards research and lack of devotion to the profession. According to him, the status of a teacher in the society is average, that is, neither good nor bad. The relationship between the teacher and the student is marked by their indifferent attitude towards each other. In cases, where teachers are negligent about their duties, he prefers to persuade them to perform their roles effectively. In the case of extreme negligence, he issues a warning to them. The students share both personal and academic problems with him. He does not find any difficulty in communicating with his colleagues as well as with the students. He faces no problem in managing the department. In his opinion, the role of teachers can be made more effective by creating interest and devotion in them towards the profession. Further, there is a need to increase their interaction with the students.

Case-8

The Principal of the Government college is 57 years old, and holds a post graduate degree. He started his teaching career in 1967 and his association with this college is since 1991. He is satisfied with the organizational set up of the college as well as with the willingness of his colleagues to help each other in serving the cause of the students. He has no difficulty in exchanging views about professional matters with members of his college as well as with Director Public Instructions (U.T) and members of the Panjab University, Chandigarh. According to him, the college is functioning to his satisfaction.

His main expectation from the teachers is that they should be dedicated and committed to serve the interest of the students. By and large, he feels that the performance of teachers matches with his expectations. In his opinion, the teacher is not enjoying that status which he or she should be given. Keeping in view, the nature of job and salary of the teacher he or she should be given a better status in the society. The relationship between the students and the teachers are not very congenial as they do not find it comfortable to communicate with the teachers. He is mainly annoyed with the teachers due to their irresponsible behaviour. He tries to advise the teachers when they do not devote enough time towards the students and indulge in other activities. The students do share their problems regarding the teachers and the college with him. He has no difficulty in communicating either with his colleagues or with the students. Besides, he has hardly any problem in managing the college. In order to make the role of a teacher effective, he suggests that teachers should keep their knowledge up-to-date and come prepared for the lectures. Besides, they should treat students as their own children. However, they should not compromise on matters related to discipline and have faith in the students so that they, in turn, have faith in them.

Case-9

The Principal of the Private college is 56 years old and holds a post graduate degree. He started his career as a teacher in 1969 and is continuing in the same college since then. He is not fully satisfied with the organizational set-up of his college. The main reasons for his dissatisfaction are disproportionate secretariat staff, over-staffing in laboratories, shortage of eligible teachers in the computer science department, interference by some governing committee members in day to day administration and inadequate funds for the smooth functioning of the college. He is not satisfied with the willingness of his colleagues to help each other to serve the interest of the students.

In his opinion, the majority of the colleagues just shirk work and they are not willing to take extra pains to do the tasks assigned to them. Further, materialism always weighs heavy on the minds of some of them. They are not so willing to assist each other except for trade union activities. He has no difficulty in exchanging views and information about professional matters with his colleagues in the college as well as with other important functionaries such as Director Higher Education, Secretary Education, UGC and the university. He feels that the college is making an all-round progress in academics, sports and extra-circular activities. He expects that teachers should be punctual, regular, well-equipped with the latest knowledge related to their subjects. They should prepare themselves fully before teaching the students. Besides, they should co-operate also in other activities of the college.

He does not think that his expectations match with the performance of the teachers. The main reasons for his dissatisfaction with performance of teachers are absenteeism, criticism and vilification. Besides, many are indifferent towards their classroom teaching and they consider it as burden to perform any other duty assigned to them. As regards status of teacher in the society, he thinks it is not the same as it used to be in the past. But, financially, teachers are much better off than their counterparts in the past.

In his opinion, the relationship between the teachers and students is not very good as the majority of the teachers command no respect and students also have an indifferent attitude towards them. He is mainly annoyed with the teachers due to their carelessness, irresponsible behaviour, absenteeism, impertinence and disrespect to the seniors. In ordinary circumstances, he ignores such behaviours after cautioning a teacher but in extreme cases, he issues warning and takes disciplinary action. The students invariably share their problems with him regarding amenities like water, toilets, electricity, canteen and accommodation in the hostel. In some cases, they also report about the indifferent attitude of their teachers towards class-room teaching. He has no difficulty in communicating with his colleagues as well as with the students.

The main difficulties faced by him in managing the college are non availability of funds, inadequate staff for certain essential services and non-serious attitude of some of the staff members towards their duties. According to him, the role of teachers can be made more effective if they have proper orientation before taking up their job as teacher. Besides, they should have proper aptitude for teaching and there should be fixing up of responsibility and accountability to the job. They should be guided by their conscience while performing their duties and they should indulge in self-appraisal of their work. Besides, there should also be appraisal done by students on their work. An appraisal system should also be evolved by the university for the examination work undertaken by the teachers. Moreover, they should get themselves involved in the administration and other additional duties.

On the basis of qualitative data presented above, in regard to views of Chairpersons of the university departments/Principals of the colleges, one can draw a few inferences. Most of them are for status-quo in the organizational setup of their departments or colleges. By and large, there is emphasis laid on instrumental roles of teachers such as teaching, research while some of the expressive roles such as to have cordial relationship with colleagues and communication with colleagues and students, have been taken for granted. Most of them expect teachers to take up their classes regularly, exhibit responsible behaviour and show more commitment and dedication towards the tasks assigned to them. Besides, they are also expected to interact more with the students and keep their knowledge updated on the subject to serve their interests in a better way. There appears more organizational and management problems in the Private than in the Government college. However, the difficulties faced by Chairpersons in the university for managing their departments are more or less similar to that of the Principals in the colleges.

4. Emphasis on Different Jobs laid by the Chairperson of the Department/Principal of the College

The teachers in the university belonging to different streams of courses as well as those in the colleges were asked whether their supervisors, that is, the Chairperson of the university department or the Principal of the college, was laying emphasis on different jobs; sometimes even stressing more on the non-academic than academic activities.

It is observed that among the university teachers, nearly one fifth of them (20.45 per cent) mentioned that the Chairpersons of their respective departments have been laying emphasis on different jobs whereas the majority of them (79.55 per cent) do not think so.

The faculty-wise analysis brings out that a higher number of male (22) than female (5) teachers in the different courses (science, social sciences and professional) feel so. On the other hand, in the case of college teachers, it is observed that nearly one-fourth of them (26.67 per cent) think that the respective Principals of their colleges are laying emphasis on different jobs. As compared to Private college, where only 3 females have expressed so, 5 male and 4 female teachers in the Government college are of this opinion.

The teachers in the university and colleges who responded positively to the above question, were asked to specify the jobs emphasized by their supervisors. In view of a small number of responses to this, the same is presented below in the combined form for both the male and female teachers, in the university and the colleges.

1. University Teachers—By and large, they are asked by their supervisors to do administrative and completely non-academic activities (8). Besides, they are required to do those activities that suit the Chairperson and help him or her in building personal relationships for his or her gains (3). There is also emphasis laid on involvement in cultural activities (3). They are also asked to perform election duties, set date-sheets, frame time-table, attend meetings and make purchases for the requirements of the department (2each). Some of the Chairpersons, especially in the science departments, also want to lay more emphasis on research than on teaching(2). They are also asked to help them in admissions (1).

2. College Teachers—The Principals lay more emphasis on cultural activities, especially the female teachers are required to make arrangements for these (6). They are also asked to help maintain discipline in the college (3). Besides, the Principals ask them to do election duty, print college magazine, admit students with low merit, prepare students for cultural events, maintain the attendance sheet for calculating shortage of lectures, attend too many meetings and follow them blindly (one each).

As is evident from the above analysis, it appears many of the teachers in the university as well as in the colleges do not consider some of these jobs emphasized by their supervisors as an integral part of their roles. This may be due to their inadequate preparedness to take up these responsibilities. The teachers appear to have this feeling that their roles are getting diffused rather than being specific. This brings in an element of role ambiguity in their roles and unless this is taken care of by their respective supervisors through counselling and advice, the role of the teachers may not become functional. From teachers' point of view, it is also expected that their supervisors should not make unnecessary demands on them to do certain activities which are not desirable in the academic interest.

J. Expectations of Students as Perceived by Teachers—

A set of roles such as taking the classes regularly, guiding students for difficulties in studies, responding to their greetings, discussing with the students their personal problems etc. was provided to the teachers and they were asked to rate these in terms of students' expectations of them, on the scale of importance. A role rated as most important was assigned a score of 5, while that considered as least important was given a score of 1. Those roles which were rated as fairly important, important and less important were given a score value of 4,3 and 2 respectively. A mean score value was worked out for each of these roles sex-wise, within each of the three faculties (science, social science and professional) in respect of university teachers as well as for the college teachers. A combined mean score was worked out for these roles separately faculty-wise for the university teachers and for teachers in the two colleges and these were compared with the overall mean score values for the various roles.

An examination of Table 4.6 shows that on the basis of the overall mean score values, in the perception of university teachers, students expect them to 'take the classes regularly' (4.56), ' guidance for difficulties in studies' (4.32), 'encourage them to express their views' (4.13), 'encourage participation in classroom discussion' (4.12), 'respond to their greetings' (3.83), 'don't keep them waiting if they want to meet' (3.81), 'friendly attitude' (3.76), 'discuss with them their personal problems' (3.10), 'not to turn them out of class' (2.98) and 'take a class even on the unscheduled time' (2.50). These roles rated by teachers have been arranged in the descending order on the basis of the overall mean score values. The greater the mean score value, the higher is the importance given to that role in the expectations of the students as perceived by the teachers.

We can classify roles such as 'take the classes regularly, 'guidance for difficulties in studies,' 'encouraging them to express their views' and 'take a class even on the unscheduled time' as instrumental roles while the roles such as 'respond to their greetings,' 'don't keep them waiting if they want to meet,' 'friendly attitude,' 'discuss with them their personal problem,' and 'not to turn them out of class' as expressive roles.

The facultywise analysis of university teachers shows that the science teachers have given more importance to 'friendly attitude' than 'respond to their greetings' and 'don't keep them waiting if they want to meet'. The sex-wise analysis within this group shows that the male teachers have placed 'don't keep them waiting if they want to meet' (3.89) higher than 'respond to their greetings' (3.87). Again, they have given more importance to 'not to turn them out of class' (3.23) than 'discuss with them their personal problems' (3.05). However, female teachers in this group have given more importance to an expressive role like 'friendly attitude' (4.00) and bracketed it along with an instrumental role 'encourage participation in classroom discussion' (4.00) than 'encourage them to express their views' (3.94). This may be because females tend to be more friendly than males in their gender behaviour.

In the case of social science teachers, the rating pattern of these roles is same as given in the overall analysis. However, the male teachers in this group are placing 'don't keep them waiting if they want to meet' (3.90) and 'friendly attitude' (3.64) above 'respond to their greetings' (3.58). Female teachers in this group are placing 'guidance for difficulty in studies' (4.56) higher than 'take the classes regularly' (4.52). Again they are placing 'friendly attitude' (3.96) above 'don't keep them waiting if they want to meet' and 'not to turn them out of class' (3.04) above 'discuss with them their personal problems' (2.96).

Table 4.6

Relationship between the Sex of the Teachers and Expectations of Students as perceived by Teachers.

S. No.	Expectations of Students as perceived by Teachers	Overall Mean Score Value	Rank	University Teachers								
				Science (Mean Score Value)			Social Science (Mean Score Value)			Professional (Mean Score Value)		
				Male	Female	Combined Mean	Male	Female	Combined Mean	Male	Female	Combined Mean
1.	Take Classes regularly	4.56	1	4.51	4.47	4.49	4.51	4.52	4.51	4.90	5.00	4.94
2.	Guidance for difficulties in studies	4.32	2	4.12	4.31	4.18	4.29	4.56	4.41	4.54	4.42	4.49
3.	Encouraging them to express their views	4.13	3	4.07	3.94	4.02	4.09	4.40	4.22	4.27	4.14	4.22
4.	Encourage participation in classroom discussion	4.12	4	3.89	4.00	3.93	4.06	4.40	4.21	4.54	4.42	4.48
5.	Respond to their greetings	3.83	5	3.87	3.57	3.77	3.58	4.32	3.91	3.81	3.85	3.82
6.	Don't keep them waiting if they want to meet	3.81	6	3.89	3.52	3.76	3.90	3.88	3.89	3.63	4.00	3.77
7.	Friendly attitude	3.76	7	3.69	4.00	3.79	3.64	3.96	3.78	3.90	3.14	3.60
8.	Discuss with them their personal problems	3.10	8	3.05	3.15	3.08	3.38	2.96	3.19	2.81	3.00	2.88
9.	Not to turn them out of class	2.98	9	3.23	2.68	3.05	2.58	3.04	2.78	3.36	3.42	3.38
10.	Take a class even on the unscheduled time	2.50	10	2.28	2.42	2.32	2.38	2.80	2.56	3.00	2.85	2.94

(Contd.)

(Contd. Table 4.6)

S.No.	Expectations of Students as perceived by Teachers	Overall mean Score Value	Rank	College Teachers					
				Government (Mean Score Value)			Private (Mean Score Value)		
				Male	Female	Combined Means	Male	Female	Combined Means
1.	Take Classes regularly	4.61	1	4.70	4.69	4.69	4.37	4.64	4.54
2.	Guidance for difficulties in studies	4.57	2	4.60	4.76	4.69	4.25	4.57	4.45
3.	Encouraging them to express their views	4.39	3	4.40	4.38	4.39	4.62	4.28	4.40
4.	Encourage participation in classroom discussion	4.10	4	4.40	3.76	4.03	4.12	4.21	4.18
5.	Friendly attitude	4.04	5	4.10	4.00	4.04	4.25	3.92	4.04
6.	Respond to their greetings	3.97	6	3.70	4.07	3.90	4.12	4.00	4.04
7.	Don't keep them waiting if they want to meet	3.95	7	4.40	3.69	3.99	4.12	3.78	3.90
8.	Discuss with them their personal problems	3.33	8	3.10	3.30	3.21	3.87	3.21	3.45
9.	Not to turn them out of class	2.97	9	3.70	3.07	3.34	3.37	2.14	2.58
10.	Take a class even on the unscheduled time	2.19	10	2.60	2.07	2.30	1.62	2.35	2.08

In the case of professional group, teachers are giving more importance to roles such as 'not to turn them out of class' and 'take a class even on the unscheduled time' than 'discuss with them their personal problems'. The male teachers in this group are placing, 'encourage participation in classroom discussion' (4.54) above 'encouraging them to express their views' (4.27). Besides, they have given a higher rating to the 'friendly attitude' (3.90) than 'respond to their greetings' (3.81) and 'don't keep them waiting if they want to meet' (3.63). Even, they have rated 'not to turn them out of class' (3.36) and 'take a class on unscheduled time' (3.00) higher than 'discuss with them their personal problems' (2.81). However, female teachers have given a higher rating to 'encouraging participation in classroom discussion' (4.42) than 'encouraging them to express their views' (4.14) and 'don't keep them waiting if they want to meet' (4.00) than 'respond to their greetings' (3.85) and below this they have placed 'not to turn them out of class' (3.42).

The above analysis suggests that among the university teachers, by and large, there is more importance given to instrumental roles, except 'take a class on unscheduled time' than expressive roles. However, females seem to be having more of a humane approach than the male teachers.

The college teachers have rated 'take the classes regularly'(4.61), 'guidance for difficulties' (4.57), 'encouraging them to express their views' (4.39), 'encourage participation in classroom discussion' (4.10), 'friendly attitude' (4.04), 'respond to their greetings' (3.97) 'don't keep them waiting if they want to meet' (3.95), "discuss with them their personal problems' (3.33), 'not to turn them out of class' (2.97) and 'take a class even on the unscheduled time' (2.19) in the above order of importance.

In the case of Government college teachers, it is observed that they have given more importance to 'friendly attitude' than 'encourage participation in class room discussion'. Even, 'don't keep them waiting if they want to meet' has been placed higher than 'respond to their greetings'. Again 'not to turn them out of class' gets a higher rank order' than 'discuss with them their personal problems'. The sex-wise analysis in this college shows that male teachers have assigned a higher rating to 'don't keep them waiting if they want to meet' (4.40) than 'friendly attitude' (4.10). Again, they have given a higher rating to 'not to turn them out of class' (3.70) than 'discuss with them their personal problems' (3.10). There appears a more varied response given to expressive than instrumental roles. Interestingly, in the case of female teachers, the most important role for them is 'guidance for difficulties in studies' (4.76) than 'take the classes regularly' (4.69). They have also given higher ranking order to 'respond to their greetings' (4.07) than 'friendly attitude' (4.00) whoreas an instrumental role such as 'encourage participation in class room discussion' (3.76) has been placed below the above two roles. This again shows that female teachers as compared to males are giving more importance to the expressive roles.

In the case of the Private college, again, the teachers have bracketed 'respond to their greetings' alongwith 'friendly attitude'. The sex-wise analysis in this college shows that male teachers have placed 'encouraging them to express their views' (4.62) at the top whereas 'friendly attitude'(4.25) has also been placed above 'encourage participation in classroom discussion,' 'respond to their greetings' and 'don't keep them waiting if they want to meet' (4.12). A higher rank order to 'encouraging them to express their views' may be because male teachers perceive that students are less communicative with them. In the case of female teachers, they have rated 'respond to their greetings' (4.00) higher than 'friendly attitude' (3.92). They have even given a higher position to 'take a class on unscheduled time' (2.35) than 'not to turn them out of class' (2.14). This may be due to their personal experience or willingness to take the unscheduled classes.

The sex-wise analysis of teachers in the university and colleges brings out that there are varied responses towards various roles of teachers from the perspective of students. This lends support to our hypothesis that the gender status of teachers influences the role expectations of students from them.

5 (a). Relationship between Status (Designation Held) of Teachers and Students' Expectations as Perceived by Teachers

An attempt was also made to find out if the status designation of teachers in the university and colleges had any influence on students' expectations about their roles, in the perception of the teachers. A set of roles was provided to the teachers and they were asked to rate these on the scale of importance ranging from most important to the least important. The scoring procedure followed was same as given in the analysis pertaining to Table 4.6.

An examination of Table 4.7 shows that on the basis of the overall mean score values, the teachers in the university have given importance to roles such as 'take the classes regularly'(4.58), 'guidance for difficulties in studies'(4.31), 'encouraging them to express their views'(4.16), 'encourage participation in classroom discussion'(4.13), 'respond to their greetings'(3.84), 'friendly attitude'(3.81), 'don't keep them waiting if they want to meet'(3.81), "discuss with them their personal problems'(3.07) 'not to turn them out of class'(2.94) and 'take a class on the unscheduled time'(2.53) in that order.

Among the science teachers in the combined form 'friendly attitude' has been placed higher than 'don't keep them waiting if they want to meet' as well as 'respond to their greetings'. Even, 'not to turn them out of class' has been given a higher position than 'discuss with them their personal problems'. The status-wise analysis in this group shows that Professors have given more importance to 'encouraging them to express their views'(4.06) than 'guidance for difficulties in studies'(4.00). They have also placed 'don't keep them waiting if they want to meet'(3.62) higher than 'friendly attitude'(3.56). Again, 'not to turn them out of class'(3.25) has been assigned a higher rank than 'discuss with them their personal problems' (3.00). Further, Readers in this group have given more importance to 'friendly attitude'(4.00) and 'don't keep them waiting if they want to meet'(4.00) than 'encourage participation in classroom discussion'(3.82). In the case of Lecturers, it is observed they have placed 'friendly attitude'(3.92) higher than 'respond to their greetings'(3.80) as well as 'not to turn them out of class'(3.16) higher than 'discuss with them their personal problems'(3.04). As compared to Professors and Lecturers, Readers are giving more importance to expressive roles.

In the case of social science teachers, it is observed that they have given more importance to 'don't keep them waiting if they want to meet' than 'friendly attitude'. The status-wise analysis of teachers in this group shows that Professors have given more importance to roles such as 'encouraging them to express their views'(4.25) and 'encourage participation in class room

Table 4.7

Relationship between Status (Designation Held) of Teachers and their perceived Role Expectations of Students.

S. No.	Expectations of students as Perceived By Teachers	Overall Mean Score Value	Rank	University Teachers: Science (Mean Score Value) P	R	L	Combined Mean	Social Science (Mean Score Value) P	R	L	Combined Mean	Professional (Mean Score Value) P	R	L	Combined Mean
1.	Take Classes regularly	4.58	I	4.62	4.58	4.40	4.51	4.56	4.50	4.50	4.52	4.87	5.00	5.00	4.94
2.	Guidance for difficulties in studies	4.31	2	4.00	4.11	4.36	4.18	3.93	4.55	4.60	4.39	4.62	4.50	4.25	4.49
3.	Encouraging them to express their views	4.16	3	4.06	4.05	4.04	4.05	4.25	4.05	4.45	4.25	4.50	4.33	3.75	4.27
4.	Encourage participation in classroom discussion	4.13	4	3.87	3.82	4.04	3.92	4.06	4.25	4.35	4.23	4.75	4.50	4.00	4.50
5.	Respond to their greetings	3.84	5	3.75	3.76	3.80	3.77	3.87	3.65	4.25	3.92	3.87	3.83	3.75	3.83
6.	Don't keep them waiting if they want to meet	3.81	6	3.56	4.00	3.92	3.84	3.37	4.00	3.90	3.78	3.75	4.16	3.50	3.83
7.	Friendly attitude	3.81	6	3.62	4.00	3.72	3.78	3.81	3.75	4.05	3.87	3.37	4.16	4.00	3.77
8.	Discuss with them their personal problems	3.07	8	3.00	3.05	3.04	3.03	3.31	3.50	2.85	3.21	2.87	2.50	3.00	2.77
9.	Not to turn them out of class	2.94	9	3.25	2.70	3.16	3.05	2.50	2.85	2.85	2.75	2.50	4.16	3.25	3.22
10.	Take a class even on the unscheduled time	2.53	10	2.50	2.11	2.36	2.32	2.31	2.85	2.70	2.64	3.12	2.50	3.00	2.88

Note : P = Professor, R = Reader, L = Lecturer

(Contd.)

(Contd. Table 4.7)

S. No.	Expectations of Students by Teachers	Overall Mean Score Value	Rank	College Teachers							
				Government (Mean Score Value)				Private (Mean Score Value)			
				Senior Lecturer	Lecturer	Guest Faculty	Combined means	Senior Lecturer	Lecturer	Guest Faculty	Combined mean
1.	Take Classes regularly	4.61	1	4.57	4.76	4.66	4.68	4.90	4.45	2.00	4.54
2.	Guidance for difficulties in studies	4.57	2	4.71	469	4.66	4.69	4.40	4.45	5.00	4.45
3.	Encouraging them to express their views	4.41	3	4.71	4.53	4.00	4.51	4.20	4.54	3.00	4.31
4.	Encourage participation in classroom discussion	4.14	4	3.85	4.38	3.66	4.12	4.00	4.45	3.00	4.17
5.	Don't keep them waiting if they want to meet	4.05	5	4.28	4.07	4.00	4.12	3.90	4.27	2.00	3.99
6.	Friendly attitude	4.02	6	4.28	3.84	4.33	4.04	4.10	4.00	3.00	4.00
7.	Respond to their greetings	3.94	7	4.42	3.69	3.66	3.90	4.00	4.00	4.00	4.00
8.	Discuss with them their personal problems	3.36	8	3.42	3.30	3.00	3.29	4.00	3.09	2.00	3.45
9.	Not to turn them out of class	3.08	9	3.57	3.07	3.00	3.21	3.00	3.09	1.00	2.95
10.	Take a class even on the unscheduled time	2.21	10	2.71	2.30	2.00	2.38	2.10	2.09	1.00	2.04

discussion'(4.06) than 'guidance for difficulties in studies'(3.93). Again, they have placed 'don't keep them waiting if they want to meet'(3.81) higher than 'friendly attitude'(3.37). As regards Readers in this group, they have assigned the highest rank to 'guidance for difficulties in studies'(4.55) than 'take the classes regularly'(4.50). Even, they have placed 'encourage participation in classroom discussion'(4.25) higher than 'encouraging them to express their views'(4.05). Further, they have given higher rating to 'friendly attitude'(4.00) and 'don't keep them waiting if they want to meet'(3.75) than 'respond to their greetings'(3.65). In the case of Lecturers, it is observed that like Readers, they have also given the highest rank to 'guidance for difficulties in studies'(4.60) than 'take the classes regularly'(4.50). They have also given a higher position to 'don't keep them waiting if they want to meet'(4.05) than 'friendly attitude'(3.90). Professors as compared to Readers in this group are giving more emphasis on 'encouraging them to express their views' whereas Readers and Lecturers have stressed more on 'guidance for difficulties in studies' than Professors, as part of the instrumental roles.

In the case of professional group, it is observed that teachers have given more importance to 'encourage participation in classroom discussion' than 'guidance for difficulties in studies'. Further, they have given a higher rank to 'not to turn them out of the class' and 'take a class even on unscheduled time' than 'discuss with them their personal problems'. The status-wise analysis of teachers in this group shows that Professors have given more importance to 'encourage participation in the classroom discussion'(4.75) than 'guidance for difficulties in studies'(4.62). Again, they have placed 'take a class even on unscheduled time'(3.12) higher than 'discuss with them their personal problems'(2.87). In the case of Readers, 'encouraging participation in the classroom discussion'(4.50) has been placed over 'encourage them to express their views'(4.33). Besides, 'friendly attitude', 'don't keep them waiting if they want to meet' and 'not to turn them out of the class' all bracketed together (4.16), have been given more importance than 'respond to their greetings'(3.83). However, Lecturers have given more importance to 'don't keep them waiting if they want to meet'(4.00) than 'encouraging them to express their views'(3.75) and 'respond to their greetings'(3.75). In this group, Professors as compared to Readers and Lecturers, are emphasizing more on 'encourage participation in classroom discussion' and 'take a class even on the unscheduled time' than on some of the other instrumental and expressive roles.

On the basis of the overall mean score values, the college teachers have given importance to 'take the classes regularly'(4.61) 'guidance for difficulties in studies'(4.57), 'encouraging them to express their views'(4.41), 'encourage participation in classroom discussion'(4.14). 'don't keep them waiting if they want to meet'(4.05), 'friendly attitude'(4.02), 'respond to their greetings'(3.94), 'discuss with them their personal problems'(3.36), 'not to turn them out of class'(3.08) and 'take a class even on unscheduled time'(2.21) in that order.

In the case of Government college, it is observed that teachers in the combined form have given more importance to 'guidance for difficulties in studies' than 'take the classes regularly'. The status-wise analysis in this college shows that the Senior Lecturers have given more importance to 'guidance for difficulties in studies' along with 'encouraging them to express their views(4.71each) than to 'take the classes regularly' (4.57). Interestingly, they have assigned a higher rank to 'respond to their greetings'(4.42), 'don't keep them waiting if they want to meet'(4.28) and 'friendly attitude'(4.28) than 'encourage participation in the classroom discussion'(3.85). Even, 'not to turn them out of the class'(3.57) has been placed higher than 'discuss with them their personal problems'(3.42). In the case of Lecturers, it is observed that they have given the highest rank to 'take the classes regularly'(4.76). However, the Guest Faculty in this college has given more importance to 'friendly attitude'(4.33) than 'encouraging them to express their views' bracketed along with 'don't keep them waiting if they want to meet'(4.00).

In the case of the Private college, in the combined form, teachers have given more importance to 'encourage participation in classroom discussion' than 'respond to their greetings' and 'friendly attitude'. As compared to senior Lecturers in the Government college, Senior Lecturers in this college have given the highest rank to 'take the classes regularly'(4.90). However, they are placing 'friendly attitude'(4.10) higher than 'encourage participation in classroom discussion,' 'respond to their greetings' and "discuss with them their personal problems' all bracketed together(4.00). On the other hand, the Lecturers in this college have considered 'encouraging them to express their views(4.54) as the most important role. However, the Guest faculty considers 'guidance for difficulties in studies' as the most important role. Besides, he or she has given more importance to 'respond to their greetings'(4.00) 'encourage participation in classroom discussion,' 'encouraging them to express their views,' and 'friendly attitude' all bracketed together(3.00). Surprisingly they have given a lower rating to 'take the classes regularly'(2.00). It appears, the only Guest Faculty in this college considers 'guidance for difficulties in studies' more important than classroom teaching.

On the basis of above analysis, it is observed that teachers holding different status or designation in the university as well as in the colleges have given different importance to various roles expected of them by the students. This lends support to our hypothesis that the status of teachers influences their role expectations. Although, by and large, teachers have given more importance to the instrumental than expressive roles, yet many of them have emphasized on expressive roles such as, 'respond to their greetings,' 'friendly attitude,' 'not to keep them waiting if they want to meet' and 'discussing personal problems' etc. However, one instrumental role, 'take a class even on unscheduled time' has invariably been given the least importance. This may be because this kind of role has not become an integral part of their duties.

6. Perceived Expectation of Students from the Teachers

The students in the university as well as in the colleges were also provided with a set of roles. This analysis is presented here along with the perceived role expectations of teachers from the students for comparative purposes.

The students were asked to rate this set of roles on a five point scale of importance. A role rated as most important was assigned a score of 5 while the one rated as least important was given a score of 1. The roles which were rated as fairly important, important and less important were assigned a score of 4, 3, 2 respectively. A mean score value was worked out separately for university and college students and the roles were arranged in the descending order, the greater the mean score value, the higher was the role rated.

In order to show relationship between the sex of the students and their perceived expectations from the teachers, a mean score value was worked out for these roles, sex-wise within different faculties (science, social science and professional) in the university as well as in the two colleges. A combined mean score was also worked out for males and females in these groups. For comparative analysis, an overall mean score value for these roles was also calculated.

An examination of Table 4.8 reveals that students in the university on the basis of the overall mean score values have rated 'clarifying the doubts and misapprehensions in the class' (4.54), 'communicating/lecturing effectively in class' (4.53), 'not to be rude and autocratic towards the students' (4.22), 'having liberal and democratic relationship with the students' (4.13), 'covering the syllabi/courses in time' (4.05), 'easy accessibility' (4.04), 'special guidance and counselling to students' (3.97), 'delivering lectures regularly' (3.83), 'giving time for research work'(3.63), 'checking the assignments in time' (3.31), and 'lenient and moderate in the evaluation of scripts' (3.16), in the order of their importance.

It may be pointed out here that the above stated roles content-wise are similar to what have been provided to teachers for rating their perceived expectations of students. However, in the case of students these have been spelled out more explicitly for their better understanding.

In the case of science students in the university, it is observed that they have given more importance to 'communicating/lecturing effectively in class' than 'clarifying the doubts and apprehensions in the class'. Further, they have given a higher position to 'covering the syllabi/courses in time' than 'having liberal and democratic relationship with the students.' They have also given more importance to 'giving time for research work' than 'easy accessibility'. Even, 'lenient and moderate in the evaluation of scripts' has been placed higher than 'checking the assignments'.

The sex-wise analysis in this group shows that male students have assigned the highest rank to 'giving time for research work' (4.92). This is followed by 'not to be rude and autocratic to students' (4.30). The roles such as 'clarifying the doubts and apprehensions in class,' 'having liberal and democratic relationships with the

Table 4.8

Relationship between the Sex of the Students and their perceived Expectations from the Teachers.

S. No.	Expectations from Teachers as perceived by Students	Overall Mean Score Value	Rank	University Teachers								
				Science (Mean Score Value)			Social Science (Mean Score Value)			Professional (Mean Score Value)		
				Male	Female	Combined Mean	Male	Female	Combined Mean	Male	Female	Combined Mean
1.	Clarifying the doubts and misapprehensions in the class	4.54	1	4.15	4.50	4.34	4.60	4.75	4.67	4.75	4.50	4.62
2.	Communication/Lecturing effectively in class	4.53	2	4.00	4.68	4.37	4.70	4.65	4.67	5.00	4.00	4.50
3.	Not to be rude and autocratic towards the students	4.22	3	4.30	4.06	4.17	4.20	4.15	4.17	5.00	4.25	4.62
4.	Having liberal and democratic relationship with the students	4.13	4	4.15	4.00	4.07	4.10	4.40	4.25	3.75	3.75	3.75
5.	Covering the syllabi/courses in time	4.05	5	4.07	4.25	4.16	4.00	4.05	4.02	4.00	3.75	3.87
6.	Easy accessibility	4.04	6	4.15	3.81	3.96	3.95	4.35	4.15	3.75	4.00	3.87
7.	Special guidance and counseling to students	3.97	7.	3.69	4.00	3.86	4.25	3.90	4.07	3.50	4.25	3.87
8.	Delivering lectures regularly	3.83	8	3.69	3.68	3.68	3.85	3.85	3.85	4.75	3.75	4.25
9.	Giving time for research work	3.63	9	4.92	3.37	4.06	3.55	3.30	3.42	3.50	2.75	3.12
10.	Checking the assignments in time	3.31	10	3.76	3.00	3.34	3.40	3.20	3.30	3.50	3.00	3.25
11.	Lenient and moderate in the evaluation of scripts	3.16	11	3.92	2.93	3.37	2.80	3.55	3.17	2.25	2.50	2.37

(Contd.)

(Contd. Table 4.8)

S.No.	*Expectations from Teachers as perceived by Students*	*Overall mean Score Value*	*Rank*	*College Teachers*					
				Government (Mean Score Value)			*Private (Mean Score Value)*		
				Male	*Female*	*Combined Mean*	*Male*	*Female*	*Combined Mean*
1.	Clarifying the doubts and misapprehensions in the class	4.34	1	4.42	4.50	4.46	4.28	4.18	4.23
2.	Communication/Lecturing effectively in class	4.21	2	3.94	4.25	4.08	4.47	4.18	4.34
3.	Not to be rude and autocratic towards the students	4.09	3	3.78	4.56	4.14	3.71	4.50	4.05
4.	Having liberal and democratic relationship with the students	4.08	4	3.68	4.43	4.02	3.66	4.75	4.13
5.	Covering the syllabi/courses in time	4.08	4	4.15	3.75	3.96	4.33	4.06	4.21
6.	Easy accessibility	4.06	6	3.84	4.25	4.03	4.09	4.06	4.07
7.	Special guidance and counseling to students	4.05	7	4.10	3.75	3.94	4.38	3.87	4.16
8.	Delivering lectures regularly	3.87	8	3.47	3.62	3.54	4.14	4.25	4.19
9.	Giving time for research work	3.55	9	3.42	2.62	3.05	3.95	4.12	4.02
10.	Checking the assignments in time	2.97	10	2.63	2.93	2.77	3.42	2.81	3.16
11.	Lenient and moderate in the evaluation of scripts	2.87	11	3.10	3.06	3.08	2.33	3.12	2.67

students' and 'easy accessibility' (4.15each) have been placed next in order of importance above 'communicating/lecturing effectively in class' (4.00). Besides, they have also given a higher rating to 'lenient and moderate in the evaluation of scripts' (3.92) and 'checking assignments in time' (3.76) than 'special guidance and counselling to students' (3.69). On the other hand, female students in this group have given the highest rank to 'communicating/lecturing effectively in class' (4.68) while 'covering the syllabi/courses in time' has been placed higher than 'not to be rude and autocratic towards the students' (4.06). Even, 'special guidance and counselling to students' (4.00) has been given a higher rank than 'easy accessibility' (3.81). It is clear from the above analysis that male students in this group are giving overriding importance to 'giving time for research work' whereas female students are for 'communicating and lecturing effectively in class'. This may be indicative of a greater inclination of male than female students towards research.

In the case of social science students, it is observed that having 'liberal and democratic relationship with the students' has been placed higher than 'not to be rude and autocratic towards the students'. Further, 'easy accessibility and 'special guidance and counselling to students' have been given higher rating to 'covering the syllabi/courses in time'. The sex-wise analysis in this group shows that male students consider 'communicating/lecturing effectively in class' (4.70) as the most important role, followed by 'clarifying the doubts and misapprehensions in the class' (4.60). Even, 'special guidance and counselling to students' (4.25) has been placed higher than 'not to be rude and autocratic towards the students' (4.20). However, female students have assigned a higher rank to 'having liberal and democratic relationship with the students' (4.40) and 'easy accessibility' (4.35) than 'not to be rude and autocratic towards the students' (4.10). Further, they have given a higher rating to 'lenient and moderate in the evaluation of scripts' (3.55) than 'giving time for research work' (3.30).

In regard to students in the professional group, they have rated 'not to be rude and autocratic towards the students' higher than 'communicating/lecturing effectively in the class'. Again, they have placed 'delivering lectures regularly' higher than 'covering the syllabi/courses in time,' 'easy accessibility' and 'special guidance and counselling to the students' whereas 'having liberal and democratic relationship with the students' has been placed below them. Even, 'checking the assignments in time' has been placed higher than 'giving time for research work.'

The sex-wise analysis of students in this group shows that male students have given higher rank to 'communicating/lecturing effectively in the class' (5.00) and 'not to be rude and autocratic towards the students' (5.00) than 'clarifying the doubts and misapprehensions in the class' as well as 'delivering lectures regularly' (4.75each). On the other hand, female students have given a higher rating to 'not to be rude and autocratic towards the students' and 'special guidance and counselling to students' (4.25 each) than 'communicating/lecturing effectively in class' as well as 'easy accessibility' (4.00each). In their case 'checking the assignments in time' (3.00) has also been placed higher than 'giving time for research work' (2.75).

In the case of college students, on the basis of overall mean score values, it is observed that they have given importance to roles of teachers such as 'clarifying the doubts and misapprehensions in the class'(4.34), 'communicating/lecturing effectively in the class'(4.21), 'covering the syllabi/courses in time'(4.09), 'delivering lectures regularly'(4.08), 'having liberal and democratic relationship with the students'(4.08), 'special guidance and counselling to students' (4.06), ' not to be rude and autocratic towards the students' (4.05), ' easy accessibility' (3.87), 'lenient and moderate in the evaluation of scripts' (3.55), 'giving time for research work' (2.97), 'checking the assignment in time' (2.87) in that order. However, in the case of Government college, it is observed that 'covering the syllabi/courses in time' has been placed higher than 'communicating/lecturing effectively in class' while 'special guidance and counselling to students' has been placed higher than 'delivering lectures regularly'. Even, 'checking the assignments in time' has been placed higher than 'lenient and moderate in the evaluation of scripts'. The sex-wise analysis of students in this college shows that male students have given a higher rating to 'having liberal and democratic relationship with the students' (4.15) and 'not to be rude and autocratic towards the students' (4.10) than 'communicating/lecturing effectively in the class' (3.94). Further, they have given a higher rating to 'special guidance and counselling to students' (3.84) than 'covering the syllabi/courses in time' (3.78). Even, 'checking the assignments in time' (3.10) has been placed higher than 'giving time for research work' (2.63).

On the other hand, female students in this college have given the first rank to 'covering the syllabi/courses in time' (4.56). Further, they have rated 'delivering lectures regularly' (4.43) higher than 'communicating/lecturing effectively in class' and 'special guidance and counselling to students' (4.25each). Even, 'checking the assignment in time' (3.06) and 'giving time for research work' (2.93) have been placed higher than 'lenient and moderate in the evaluation of scripts' (2.62).

In the case of the Private college, it is observed that students have given the highest rank to 'communicating/lecturing effectively in class'. However, they have given a higher rating to 'having liberal and democratic relationship with the students,' 'easy accessibility,' 'not to be rude and autocratic towards the students' than 'delivering lectures regularly'. Further, 'special guidance and counselling to students' has been placed higher than 'covering the syllabi/courses in time'. The sex-wise analysis of students in this college shows that male students have given more importance to 'communicating/lecturing effectively in the class' (4.47) 'not to be rude and autocratic towards the students' (4.38) and 'having liberal and democratic relationship with the students' (4.33) than 'clarifying the doubts and misapprehensions in the class' (4.28). Even 'easy accessibility' (4.14) and 'lenient and moderate in the evaluation of scripts' (3.95) have been placed higher than 'covering the syllabi/courses in time' (3.71). In the case of female students in this college, they have given first rank to 'delivering lectures regularly' (4.75). Surprisingly, 'easy accessibility' (4.25) has been placed higher than 'clarifying the doubts and misapprehensions in the class' and 'communicating/lecturing effectively in the class' (4.18each). Again, 'lenient and moderate in the evaluation of scripts' (4.12) has been placed higher than 'having liberal and democratic relationship with the students' (4.06) and 'special guidance and counselling to students' (4.06).

The above analysis in regard to perceived role expectation of students from the teachers in the university as well as in the colleges, clearly shows that there is differential importance given to various roles by the male and the female students. This supports our hypothesis that the gender-status of students also influences their role expectations from teachers.

If we categorize the above roles expected by students from their teachers, we can broadly classify roles such as 'clarifying the doubts and misapprehensions in the class' and 'communicating/ lecturing effectively in the class' 'covering the syllabi/courses in time, 'delivering lectures regularly,' 'special guidance and counselling to students' 'giving time for research work' and 'checking the assignments in time' as instrumental while 'having liberal and democratic relationship with the students 'not to be rude and autocratic towards the students,' 'easy accessibility' and 'lenient and moderate in the evaluation of scripts' as expressive roles.

The sex-wise analysis among the university students shows that as compared to science students those in social sciences and professional groups, especially females, have to a certain extent given more importance to some of the expressive than instrumental roles. Again, in the case of sex-wise analysis of students in the colleges, more female than male students especially in the Private college, are giving importance to some of the expressive roles. Even, male students in the Private college are giving more importance to some of the expressive than instrumental roles.

In the foregoing analysis, it is observed that in the perceived expectations of teachers from the Chairpersons of the departments in the university as well from the Principals of the colleges, there is greater emphasis laid on the instrumental roles including some of the bureaucratic roles such as 'conform to the rules,' 'obey the order and carry out the task assigned' etc than expressive roles such as 'cordial relationships with colleagues'. Besides, some teachers expressed that their supervisors (Chairpersons of the departments and Principals of the colleges) do emphasis on different jobs. This diffuseness in jobs brings in some element of role ambiguity. Further, it is observed that in regard to teachers' perceived expectations of students, there is again a greater importance given to instrumental than expressive roles. However, in the case of perceived expectations of students from the teachers both in the university and colleges, there appears inconsistency in regard to importance given to various roles. Quite a number of students, appear to be giving more importance to some of the expressive than instrumental roles.

Further, the qualitative analysis through caselets of Chairpersons of the university departments/Principals of the colleges clearly shows that they expect teachers to take up instrumental roles such as taking classes regularly, to cover syllabi/ courses on time. However, they seem to be taking the expressive roles such as cordial relationship with colleagues and tackling the personal problems of students, for granted. In other words, there appears to be different set of expectations of teachers, Chairpersons, Principals and students, both in the university and colleges from each other. This may generate role conflict which often occurs when there isa difference between what others expect of one and what one expects of one self (Lindgren, 1974).

It is observed that the role conflict arises when one expectation requires behaviour which to a certain degree is not congruent with the behaviours required with another expectation within that sector or in another sector of a particular role. There are two types of role-conflicts namely intra-role and inter role. The intra role conflict involves contradictory expectations held by two or more groups of relevant 'others' regarding the same role whereas the inter-role conflict arises due to the occupancy of two or more positions having incompatible role expectations.

In short, it may be pointed out that some element of role ambiguity due to intra-role conflict was there due to varying perception of teachers and expectation of students as well as that of supervisors from each other. Besides, intra-role conflict may have some bearing on the role performance of teachers, along with other factors which hitherto will be analysed subsequently.

5

Role Performance of Teachers

Role performance of individuals in an organization is not always in correspondence with their prescribed or expected roles. Infact, it is not possible to have complete conformity of actual behaviour to the expected one. It is observed that members of the group may appear alike in the norms they hold than in their overt behaviour (Homans, 1961).

Further, a judicious mix of "Challenge on the job" and "Social hygiene" factors may affect the role performance of individuals in an organization. In this respect, it may be worthwhile to refer to the work of Maslow (1954) who suggested a hierarchy of needs such as security (psychological and economic), social (need to affiliate), esteem (prestige). autonomy(authority, independent thought and action) and self-actualization (feeling of self-fulfillment or worthwhile accomplishment), for achieving goals within the organization. The first two needs are mainly concerned with extrinsic or hygiene type needs while the last three relate to intrinsic or motivation type rewards. Persons may be guided by different set of motives related to these needs and this may have varied effect on their performance.

McClelland et al (1953) provided a need for achievement (nAch) factor significant for motivating individuals to perform adequately. Based on this factor, people may interact with their environment, depending upon their attitudes and values. Those persons who have a higher nAch factor. enjoy problem solving issues and are task oriented while those with low rating on this, avoid problems and consider them as sources of anxiety and irritation.

Apart from these personal factors, Parsons (1951) points out that if roles are to be enacted in a manner that fits the needs of the social system, then persons have to be motivated to perform according to the roles prescribed for them. The performance of roles, in that sense becomes contingent upon the rewards and sanctions that exist between actor and "others". Even, the exchange theorists (Homans, 1961; Blau, 1964) suggest that once a person finds it rewarding to behave in a certain way, he or she continues with the same form of behaviour in a similar situation. It is further observed that no exchange continues to take place between people unless persons involved in the interacting situations think it profitable. As such, either in terms of psychic gratification or some other rewards, there is a need for some kind of motivation for role performance.

In the light of the above, the role facilities and the reward system available to persons within the organization will influence their role performance. We have earlier stated about the effect of role ambiguity and role conflict influencing the performance of individuals. For analyzing the role performance of teachers in our society, it needs to be examined as part of socio-cultural milieu in which they have their life experiences. (Gandhi, 1983).

Thus, in addition to personal and organizational factors, one must also take into account some familial and societal influences that may effect the role performance of teachers. The focus over here will be to analyse the main duties that teachers actually perform in their day to day functioning, gaps between educational training and jobs expected by teachers, matching of performance of teachers with the expectations of students etc, as well as the various factors affecting their role performance.

1. Main Duties that Teachers Actually Perform in their Day to Day Functioning

A set of roles (main duties) such as classroom teaching, guidance to students on research problems, conducting of examination etc. that teachers actually perform was provided to the teachers and they were asked to rate these on a scale of importance. A role rated as most important was assigned a score of 5 while that rated as least was given a score of 1. Those roles which were rated as fairly important, important, and less important were given a score of 4, 3, 2 respectively. A mean score value was worked our for each of these duties sex-wise and in the combined form for university teachers in the different faculties (science, social sciences and professional) as well as for the two colleges. An overall mean score value was worked out separately for the university and the college teachers. The mean score values were arranged in the descending order and the various roles were assigned ranks according . The higher the mean score value, the greater was the importance given to the role being performed.

An examination of Table 5.1 reveals that on the basis of overall mean score values, teachers in the university have given importance to class room teaching (4.95), clarification of doubts of students in and after the class (4.76), guidance to students on research problem (4.35). encouraging students to write research papers (3.74), involving students in seminars (3.72), guidance and counselling to stüdents on personal problems (3.45), involvement in preparation of syllabi (3.28), evaluation of answer books (3.15) and conducting of examination (2.85) in that order.

It is apparent from the above that teachers, by and large, have given more importance to instrumental than expressive roles such as guidance and counselling to students on personal problems as a part of their role performance. Interestingly, the examination oriented roles have been given the least importance.

In the case of science teachers except for 'evaluation of answer books' which has been given a higher rating than 'involvement in preparation of syllabi,' the rating pattern of other duties is similar to that based on the overall mean score values. The sex-wise analysis in this group shows that in case of male teachers except for 'evaluation of answer books' (3.41), which has been given a higher rank than 'involvement in preparation of syllabi' (3.28), the ranking of other roles remains the same. Even for female teachers, the ranking pattern is same as that of males.

In the case of social science teachers, they have given a higher position to 'involving students in seminar' than 'encouraging students to write research papers'. The sex-wise analysis in this group shows that male-teachers are giving more importance to 'involving students in seminars' (3.80) and 'involvement in preparation of syllabi' (3.77) than 'encouraging students to write research papers' (3.61) while female teachers are giving more importance to 'involving students in seminars' (3.80) than 'encouraging students to write research papers' (3.56).

In the case of professional group, it is observed that teachers have given more importance to 'evaluation of answer books' and

Table 5.1
Relationship between the Sex of the Teachers and the main duties that they actually perform in the day to day functioning

S. No.	Main duties actually performed by Teachers	Overall Mean Score Value	Rank	University Teachers								
				Science (Mean Score Value)			Social Science (Mean Score Value)			Professional (Mean Score Value)		
				Male	Female	Combined Mean	Male	Female	Combined Mean	Male	Female	Combined Mean
1.	Classroom teaching	4.95	1	4.94	4.94	4.94	4.93	4.96	4.94	5.00	5.00	5.00
2.	Clarification of doubts of students in and after the class	4.76	2	4.74	4.94	4.80	4.74	4.68	4.71	4.72	4.85	4.77
3.	Guidance to students on research problems	4.35	3	4.33	4.57	4.41	4.38	4.36	4.37	4.45	3.70	4.16
4.	Encouraging students to write research papers	3.74	4	3.92	3.84	3.89	3.61	3.56	3.58	3.72	3.85	3.77
5.	Involving students in seminars	3.72	5	3.82	3.57	3.73	3.80	3.80	3.80	3.27	3.85	3.50
6.	Guidance and counseling to students on personal problems	3.45	6	3.41	3.63	3.48	3.38	3.56	3.46	3.36	3.42	3.38
7.	Involvement in preparation of Syllabi	3.28	7	3.28	3.00	3.18	3.77	3.04	3.44	3.18	3.14	3.16
8.	Evaluation of answer books	3.15	8	3.41	3.21	3.34	3.03	2.76	2.90	2.90	4.00	3.32
9.	Conducting of examination	2.85	9	3.02	3.05	3.03	2.77	2.32	2.56	2.81	3.85	3.21

(Contd.)

(Contd. Table 5.1)

S.No.	Main duties actually performed by Teachers	Overall mean Score Value	Rank	College Teachers					
				Government (Mean Score Value)			Private (Mean Score Value)		
				Male	Female	Combined Means	Male	Female	Combined Means
1.	Classroom teaching	4.79	1	4.60	5.00	4.82	4.75	4.78	4.76
2.	Clarification of doubts of students in and after the class	4.63	2	4.50	4.53	4.51	4.75	4.78	4.76
3.	Guidance to students on research problems	3.74	3	3.80	3.92	3.86	4.25	3.28	3.63
4.	Encouraging students to write research papers	3.39	4	3.60	2.92	3.21	4.00	3.35	3.58
5.	Involving students in seminars	3.17	5	3.50	2.92	3.17	3.37	3.07	3.17
6.	Guidance and counselling to students on personal problems	3.12	6	3.00	3.46	3.26	2.87	3.07	2.99
7.	Involvement in preparation of Syllabi	3.03	7	3.40	2.76	3.03	3.25	2.92	3.04
8.	Evaluation of answer books	2.81	8	2.30	3.15	2.78	2.87	2.85	2.86
9.	Conducting of examination	2.70	9	2.60	3.15	2.91	3.12	2.14	2.49

'conducting of examination' than 'involvement in preparation of syllabi.' The sex-wise analysis in this group suggests that male teachers give more preference to 'guidance and counselling to students on personal problems' (3.36) than 'involving students in seminars' (3.27). On the other hand, female teachers have placed 'evaluation of answer books' (4.00), 'encouraging students to write research papers' (3.85), 'involving students in seminar' (3.85) and 'conducting of examination' (3.85) higher than 'guidance to students on research problem'(3.70). It shows that female teachers have less inclination to guide students on research problems than the males.

In the case of college teachers, the important duties performed by them are 'classroom teaching' (4.79), 'clarification of doubts of students in and after the class' (4.63), 'guidance and counselling to students on personal problems' (3.74), 'conducting of examination' (3.39), 'evaluation of answer books' (3.17), 'involving students in seminars' (3.12), 'involvement in preparation of syllabi (3.03), 'guidance to students on research problems' (2.81) and 'encouraging students to write research papers' (2.70) in the above order. Barring the first two duties, the remaining ones are entirely in a different order than those actually performed by the university teachers.

In respect of Government college, teachers have assigned a higher rank to 'involving students in seminars' than 'conducting of examination' as well as 'encouraging students to write research papers' than 'guidance to students on research problems'. Male teachers in this college have given a higher place to 'involvement in preparation of syllabi' (3.40) than 'involving students in seminars' (3.00). Again they have rated 'encouraging students to write research papers' (2.60) higher than 'guidance to students on research problems' (2.30). However, female teachers have given more importance to 'involving students in seminars' (3.46), 'guidance to students on research problems' and 'encouraging students to write research papers' (3.15 each) than 'conducting of examination' (2.92).

On the other hand, in the case of the Private college, the teachers have given more importance to 'involvement in preparation of syllabi' than 'involving students in seminars'. The sex-wise analysis in this group also shows that male teachers, have given more importance to 'involvement in preparation of syllabi' (3.25) than 'involving students in seminars' (2.87). However, female teachers have placed 'conducting of examination' (3.35) higher than 'guidance and counselling to students on personal problems' (3.28). Teachers in the colleges appear to be giving more importance to expressive than many of the instrumental roles.

The varied responses to the different duties actually performed by the teachers both in the university and colleges on sex-basis shows that role performance is influenced by the gender-status of the teachers. This lends support to our hypothesis.

1. (a) Relationship between the status (Designation Held) of Teachers and the Main Duties Actually Performed by them

An attempt was also made to find out the relationship between the status of teachers in the university and colleges and the main duties actually performed by them. A set of duties was provided to them and they were asked to rate these on a scale of importance, ranging from 'most important' to 'least important'. The scoring procedure followed is the same as that given for the previous table.

On the basis of the overall mean score values, as revealed in Table 5.2, the university teachers have given the same rank order to the roles that they actually perform, as given in the analysis of the previous table,

In the science group, we observe that teachers have also given the same rank older to the roles being performed by them except 'evaluation of books' as is apparent in Table 5.2. This has been placed higher than 'involvement in preparation of syllabi'. The status-wise analysis in this group shows that Professors have rated these roles on same pattern as observed on the basis of the overall mean score values. However, Readers have placed 'guidance and counselling to students on personal problems' (3.82) and 'involving students in seminars' (3.70) higher than 'encouraging students to write research papers' (3.64). However, Lecturers have given a higher rating to 'evaluation of answer books' (3.48) than 'guidance and counselling to students on personal problems' (3.24) as well as 'conducting of examination' (3.08) higher than 'involvement in preparation of syllabi' (2.72). This may be due to their lower position in the hierarchy of status of teachers.

Table 5.2

Relationship between the Status (Designation Held) of the Teachers and the Main Duties that they actually perform in the day to day functioning

S. No.	Main duties actually performed by Teachers	Overall Mean Score Value	Rank	University Teachers: Science (Mean Score Value) P	R	L	Combined Mean	Social Science (Mean Score Value) P	R	L	Combined Mean	Professional (Mean Score Value) P	R	L	Combined Mean
1.	Classroom teaching	4.94	1	5.00	4.82	5.00	4.94	5.00	4.90	4.95	4.94	5.00	5.00	5.00	5.00
2.	Clarification of doubts of students in and after the class	4.76	2	4.87	4.76	4.80	4.80	4.81	4.70	4.65	4.71	5.00	4.50	4.75	4.77
3.	Guidance to students on research problems	4.10	3	4.62	4.41	4.28	4.41	4.50	4.60	2.40	3.78	4.50	4.33	3.25	4.16
4.	Encouraging students to write research papers	3.73	4	4.31	3.64	3.80	3.89	3.81	3.40	3.55	3.57	3.87	3.66	3.75	3.77
5.	Involving students in seminars	3.72	5	4.00	3.70	3.60	3.74	3.93	3.55	3.90	3.78	3.25	3.66	3.75	3.50
6.	Guidance and counselling to students on personal problems	3.47	6	3.50	3.82	3.24	3.48	3.62	3.40	3.40	3.46	3.62	3.33	3.50	3.49
7.	Involvement in preparation of Syllabi	3.29	7	3.50	3.41	2.72	3.13	3.56	3.75	3.20	3.50	3.50	2.83	3.00	3.16
8.	Evaluation of answer books	3.15	8	3.37	3.05	3.48	3.32	2.50	3.25	2.85	2.89	3.00	4.00	3.50	3.44
9.	Conducting of examination	2.88	9	3.18	2.76	3.08	3.01	2.50	2.85	2.50	2.62	3.25	3.33	3.50	3.33

(Contd.)

Note P = Professor, R = Reader, L = Lecturer

(Contd. Table 5.2)

S. No.	Main duties actually performed by Teachers	Overall Mean Score Value	Rank	College Teachers: Government (Mean Score Value)				College Teachers: Private (Mean Score Value)			
				Senior Lecturer	Lecturer	Guest Faculty	Combined mean	Senior Lecturer	Lecturer	Guest Faculty	Combined mean
1.	Classroom teaching	4.77	1	5.00	4.76	4.66	4.82	5.00	4.63	3.00	4.72
2.	Clarification of doubts of students in and after the class	4.65	2	4.57	4.53	5.00	4.60	4.70	4.72	5.00	4.72
3.	Guidance to counseling to students on personal problems	3.74	3	4.28	3.84	3.00	3.86	3.80	3.45	4.00	3.63
4.	Conducting of examination	3.37	4	3.28	3.38	2.33	3.21	3.80	3.45	2.00	3.54
5.	Evaluation of answer books	3.19	5	3.42	3.30	2.33	3.21	3.20	3.27	2.00	3.18
6.	Involving students in seminars	3.12	6	2.57	3.53	3.66	3.25	3.20	2.81	3.00	2.99
7.	Involvement in preparation of Syllabi	2.97	7	3.00	3.15	2.66	3.04	3.10	2.72	3.00	2.90
8.	Guidance to students on research problems	2.90	8	2.28	3.00	4.66	2.99	2.60	3.18	1.00	2.81
9.	Encouraging students to write research papers	2.63	9	2.14	3.15	3.66	2.90	2.40	2.36	2.00	2.36

In the case of social science group, the teachers have given more importance to 'involving students in seminars' than 'encouraging students to write research papers'. Again, they have ranked, 'involvement in preparation of syllabi' higher than 'guidance and counselling to students on personal problems'. The status-wise analysis in this group shows that Professors attach more importance to "involving students in seminars' (3.93) than 'encouraging students to write research papers' (3.81) but Readers in this group in their day to day functioning give more importance to 'involvement in preparation of syllabi' (3.75) and 'involving students in seminars' (3.55) than 'encouraging students to write research papers' (3.40). However, Lecturers in this group have assigned a higher rating to 'involving students in seminars' (3.90) than 'encouraging students to write research papers' (3.55). Interestingly, they have given lowest rank order to 'guidance to students on research problems' (2.40). This may be due to their lower position and less experience to guide students on research.

The teachers in the professional group seem to be giving more importance to 'evaluation of answer books' and 'conducting of examination' than 'involvement in preparation of syllabi'. The status-wise analysis shows that Professors in this group are giving more importance to 'guidance and counselling to students on personal problems' (3.62) and 'involvement in preparation of syllabi' (3.50) than 'involving students in seminars' along with 'conducting of examination' (3.25 each). However, Readers have rated 'evaluation of answer books' (4.00) higher than 'encouraging students to write research papers' (3.66) whereas 'conducting of examination' (3.33) has been given more importance than 'involvement in the preparation of syllabi' (2.83). Lecturers in this group have given more importance to 'encouraging students to write research papers' 'involving students in seminars' (3.75 each) than 'guidance and counselling to students on personal problems,' 'evaluation of answer books' and 'conducting of examination (3.50 each). 'Guidance to students on research problems' (3.25) is placed below them. This may be because of their lesser experience than the senior teachers that they do not give much importance to this role.

In the case of college teachers on the basis of overall mean score value, it is observed that they have given importance to 'classroom teaching' (4.77). 'clarification of doubts in and after the class' (4.65), 'guidance and counselling to students on personal problems' (3.74), 'conducting of examination' (3.37), 'evaluation of answer books' (3.19), 'involving students in seminars' (3.12), 'involvement in the preparation of syllabi' (2.97), 'guidance to students on research problems' (2.90) and 'encouraging students to write research papers' (2.63) in that order while performing their duties.

In respect of the Government college, the teachers have given more importance to "involving students in seminars' than 'conducting of examination' and 'evaluation of answer books'. The status-wise analysis in this college shows that Senior Lecturers attach more importance to 'evaluation of answer books' (3.42) than 'conducting of examination' (3.28), while 'involving students in seminars' (2.57) has been placed below 'involvement in the preparation of syllabi' (3.00). However, Lecturers have given more importance to 'involving students in seminars' (3.53) than 'conducting of examination' (3.38). Further, 'encouraging students to write research papers' (3.15) has been placed higher than 'guidance to students on research problems' (3.00). The Guest Faculty in this college appears to be quite inconsistent in his or her rating pattern. He or she has importance to 'clarification or doubts in and after the class' (5.00) than 'classroom teaching' and 'guidance to students on research problems' (4.66 each). Even, 'involving students in seminars' bracketed alongwith 'encouraging students to write research papers' (3.66) has been given more importance than 'guidance and counselling to students on personal problems' (3.00) and 'involvement in the preparation of syllabi' (2.66). He or she has given least importance to 'conducting of examination' and 'evaluation of answer books' (2.33). This may be because he or she being on temporary basis, is not eligible to evaluate the answer books.

On the other hand, in the case of the Private college, the teachers have rated 'evaluation of answer books' higher than 'involving students in seminars'. The status-wise analysis in this college shows that Senior Lecturers have given importance to various duties in the same manner as observed on the basis of overall mean score values. However, Lecturers seem to be giving more importance to 'clarification of doubts in and after the class' (4.72) than 'classroom teaching' (4.63). Besides, they are giving more importance to 'evaluation of answer books' (3.27) and 'guidance to the students on research problems' (3.18) than 'involving students in seminars'(2.81). Again, the Guest Faculty members in this college have given more importance to 'clarification of doubts in and after the class' (5.00) and 'guidance and counselling to students on personal problems' (4.00) than 'classroom teaching,' 'involving students in seminars' and 'involvement in the preparation of syllabi' (3.00each) while 'guidance to students on research problems' (1.00) has been given the lowest rank order.

It is apparent from the above analysis that teachers both in the university and colleges holding different statuses or ranks have given varied responses in order of importance to various duties being performed by them. As such, we can infer that the status of teachers influences their role performance. This is in support of our hypothesis that the status or designation held by teachers has some bearing on their role performance.

2. Gaps between Educational Training and Jobs Expected of Teachers

An attempt is made to find out from teachers in the university and colleges whether or not they experience any gap between their educational training and jobs expected of them. It is observed that out of 132 teachers in the university, only 7 of them (2 males and 1 female in science, one male in social science and one male and two females in the professional group), mentioned that they experienced this gap. Again, in the case of college teachers, out of 45 teachers only 6 of them (one male in Government college and one male and four females in the Private college) stated that they observed this gap between the educational training and jobs expected of them. It is apparent from the above that the majority of the teachers feel that they have adequate educational training to match the jobs expected of them.

3. Gaps between Jobs Expected and Performed by Teachers

The teachers in the university and colleges were asked to specify whether or not there was any gap felt by them between the jobs expected and performed.

Out of 132 teachers, only 11 in the university (6 males in the science, 2 males and 1 female in the social science and 1 male and 1 female in the professional group) expressed that there was a gap experienced by them between the jobs expected and performed. Again, in the case of colleges, out of 45 teachers only 4 (1 male in the Government college and 3 females in the Private college) replied in affirmative to the above question. In view of small number of responses the gaps experienced by the teachers in the university as well as in the colleges have been clubbed together and these are as stated below.

In the case of university teachers, some teachers mentioned that they had more expectation from themselves and their actual performance could not match with it. In a way, this may act as a motivating factor for improving their performance. It is also mentioned that there is a gap experienced while applying theoretical knowledge to certain practical aspects. Due to increase in knowledge and techniques, a need is now felt for new equipments to carry out advanced research and for conducting frequent laboratory tests. It is also stated that there is inadequate time for research work due to too many teaching hours.

On the other hand, in the case of college teachers, it is pointed out that the Principals treat every faculty with the same yardstick without understanding the nature of work involved. This increases the gap between the jobs expected and performed by them. Further, it is mentioned that although teachers have acquired a higher level of knowledge, yet students want them to stick to the set syllabi. It is also stated that the newly appointed teacher is just handed over the time-table and attendance register without any formal orientation or training. Some talented teachers may cope with it while others may not be able to do so.

4. Gaps in Jobs Expected and Performed by Teachers affecting their performance

The teachers in the university and colleges were further asked whether or not the gaps in jobs expected and performed by them affected their performance.

It is found out that of 132 teachers in the university, only 6 of them (two males in science, one male and one female in social science and one male and one female in the professional group) replied affirmatively to the above question. It is suggested by these teachers that, by and large, the gaps observed between jobs expected and performed by them lower their efficiency.

On the other hand, in the case of college teachers, out of 45, three of them (one male in Government college and two females in the Private college) feel that the gaps expected and performed by them affect their performance.

It is argued that a teacher is expected to develop the all-round personality of students but in reality, he or she is not able to do so. Even, because of the gaps observed in between the two, the output of teachers is less. Further, in order to complete the syllabus in time, a teacher is compelled to follow it rather than covering wider issues.

5. Matching of Performance of Teachers with the Expectations of Students

The teachers in the university and colleges were asked to specify whether or not, in their perception, there is matching of their performance with the expectations of students.

Again out of 132 teachers in the university, only three of them (2 males in science and 1 male in the professional group) state that there is no matching of their performance with the expectations of students. It is expressed by these teachers that students do not appreciate that they should ask the students to work hard for carrying out research. Besides, they expect teachers to give them notes as well as not to ask them questions in the class. On the other hand, in the case of college teachers, out of 45, only one teacher feels that there is no matching of her performance with the expectations of students (one female in the Private college).

It is clear from the above that almost all teachers feel that there is matching of their performance with the expectations of students. However, the only female teacher in the Private college feels that the contact of teachers with the students on personal level is less. As such, it affects adversely the matching of performance of teachers with the expectations of students.

6. Response of Students towards Gaps Observed in the Tasks Expected and Performed by the Teachers

In addition to the perception of teachers regarding gaps between the jobs expected and performed by them and the matching of their performance with the expectations of students, it may be worthwhile to bring in here the analysis pertaining to the response of students towards the gaps observed in the tasks expected and performed by the teachers for comparative purposes.

Out of 77 university students, nearly three-fourth of them (76.62 per cent) express that they do observe gaps in the task expected and performed by their teachers. The sex-wise analysis of students attending various courses, again confirms that nearly three-fourth of them belonging to both the sexes in the science group experience this gap. Further, a higher proportion of male (90 per cent), than female (75 per cent) students in the social science group and higher number of female (3) than (1) male students in the professional group feel that there are gaps observed in the tasks expected and performed by teachers.

On the other hand, in the case of college students, out of 72, as many as 52 (72.22 per cent) have mentioned that they do experience gaps in tasks expected and performed by teachers. The sex-wise analysis of students shows that in the case of Government college, a higher proportion of female (75.00 per cent) than male (63.16 per cent) students have expressed this gap. However, in respect of the Private college, we find a higher proportion of male (80.95 per cent) than female (68.75 per cent) students observing the gap between tasks expected and performed by teachers. By and large, it is the male students except in the case of professional group in the university and the Government college where female students show pre-ponderence over them, who are responding more positively about this gap.

7. Response of those Students, who think that the Gaps Observed in the Tasks Expected and Performed by Teachers make their Role Ineffective

All those students in the university and colleges who stated that they observed gaps in the task, expected and performed by the teachers, were asked to respond whether or not these gaps made the role of teachers ineffective.

It is observed that out of 59 students in the university, as many as 48 (81.36 per cent) expressed that the gaps observed made the role of their teachers ineffective. The sex-wise analysis of students attending different courses in the university suggests that in the science and social sciences groups in the combined form, there is higher number of female (23) than male (21) students who expressed that the gaps observed have made the role of teachers ineffective. In the case of professional group, all students (one male and three females) support the above statement.

In the case of college students, out of 52, the majority of them 44 (84.62 per cent) have replied in affirmative to the existence of gaps between the tasks expected and performed by the teachers. The sex-wise analysis of students in the colleges suggests that a higher number of male (10) than female (9) students in the Government college while a higher proportion of female (90.91 per cent) than male (88.24 per cent) students in the Private college, feel that the gaps observed in the tasks expected and performed by teachers make their role ineffective.

If we compare the results of teachers regarding the gaps observed between the jobs expected and performed by them, and matching of their performance with the expectations of students, with those of students in regard to the gaps observed in the tasks expected and performed by the teachers, we observe contradictory findings.

On the one hand, teachers in the university as well as in the colleges hardly observe any gaps between the jobs expected and performed by them while students express otherwise. Teachers, by and large, stick to syllabi and courses, which are hardly updated and revised to meet the changing needs of the students. Often, these syllabi are teacher rather than student oriented. The teachers want to give to the students what they have rather than basing their courses on the needs of the students. In this scenario of globalization, information technology, computerization, bio-diversity, advances in physical and biomedical sciences, engineering and management, there are newer developments which need to be brought home to the students. This can prepare them adequately to find avenues of employment and have better control of their environments. Even, in the case of liberal arts and social sciences as well as in the profession like laws, there are newer developments and futuristic trends which need to be accumulated and transmitted to the students. There is also a need to bring in innovative methods of teaching as well as to restructure the examination system so that the teaching and the research components become more relevant to the requirements of the students.

It is also possible that students may have a higher set of expectations from their teachers and this may not be matching, to a large extent, to their actual performance. As it is often reported by students that teachers especially in the colleges, do not take classes regularly and are not serious about their jobs. On the other hand, teachers blame students for their non-seriousness. In order to make the role of teachers more effective, the gaps observed between the expectations of teachers and those of students from each other need to be bridged by bringing in certain changes in the educational structure.

Whenever there are different set of expectations of teachers and students from each other, these are bound to give rise to role conflict. It is observed that with so many role demands to satisfy, it is difficult to comply with all. The only way one can cope up with this role conflict is by yielding to pressure, sticking to professional standards, making compromises or avoiding the responsibility of making relevant decisions (Lindgren, 1974).

8. Difference with Colleagues regarding Teaching Components of the Students

An attempt is made to find out whether there is any difference of opinion on the part of teachers with their colleagues regarding teaching components to be given to the students. This may have some bearing on their role performance.

Nearly half of the teacher in the university (49.24 per cent) and two thirds in the colleges (68.89 per cent) have expressed that they have difference of opinion with their colleagues in regard to teaching components. The faculty-wise analysis in the university suggests that a higher proportion of teachers (63.79 per cent) in the science group belonging to both the sexes, show difference with their colleagues on this aspect. However, in the social science group, only 41.08 per cent teachers have expressed difference, with their colleagues and a higher proportion of male (45.16 per cent) than female (36.0 per cent) teachers appear to be doing so. But, in the case of professional teachers, nearly one-fourth of them have expressed difference of opinion with their colleagues and again we have more male (4) than female (1) teachers expressing so.

On the other hand, in the case of colleges, more number of teachers in the Private college (18) than those in the Government college (13) have stated difference of opinion with their coileagues in regard to teaching components to be given to the students. Again, a higher proportion of male than female teachers in both the colleges are expressing difference of opinion with their colleagues.

8 (a) Extent Of Cordial Relationships with the Colleagues

All the teachers in the university (65) and in the colleges (31) who expressed that they had difference of opinion with their colleagues regarding teaching components to be given to the students, were asked to indicate the extent of cordial relationships they had with their colleagues. They were asked to specify their relationships in terms of most cordial/fairly cordial/cordial/less cordial/least cordial. A score of 5 was given to those respondents who specified their relationship as 'most cordial' while a score of one was assigned to relationship mentioned as 'least cordial'. Those who stated fairly cordial/cordial/less cordial were assigned a score of 4, 3 and 2 respectively. A mean score value was worked out sex-wise within each faculty in the university as well as in the two colleges to show gender-differences. An overall mean score value was also worked out in the university and in the two colleges for comparative purposes.

On the basis of overall mean score values, the teachers in the university exhibit a better cordial relationship (3.99) than those in the colleges (3.76). Within the university, we observe a higher extent of cordiality among female (4.08) than male teachers (3.96).

Again, the faculty wise analysis suggests that as compared to science (3.69) and professional groups (3.80), the teachers in the social science group (4.53) are showing a higher extent of cordial relationship with their colleagues. However, sex-wise analysis within each faculty shows that more female (3.90) than males (3.61) in the science group and also more female (4.00) than males (3.75) teachers in the professional group have expressed greater extent of cordial relationships. However, in the case of social science group, more male (4.67) than female (4.33) teachers have shown a larger extent of cordiality towards their colleagues.

The college-wise analysis suggests that teachers in the Government college (3.84) than those in the Private college (3.71) appear to have more cordial relationships with their colleagues. In the case of Government college, more female (4.16) than male teachers (3.57) have expressed a greater extent of cordial relationships with their colleagues. However, this is vice-versa the case in respect of teachers in the Private college.

The above analysis suggests that except for social science group in the university and the Private college teachers, female teachers tend to show a higher degree of cordiality in their relationships with their colleagues. This may be due to their gender role. As suggested by various researches, females prefer activities involving social interaction and ingratiation (Lindgren, 1974). Thus, it appears that although, by and large, the relationships of teachers with colleagues are cordial, yet in some cases discordiality has been mentioned. The various factors leading to lack of cordiality are discussed below.

9. Factors/Reasons Causing Problems with Colleagues

It is observed that teachers both in the university as well as in the colleges cannot work as a team for the growth and development of their departments/colleges. They were asked to respond to a number of factors causing problems with their colleagues for working as a team. These factors often affect the role performance of teachers.

An examination of Table 5.3 shows that among the university teachers, the most important factor causing problem with the

Table 5.3

Factors causing Problems with Colleagues to Work as a Team

S.No.	Factors causing problems with colleagues	University Teachers			Combined Total (N=132)*	College Teachers		Combined Total of Colleges (N=45)*
		Science (N=58)	Social Science (N=56)	Professional (N=18)		Government (N=23)	Private (N=22)	
1.	Adamant attitude of some	33 (56.90)	29 (51.78)	10 (55.55)	72 (54.54)	12 (52.17)	9 (40.90)	21 (46.66)
2.	Ego Involvement or Hassles	24 (41.37)	29 (51.78)	12 (66.66)	65 (49.24)	6 (26.08)	8 (36.36)	14 (31.11)
3.	Personal Interests	25 (43.10)	32 (57.14)	8 (44.44)	65 (49.24)	11 (47.82)	9 (40.90)	20 (44.44)
4.	Group alignment or Factional Politics	20 (34.48)	26 (46.42)	11 (61.11)	57 (43.18)	4 (17.39)	13 (59.09)	17 (37.77)
5.	Jealousy	19 (32.75)	24 (42.85)	7 (38.88)	50 (37.87)	6 (26.08)	6 (27.27)	12 (26.66)
6.	Overlapping of duties and responsibilities	17 (29.31)	9 (16.07)	1 (5.55)	27 (20.45)	9 (39.13)	6 (27.27)	15 (33.33)
7.	Unhealthy Competition	9 (15.51)	8 (14.28)	2 (11.11)	19 (14.39)	1 (4.34)	2 (9.09)	3 (6.66)
8.	Others (Lack of interest in the profession/lack of respect for seniority/different perceptions of the collegues)	1 (1.72)	2 (3.57)	0 (0.00)	3 (2.27)			

Note : (I) * Multiple Responses

(ii) Figures within brackets represent percentages

colleagues to work as a team, is adamant attitude of some (54.54 per cent). This is followed by ego involvement or hassles and personal interests (49.24 per cent each). The other factors mentioned in order of importance are group alignment of factional politics (43.18 per cent) and jealousy (37.37 per cent). The overlapping of duties and responsibilities (20.45 per cent) and unhealthy competition (14.39 per cent) have been stated as other reasons causing problems with colleagues. A few of them (3) have also given lack of interest in the profession/lack of respect for seniority/different perceptions of the colleagues as reasons in the category of others. (These responses are multiple and have been arranged in the table in the descending order according to frequency distribution for the university teachers. However, for the college teachers these have not been arranged in the descending order but have been stated corresponding to the responses given by the university teachers).

The faculty-wise analysis among the university teachers suggests that a higher proportion of science teachers have given more importance to personal interests (43.10 per cent) than ego involvement (41.37 per cent) as a factor causing problems with colleagues. The same holds good for social science teachers. However, the teachers in the professional group consider 'group alignment or factional politics' (61.11 per cent) more significant than 'personal interests' (44.44 per cent) as a factor causing problems with colleagues. Even, more number of teachers in this group have mentioned about 'unhealthy competition' (2) than 'overlapping of duties and responsibilities' (1) as a factor contributing towards this end.

In the case of college teachers in terms of frequency distribution, we observe that 'personal interests' (20) has been placed next to 'adamant attitude of some teachers' (21). This is followed by jealousy (17), overlapping of duties and responsibilities (15), ego involvement or hassles (14), group alignment or factional politics (12) and unhealthy competition (3).

In the case of Government college, the factors identified in order are adamant attitude of some (12), personal interest (11), overlapping of duties and responsibilities (9), ego involvement and group alignment (6 each) and unhealthy competition (1). However, in the case of the Private college, more number of teachers have stated jealousy (13), adamant attitude of some and personal interests (9 each), ego involvement (8), group alignment and overlapping of duties and responsibilities (6 each) as well as unhealthy competition (2).

It is clear from the above analysis that teachers, being educated have a rational outlook and keep their personal interests above other things. Besides, their ego gets evolved and they develop adamant attitudes. In this competitive world, there is also tendency to have unhealthy competition which often gives rise to jealousy or indulgence in factional politics. Moreover, there is also overlapping of duties and responsibilities observed in day to day functioning. The above factors are not mutually exclusive and influence each other in causing problems with the colleagues to work as a team for the growth and development of their respective departments. In short, these factors affect the role performance of teachers both in the university as well as the colleges.

10. Factors (Personal, Familial, Organizational and Societal) affecting the Role Performance of Teachers

It is observed that there are a number of personal, familial, organizational and societal factors that are likely to affect he performance of teachers. A set of these factors was provided to the university and college teachers and they were asked to express their agreement or disagreement on the influence of these in their role performance. These factors were presented to them in the form of statements. Those who strongly agreed to a statement were given a score of 5, while those who strongly disagreed to the statement were assigned a score of 1. Besides, those who responded 'agree,' 'undecided' and 'disagree' to the statement, were assigned a score of 4, 3, 2 respectively. A sex-wise mean score value within science, social sciences and professional groups in the university as well as for the two colleges was worked out. A combined mean score was also worked out for teachers within the three faculties in the university and for the Government and Private colleges. An overall mean score value was also worked out for these factors to rank them in order of "extent of agreement" for comparative analysis. These were arranged in a descending order. The higher the mean score value, the greater was the extent of agreement. An attempt is made to see if there is any relationship between the sex of the teachers and the various factors that affect their role performance.

An examination of Table 5.4 brings out that teachers in the university have shown a greater extent of agreement to a societal factor 'one should give equal attention to all students irrespective of socio-economic status' (4.88). This is followed by 'one should care more to satisfy the students than seeking appreciation of the chairperson' (4.61). This relates to the organizational factor. Next in order are personal orientated factors, that is, 'one should keep away from emotional involvement of any kind with the students' (3.39) and 'one should try to meet the needs of the students and take interest in their personal problems' (3.36). This is followed by two familial factors, that is 'one should not bother about the complaint of one's spouse that one cares more for books than for her/him' (2.76) and 'one should discourage one's son/daughter to join this profession' (1.83). The last factor ranked in order is societal, that is, 'one should give extra attention to students belonging to your kin, caste, religion or region' (1.28). The least agreement on this factor shows that teachers being educated have a secular outlook.

The faculty-wise analysis among the university teachers shows that teachers in the science group have shown a greater extent of agreement with 'one should try to meet the needs of the students and take interest in their personal problems' than "one should keep away from emotional involvement of any kind with the students". The sex-wise analysis in this group shows that the extent of agreement with the statements on the part of . male teachers is same as given in the overall analysis while the female teachers have suggested a greater extent of agreement with 'one should try to meet the needs of the students and take interest in their personal problems' (3.63) than 'one should keep away from emotional involvement of any kind with the students' (3.21). The teachers in the social science group have given the same extent of agreement to these statements as observed in the overall analysis. Again, the sex-wise analysis in this group shows that both the male and female teachers are in agreement with the teachers in the science group towards ranking of these statements. However, in the case of professional group, teachers are for greater agreement on 'one should try to meet the needs of the students

Table 5.4

Relationship between sex of the Teachers and Factors (Personal, Familial, Organizational and Societal) that affect their Performance

S. No.	Factors (Personal, Familial, Organizational and Societal)	Overall Mean Score Value	Rank	Extent of Agreement — University Teachers: Science (Mean Score Value)			Social Science (Mean Score Value)			Professional (Mean Score Value)		
				Male	Female	Combined Mean	Male	Female	Combined Mean	Male	Female	Combined Mean
1.	One should give equal attention to all students irrespective of socio-economic status	4.88	1	4.89	5.00	4.92	4.80	4.88	4.83	4.90	5.00	4.93
2.	One should care more to satisfy the students than seeking appreciation of the chairperson/principal	4.61	2	4.71	4.47	4.63	4.70	4.52	4.61	4.54	4.71	4.60
3.	One should keep away from emotional involvement of any kind with the students	3.39	3	3.28	3.21	3.25	3.87	3.28	3.60	3.27	3.14	3.21
4.	One should try to meet the needs of the students and take interest in their personal problems	3.36	4	3.12	3.63	3.28	3.25	3.64	3.42	3.36	3.57	3.44
5.	One should not bother about the complaint of one's spouse that you care more for books than for her/him	2.76	5	2.74	2.68	2.72	3.09	2.64	2.88	2.72	2.28	2.54
6.	One should discourage one's son/daughter to join this profession	1.83	6	1.97	1.78	1.90	1.77	1.92	1.83	1.72	1.57	1.66
7.	One should give extra attention to students belonging to your kin, caste, religion or region.	1.28	7	1.23	1.68	1.37	1.19	1.20	1.19	1.27	1.28	1.27

(Contd.)

(Contd. Table 5.4)

S.No.	Factors (Personal, Familial, Organizational and Societal)	Extent of Agreement: Overall mean Score Value	Rank	College Teachers: Government (Mean Score Value) Male	Government Female	Government Combined Mean	Private (Mean Score Value) Male	Private Female	Private Combined Mean
1.	One should give equal attention to all students irrespective of socio-economic status	4.93	1	5.00	5.00	5.00	5.00	4.78	4.86
2.	One should care more to satisfy the students than seeking appreciation of the chairperson/principal	4.68	2	4.90	4.61	4.73	4.50	4.71	4.63
3.	One should keep away from emotional involvement of any kind with the students	3.43	3	3.50	3.76	3.64	2.75	3.50	3.22
4.	One should try to meet the needs of the students and take interest in their personal problems	3.30	4	3.10	3.15	3.12	3.50	3.50	3.50
5.	One should not bother about the complaint of one's spouse that you care more for books than for her/him	2.88	5	3.20	2.92	3.04	2.62	2.78	2.72
6.	One should discourage one's son/daughter to join this profession	1.52	6	1.40	1.76	1.60	1.25	1.57	1.45
7.	One should give extra attention to students belonging to your kin, caste, religion or region.	1.30	7	1.00	1.30	1.16	1.37	1.50	1.45

and take interest in their personal problems' than 'one should keep away from emotional involvement of any kind with the students'. The sex-wise analysis of teachers in this group shows that both the male and female teachers are in line with the extent of agreement on these statements as indicated by the combined mean score values for this group.

In the case of college teachers, interestingly, it is observed that they have stated the same extent of agreement to these statements in order of rank as given by the university teachers. Even the Government college teachers have assigned the same rank order to these statements as given in the overall analysis. However, male teachers in this college have shown greater extent of agreement with 'one should keep away from emotional involvement of any kind with the students' (3.50) and 'one should not bother about the complaint of one's spouse that one cares more for books than for him or her' (3.20) than 'one should try to meet the needs of the students and take interest in their personal problems' (3.10). However, female teachers in this college have provided the same rank to these statements as given in the overall analysis for the college teachers. On the other hand, teachers in the Private college have given a greater extent of agreement to 'one should try to meet the needs of the students and take interest in their personal problems' than 'one should keep away from emotional involvement of any kind with the students'. The male teachers in this college have given the same rank order to these statements as stated above, while the female teachers are consistently in agreement with these statements as suggested by the teachers in the overall analysis for both the colleges.

It is clear from the above analysis, that teachers both in the university and colleges are, by and large, consistent with the extent of agreement with these statements in providing a rank order except the personal factors such as 'one should keep away from emotional involvement of any kind with the students,' and 'one should try to meet the needs of the students and take interest in their personal problems', as there are variations observed on gender basis of the teachers on these. The extent of agreement or disagreement on personal, familial, organistional and societal factors expressed in terms of various statements reflect the opinions and attitudes of teachers. These may, to a certain extent, contribute towards influencing the performance of teachers.

11. Nature of Problems faced by teachers while Performing their Duties and Responsibilities

There are a number of problems which the teachers face while performing their roles. A set of these problems was provided to teachers both in the university as well as in the colleges and they were asked to specify these in order of importance. These problems can be broadly categorized as professional and organizational. The professional problems include 'competing claims of research and teaching,' 'conflicting claims of profession (meetings, conferences, examinations and teaching),' 'conflicting claims of reading, teaching and writing,' 'competing claims of students' work and one's own work,' 'competing claims of teaching and family roles,' 'lack of orientation and refresher course facilities' and 'lack of autonomy to the teachers'. On the other hand, the organizational problems faced by teachers include 'inadequate salary structure,' 'inadequate housing accommodation,' 'lack of facilities to travel abroad (fellowship and training grants),' 'lack of incentives such as promotional avenues due to stagnation in position for long,' 'inadequate medical facilities,' 'administrative difficulties such as leave rules, promotional rules etc' and 'inadequate physical surroundings not congenial for work'.

The teachers were asked to rate these problems on a scale of importance. A problem rated as most important was assigned a score of 5 while the one mentioned as least important was given a score of 1. The problems which were rated as fairly important, important and less important were given a score of 4, 3, 2 respectively. A mean score value was worked out sex-wise within each faculty for the teachers in the university as well as for the two colleges separately. A combined mean score was also worked out for these problems for teachers in the science, social science and professional groups within the university and for the two colleges. An overall mean score value for these problems was worked out for all the teachers in the university as well as for the colleges to provide comparative analysis.

In order to show relationship between the sex of the teachers and the nature of problems faced by them while performing their duties, an examination of Table 5.5 brings out that on basis of overall mean values, the teachers in the university have rated

Table 5.5 Relationship between the Sex of the Teachers and the nature of Problems faced by them while performing their duties

S. No.	Nature of Problems faced by Teachers	Overall Mean Score Value	Rank	University Teachers								
				Science (Mean Score Value)			Social Science (Mean Score Value)			Professional (Mean Score Value)		
				Male	Female	Combined Mean	Male	Female	Combined Mean	Male	Female	Combined Mean
1.	Competing claims of research and teaching	3.61	1	3.84	4.05	3.91	3.16	3.56	3.33	3.09	4.14	3.50
2.	Conflicting claims of profession (meetings/conferences/examination)	3.56	2	4.84	3.15	4.28	2.67	2.92	2.78	3.81	3.57	3.71
3.	Lack of Incentives such as promotional avenues due to stagnation	3.00	3	3.05	3.05	3.05	2.64	3.04	2.82	2.81	4.42	3.47
4.	Lack of autonomy to teachers	2.91	4	3.05	2.63	2.91	2.64	2.96	2.78	3.00	3.85	3.33
5.	Conflicting claims of reading, teaching and writing	2.80	5	2.76	2.73	2.75	2.58	3.00	2.76	3.18	3.00	3.11
6.	Inadequate physical surrounding not congenial for work	2.75	6	3.05	2.36	2.82	2.35	2.76	2.53	2.90	3.71	3.21
7.	Lack of facilities to travel abroad (fellowships and grants)	2.71	7	2.74	2.94	2.80	2.45	2.88	2.64	2.09	3.57	2.66
8.	Inadequate housing accommodation	2.69	8	2.84	2.52	2.73	2.61	2.60	2.60	2.27	3.85	2.88
9.	Competing claims of students' work and one's own work	2.68	9	2.69	2.78	2.71	2.29	2.88	2.55	2.81	3.42	3.04
10.	Administrative difficulties (leave rules/promotional rules)	2.66	10	2.82	3.05	2.89	2.22	2.60	3.39	2.09	3.85	2.77
11.	Competing claims of teaching and family roie	2.60	11	2.33	3.00	2.55	2.29	2.92	2.57	2.27	3.85	2.88
12.	Inadequate medical facilities	2.38	12	2.41	2.63	2.48	2.00	2.40	2.17	2.09	3.71	2.72
13.	Lack of orientation and refresher course facilities	2.27	13	2.51	2.42	2.48	1.67	2.44	2.01	2.18	2.85	2.44
14.	Inadequate salary structure	2.18	14	2.23	2.31	2.25	1.90	2.12	2.00	2.00	3.42	2.55

(Contd.)

(Contd. Table 5.5)

S.No.	Nature of problems faced by teachers	Overall mean Score Value	Rank	College Teachers					
				Government (Mean Score Value)			Private (Mean Score Value)		
				Male	Female	Combined Mean	Male	Female	Combined Mean
1.	Lack of Incentives such as promotional avenues due to stagnation	3.92	1	4.20	3.92	4.04	4.00	3.71	3.81
2.	Inadequate physical surrounding not congenial for work	3.86	2	4.00	3.76	3.86	4.50	3.50	3.86
3.	Lack of autonomy to teachers	3.68	3	4.30	3.15	3.65	4.12	3.50	3.72
4.	Administrative difficulties (leave rules/promotional rules)	3.39	4	3.90	3.23	3.52	3.25	3.28	3.26
5.	Inadequate medical facilities	3.32	5	3.40	3.15	3.25	3.12	3.57	3.40
6.	Competing claims of teaching and family role	3.28	6	3.20	3.69	3.47	4.00	2.57	3.09
7.	Lack of orientation and refresher course facilities	3.25	7	4.20	2.92	3.47	2.62	3.28	3.04
8.	Competing claims of students' work and one's own work	3.19	8	2.70	3.46	3.12	3.62	3.07	3.27
9.	Inadequate salary structure	3.04	9	3.30	2.80	3.01	3.37	2.92	3.08
10.	Inadequate housing accommodation	3.03	10	3.10	2.76	2.90	3.37	3.07	3.17
11.	Competing claims of research and teaching	2.99	11	3.60	2.69	3.08	2.50	3.14	2.90
12.	Conflicting claims of profession (meetings/conferences/examination)	2.96	12	3.00	2.92	2.95	2.50	3.28	2.99
13.	Lack of facilities to travel abroad (fellowships and grants)	2.94	13	3.00	3.07	3.03	2.75	2.92	2.85
14.	Conflicting claims of reading, teaching and writing	2.90	14	2.50	3.00	2.78	3.12	3.00	3.04

'competing claims of research and teaching' (3.61) 'conflicting claims of profession' (3.56), 'lack of incentives such as promotional avenues due to stagnation' (3.00), 'lack of autonomy to teachers' (2.91) 'conflicting claims of reading, teaching and writing' (2.80), inadequate physical surroundings not congenial for work' (2.75), 'lack of facilities to travel abroad' (2.71), 'inadequate housing accommodation' (2.69), 'competing claims of students' work and one's own work' (2.68) 'administrative difficulties' (2.66), 'competing claims of teaching and family role' (2.60), 'inadequate medical facilities' (2.38), 'lack of orientation and refresher courses' (2.27) and 'inadequate salary structure' (2.18), in order of their importance. It is apparent from the above analysis that most of these problems either fall in between fairly important and important or between important and less important categories. It may be indicative of the fact that many of these problems may not be hampering their performance.

The faculty wise analysis shows that teachers belonging to the science group have given more importance to 'conflicting claims of profession' (meetings, conferences, examination) than 'competing claims of research and teaching' in the area of professional issues. However, they-have rated 'administrative difficulties', 'inadequate physical surroundings not congenial for work' and 'lack of facilities to travel abroad' as a part of organistional problems, higher than 'conflicting claims of reading, teaching and writing'. The sex-wise analysis in this group shows that male teachers have given more importance to 'conflicting claims of profession' (4.84) than 'competing claims of research and teaching' (3.84). Further, they have given a higher rating to 'inadequate physical surroundings not congenial for work' (3.05), 'inadequate housing accommodating' (2.84), 'administrative difficulties' (2.82) higher than 'conflicting claims of reading, teaching and writing' (2.76). Even 'lack of orientation and refresher course facilities' (2.51) and 'inadequate medical facilities' (2.41) finds a higher ranking than 'competing claims of teaching and family role' (2.33). It is clear that male teachers in this group are giving relatively more importance to organistional issues related to facilities, incentives and reward system than professional problems. On the other hand, the female teachers in this group have given more importance to 'administrative difficulties' (3.05), 'competing claims of teaching and family role' (3.00), 'lack of facilities to travel abroad' (2.94), 'competing claims of students' work and one's own work' (2.78) and 'conflicting claims of reading, teaching and writing' (2.73) than 'lack of autonomy to teachers (2.63). Even, 'inadequate medical facilities' (2.63), 'inadequate housing accommodation' (2.52) and 'lack of orientation and refresher course facilities' (2.42) have been placed higher than 'inadequate physical surroundings' (2.36).

In the case of social science group, teachers have rated 'lack of incentives such as promotional avenues' higher than 'conflicting claims of profession,' Ever, 'lack of facilities to travel abroad', 'inadequate housing accommodation', 'competing claims of teaching and family role' and 'competing claim of students' work and one's own work' have been given more importance than 'inadequate physical surroundings not congenial for work'. The sex-wise analysis shows that male teachers have rated 'inadequate housing accommodation' (2.61) higher than 'conflicting claims of reading, teaching and writing (2.58) while 'lack of facilities to travel abroad' (2.45) has also been given higher rank than 'inadequate physical surrounding not congenial to work' (2.35). On the other hand, the female teachers in this group have given more importance to 'lack of incentives such as promotional avenues' (3.04), 'conflicting claims of reading, teaching and writing' and 'lack of autonomy to teachers' (2.96) than 'conflicting claims of profession' and 'conflicting claims of teaching and family roles' (2.92 each). Further, 'competing claims of students' work and one's own work' along with 'lack of facilities to travel abroad' (2.88 each) find a higher placing than 'inadequate physical surroundings not congenial for work' (2.76). Even in their case, 'lack of orientation and refresher course facilities' (2.44) finds a higher rating than 'inadequate medical facilities' (2.40).

In case of professional group, the 'conflicting claims of profession' finds a higher ranking than 'competing claims of research and teaching'. Further, 'inadequate physical surroundings not congenial for work' has been given a higher rating than 'conflicting claims of reading, teaching and writing'. Again, 'administrative difficulties' and 'inadequate medical facilities' find a higher placing than 'lack of facilities to travel abroad'. Even, 'inadequate salary structure' has been given a higher rating than 'lack of orientation and refresher course facilities'.

The sex-wise analysis in this group shows that male teachers tend to emphasize more on 'conflicting claims of profession' (3.81) and 'conflicting claims of reading, teaching and writing' (3.18) than 'competing claims of research and teaching' (3.09). Further, 'lack of autonomy to teachers' (3.00) and 'inadequate physical surroundings not congenial for work' (2.90) have been rated higher than 'lack of incentives such as promotional avenues' and 'competing claims of students' work and one's own work' (2.81 each). Even, 'lack of orientation and refresher course facilities' (2.18) has been placed higher than 'lack of facilities to travel abroad' (2.09), bracketed alongwith, 'administrative difficulties' and 'inadequate medical facilities'. On the other hand, the female teachers in this group have given a higher rank to 'lack of incentives such as promotional avenues' (4.42) than 'competing claims of research and teaching' (4.14). Even, 'lack of autonomy to teachers,' 'inadequate housing accommodation,' 'competing claims of teaching and family role' and 'administrative difficulties' (3.85 each), 'inadequate physical surroundings not congenial for work,' 'inadequate medical facilities' (3.71 each) have been placed higher than 'conflicting claims of profession' and 'lack of facilities to travel abroad' (3.57 each). Also, 'inadequate salary structure' (3.42) has been given a higher rating than 'lack of orientation and refresher course facilities' (2.85).

The sex-wise analysis of teachers in the three faculties shows that the nature of problems faced by them are in variance with their gender status. By and large, female teachers in all the three groups have relatively given more importance to some of the organizational issues related to facilities and incentives than male teachers. Interestingly, more female than male teachers have given higher rank order to the competing claims of teaching and family roles. This may be due to inter role conflict in between their professional and the familial role which is equally demanding for them.

In respect of college teachers, the issues faced in order of importance are 'lack of incentives such as promotional avenues' (3.92), 'inadequate physical surroundings' (3.86), 'lack of autonomy to teachers' (3.68), 'administrative difficulties' (3.39), 'inadequate medical facilities' (3.32), 'competing claims of teaching and family roles' (3.28), 'lack of orientation and refresher course facilities' (3.25), 'competing claims of students work and one's own work'

(3.19), inadequate salary structure' (3.04), 'inadequate housing accommodation' (3.03), 'competing claims of research and teaching' (2.99), 'conflicting claims of profession' (2.96), 'lack of facilities to travel abroad' (2.94) and 'conflicting claims of reading, teaching and writing' (2.90).

It is apparent from the above findings that teachers in the colleges have different set of problems than those in the university. They seem to have given higher ranking to 'lack of incentives such as promotional avenues due to stagnation' as well as 'inadequate physical surroundings not congenial for work'. These two issues which are related to facilities and incentives are organisational than professional in nature. They stagnate in their positions for long and have no separate rooms for sitting as well as for doing their professional work. They all share a common room meant for the teaching staff.

The college wise analysis suggests that teachers in the Government college have rated these problems in the same manner as observed on the basis of overall analysis except that 'inadequate medical facilities' has been placed lower than 'competing claims of teaching and family roles'. The sex-wise analysis in this college shows that male teachers have given more importance to 'lack of autonomy to teachers' (4.30) than 'lack of incentives such as promotional avenues' (4.20) bracketed alongwith 'lack of orientation and refresher course facilities' (4.20). Further, they have given a higher position to 'competing claims of research and teaching" (3.60) and 'inadequate salary structure' (3.30) than 'competing claims of teaching and family roles' (3.20). On the other hand, the female teachers have given the third rank position to 'competing claims of teaching and family roles' (3.69) after 'inadequate physical surroundings' (3.76). Further, they have given a higher rating to 'competing claims of students' work and one's own work' (3.46) than 'administrative difficulties' (3.23). Again, they have rated 'lack of facilities to travel abroad' (3.07), 'conflicting claims of reading, teaching and writing' (3.00) higher than 'lack of orientation and refresher course facilities' as well as 'conflicting claims of profession' (2.92 each).

In the case of the Private college, the teachers have given the first rank to 'inadequate physical surroundings not congenial for work'. Further, they have given a higher rating to 'inadequate medical facilities,' and 'competing claims of students' work and one's own work' higher than 'administrative difficulties'. Again, 'the inadequate housing accommodation" has been placed higher than 'competing claims of teaching and family roles'. The 'inadequate salary structure' has also been given a higher rating than 'lack of orientation and refresher course facilities' along with 'conflicting claims of reading, teaching and writing'. Even 'conflicting claims of profession' finds a higher place than 'competing claims of research and teaching.'

The sex-wise analysis for this college shows that male teachers have given more importance to 'inadequate physical surroundings' (4.50) and 'lack of autonomy to teachers' (4.12) than 'lack of incentives such as promotional avenues' alongwith 'competing claims of teaching and family roles' (4.00 each). Further, 'competing claims of students' work and one's own work' (3.62), 'inadequate salary structure' and 'inadequate housing accommodation' (3.37 each) find a higher placing than 'administrative difficulties' (3.25) whereas 'conflicting claims of reading, teaching and writing' (3.12) has been bracketed alongwith 'medical facilities'. Even, 'lack of facilities to travel abroad' (2.75) finds a higher rating than 'lack of orientation and refresher course facilities'. On the other hand, the female teachers in this college have given a higher rating to 'inadequate medical facilities' (3.57) than 'inadequate physical surroundings' (3.50). Further, they have given more importance to 'administrative difficulties,' 'lack of orientation and refresher course facilities' and 'conflicting claims of profession' (3.28 each) than 'competing claims of research and teaching' (3.14). The 'conflicting claims of reading, teaching and writing' (3.00), 'lack of facilities to travel abroad' (2.92),' 'inadequate salary structure' (2.92) and 'competing claims of teaching and family roles (2.57) have been placed below 'competing claims of students' work and one's own work' as well as 'inadequate housing accommodation' (3.07 each).

The varied responses to these problems by male and female teachers show that some of these problems may be more gender specific. The lowest rank given to 'competing claims of teaching and family roles' by female teachers in the Private college may be either due to their being a part of joint family set-up or due to help rendered by domestic servants tc take care of some of their household responsibilities.

11 (a) Relationship between Status (Designation) held by Teachers and the Nature of Problems faced by them

An attempt is also made to find out whether or not, the status of teachers has any relationship to the importance given to various problems faced by them while performing their duties in the university as well as in the colleges.The procedure for working out the mean score values on the scale of importance for various problems provided to them is same as given in the previous tables.

An examination of Table 5.6 brings out that in the case of university teachers, the problems faced by them in order of importance are 'competing claims of research and teaching' (3.63), conflicting claims of-profession' (2.95), 'lack of incentives such as promotional avenues' (2.94), 'lack of autonomy to the teachers' (2.93), 'conflicting claims of reading, teaching and writing' (2.81), 'inadequate physical surroundings' (2.79), 'lack of facilities to travel abroad' (2.69), 'competing claims of students'z work and one's own work' (2.67), 'inadequate housing accommodation' (2.65), 'administrative difficulties' (2.64), 'competing claims of teaching and family role' (2.60), 'inadequate medical facilities' (2.33), 'inadequate salary structure' (2.29) and 'lack of orientation and refresher course facilities' (2.26).

The faculty wise analysis suggests that teachers in the science group have given more importance to 'administrative difficulties' and 'lack of facilities to travel abroad' than 'inadequate physical surroundings'. Further, the 'inadequate housing accommodation' finds a higher place than 'competing claims of students' work and one's own work'. Even, 'lack of orientation and refresher course facilities' is given a higher rating than 'inadequate medical facilities'.

The status wise analysis in the science group shows that Professors have given more importance to 'lack of facilities to travel abroad' (2.87) and 'administrative difficulties' (2.75) than 'lack of incentives such as promotional avenues' (2.68) and 'conflicting claims of reading, teaching and writing' (2.43). Further they have rated 'inadequate medical facilities' (2.37) slightly higher than 'competing claims of students' work and one's own work' (2.31). The 'inadequate salary structure' (2.25) also gets a higher ranking than 'inadequate housing accommodation' (2.18) while 'lack of orientation and refresher course facilities' (2.12) is placed higher

Table 5.6
Relationship between Status (Designation Held) of Teachers and Nature of Problems faced by them while performing their duties.

S. No.	Nature of Problems faced by Teachers	Overall Mean Score Value	Rank	University Teachers											
				Science (Mean Score Value)				Social Science (Mean Score Value)				Professional (Mean Score Value)			
				P	R	L	Combined Mean	P	R	L	Combined Mean	P	R	L	Combined Mean
1.	Competing claims of research and teaching	3.63	1	4.31	3.94	3.76	3.96	2.87	3.25	3.80	3.33	3.12	3.83	3.75	3.50
2.	Conflicting claims of profession (meetings, conferences, examinations etc.)	2.95	2	3.18	2.94	3.04	3.05	2.45	2.55	2.85	2.62	4.25	3.33	3.25	3.72
3.	Lack of Incentives such as promotional avenues due to stagnation	2.94	3	2.68	3.00	3.16	2.98	2.50	3.15	2.75	2.82	2.50	3.50	4.25	3.22
4.	Lack of autonomy to teachers	2.93	4	3.00	2.70	3.00	2.91	2.50	2.80	3.15	2.84	2.50	4.16	3.75	3.33
5.	Conflicting claims of reading, teaching and writing	2.81	5	2.43	3.00	2.84	2.77	2.31	3.00	2.90	2.76	3.00	3.33	3.00	3.11
6.	Inadequate physical surroundings not congenial for work	2.79	6	2.87	2.88	2.76	2.82	2.25	2.80	2.70	2.60	2.75	3.83	3.75	3.33
7.	Lack of facilities to travel abroad (fellowships and grants)	2.69	7	2.87	2.82	2.84	2.84	2.43	2.60	2.85	2.64	1.75	2.60	3.50	2.42
8.	Competing claims of students' work and one's own work	2.67	8	2.31	2.47	3.00	2.65	2.37	2.70	2.65	2.58	2.62	3.50	3.25	3.05

(Contd.)

(Contd. Table 5.6)

S. No.	Nature of Problems faced by Teachers	Overall Mean Score Value	Rank	University Teachers: Science (Mean Score Value) P	R	L	Combined Mean	Social Science (Mean Score Value) P	R	L	Combined Mean	Professional (Mean Score Value) P	R	L	Combined Mean
9.	Inadequate housing accommodation	2.65	9	2.18	2.82	2.88	2.66	2.06	2.35	3.25	2.58	1.87	4.00	3.25	2.88
10.	Administrative difficulties (leave rules/promotional rules)	2.64	10	2.75	2.82	3.00	2.88	1.93	2.30	2.75	2.35	1.75	3.33	4.00	2.77
11.	Competing clams of teaching and family role	2.60	11	2.06	2.64	2.84	2.56	1.93	2.55	3.10	2.56	2.12	3.83	3.00	2.88
12.	Inadequate medical facilities	2.33	12	2.37	2.17	2.60	2.41	2.06	2.10	2.30	2.16	2.25	2.50	3.50	2.61
13.	Inadequate salary structure	2.29	13	2.25	2.11	2.52	2.32	2.43	1.80	2.40	2.19	1.75	3.33	3.00	2.55
14.	Lack of orientation and refresher course facilities.	2.26	14	2.12	2.70	2.48	2.44	1.43	2.05	2.40	1.99	2.12	2.83	3.00	2.55

Note P = Professor, R = Reader, L = Lecturer

(Contd.)

(Contd. Table 5.6)

S. No.	Nature of Problems faced by Teachers	Overall Mean Score Value	Rank	College Teachers							
				Government (Mean Score Value)				Private (Mean Score Value)			
				Senior Lecturer	Lecturer	Guest Faculty	Combined mean	Senior Lecturer	Lecturer	Guest Faculty	Combined mean
1.	Lack of Incentives such as promotional avenues due to stagnation	3.92	1	4.00	3.84	4.66	3.99	3.70	3.90	5.00	3.85
2.	Inadequate physical surroundings nct congenial for work	3.74	2	4.00	3.69	4.00	3.82	3.40	3.90	4.00	3.67
3.	Lack of autonomy to teachers	3.57	3	3.71	3.38	4.00	3.56	3.80	3.36	4.00	3.59
4.	Inadequate medical facilities	3.45	4	2.85	3.30	3.33	3.16	3.70	3.90	3.00	3.76
5.	Administrative difficulties (leave rules/ promotional rules)	3.32	5	3.14	3.69	2.66	3.38	3.50	3.00	4.00	3.27
6.	Competing claims of teaching and family role	3.21	6	4.14	2.92	4.00	3.43	3.50	2.72	1.00	2.99
7.	Lack of orientation and refresher course facilities	3.19	7	3.28	3.38	3.33	3.34	3.10	2.90	4.00	3.04
8.	Competing claims of students' work and one's own work	3.15	8	3.71	2.76	3.00	3.08	3.50	3.00	3.00	3.22

(Contd.)

(Contd. Table 5.6)

S. No.	*Nature of Problems faced by Teachers*	*Overall Mean Score Value*	*Rank*	*College Teachers*							
				Government (Means Score Value)				*Private (Mean Score Value)*			
				Senior Lecturer	*Lecturer*	*Guest Faculty*	*Combined mean*	*Senior Lecturer*	*Lecturer*	*Guest Faculty*	*Combined mean*
9.	Competiting claims of research and teaching	2.99	9	3.14	3.15	2.66	3.08	2.80	3.00	3.00	2.90
10.	Inadequate salary structure	2.99	9	2.57	2.84	4.00	2.90	3.90	2.45	2.00	3.08
11.	Inadequate housing accommodation	2.97	11	2.57	2.69	3.66	2.78	3.60	2.90	2.00	3.17
12.	Lack of facilities to travel abroad (fellowships and grants)	2.95	12	2.57	3.00	3.33	2.91	3.10	2.90	3.00	2.99
13.	Conflicting claims of reading, teaching and writing	2.88	13	2.85	2.76	2.33	2.73	3.40	2.81	2.00	3.04
14.	Conflicting claims of profession (meeting, conference, examination etc.)	2.85	14	2.42	2.84	3.66	2.81	2.50	3.18	4.00	2.90

than 'competing claims of teaching and family role' (2.06). On the other hand, Readers in this group have given second rank to 'lack of incentives such as promotional avenues' (3.00) along with 'conflicting claims of reading, teaching and writing' whereas 'conflicting claims of profession' (2.94), 'inadequate physical surroundings' (2.88), 'lack of facilities to travel abroad' and 'administrative difficulties' (2.82 each) have been rated higher than 'lack of autonomy to the teachers' and 'lack of orientation and refresher course facilities' (2.70 each). Even, 'competing claims of teaching and family role' (2.64) finds a higher ranking than 'competing claims of students' work and one's own work' (2.47). However, Lecturers in this group have given more importance to 'lack of incentives such as promotional avenues' (3.16) than 'conflicting claims of profession' (3.04). Further, 'lack of autonomy to the teachers,' 'competing claims of students' work and one's own work' and 'administrative difficulties' (3.00 each) find a higher place than 'inadequate housing accommodation' (2.88). Even, 'lack of facilities to travel abroad', 'competing claims of teaching and family role' and 'conflicting claims of reading, teaching and writing' have been bracketed together (2.84 each) and placed higher than 'inadequate physical surroundings' (2.76).

In the case of social science teachers, 'lack of autonomy to the teachers' finds a higher rating than 'lack of incentives such as promotional avenues'. Further, 'conflicting claims of reading, teaching and writing' and 'lack of facilities to travel abroad' have been placed higher than 'conflicting claims of profession.' Even, the 'competing claims of teaching and family role' finds a higher place than 'administrative difficulties'. The status-wise analysis in this group shows that Professors have given more importance to 'lack of incentives such as promotional avenues' and 'lack of autonomy to the teachers' (2.50 each) than 'conflicting claims of profession' (2.45). Again, they have rated 'lack of facilities to travel abroad' and 'inadequate salary structure' (2.43 each) higher than 'competing claims of students' work and one's own work' (2.37) as well as 'conflicting claims of reading, teaching and writing' (2.31) and 'inadequate physical surroundings' (2.25). Even 'inadequate medical facilities' along with 'inadequate housing accommodation' (2.06each) have been placed higher than 'administrative difficulties' (1.93). However, Readers in this group have given more importance to 'conflicting claims of reading, teaching and writing' than 'lack of autonomy to the teachers' and 'inadequate physical surroundings' (2.80 each). Even, 'competing claims of students' work and one's own work' (2.70) as well as 'lack of facilities to travel abroad' (2.60) have been placed higher than 'conflicting claims of profession' and 'competing claims of teaching and family role' (2.55 each). Again, 'lack of orientation and refresher course facilities' (2.05) finds a higher place than 'inadequate salary structure' (1.80). On the other hand, Lecturers in this group have given more importance to 'inadequate housing accommodation' (3.25) than 'lack of autonomy to the teachers' (3.15). Further, 'competing-claims of teaching and family roles' (3.10), 'lack of facilities to travel abroad,' (2.85) and 'conflicting claims of profession' (2.85) find a higher place than 'lack of incentives such as 'promotional avenues' and 'administrative difficulties' (2.75 each). Again, 'inadequate salary structure' and 'lack of orientation and refresher course facilities' (2.40 each) are rated higher than 'inadequate medical facilities' (2.30).

In the case of professional teachers, they have assigned the highest importance to 'conflicting claims of profession' followed by 'competing claims of research and teaching'. Next is 'lack of autonomy to the teachers,' 'inadequate physical surroundings' and 'lack of incentives such as promotional avenues' in that order. Again, the 'competing claims of teaching and family role' (2.88) find a higher place than 'administrative difficulties' (2.77) while 'lack of facilities to travel abroad' (2.42) has been given the lowest rank in order of its importance.

The status wise analysis in this group shows that Professors have given the highest importance to 'conflicting claims of profession' (4.25) followed by 'competing claims of research and teaching'. The 'conflicting claims of reading, teaching and writing' (3.00), 'inadequate physical surroundings' (2.75) and 'competing claims of students' work and one's own work' (2.62) have been given more importance than 'lack of incentives such as promotional avenues' and 'lack of autonomy to the teachers' (2.50 each). Even, 'inadequate medical facilities' (2.25) 'competing claims of teaching and family role,' 'lack of orientation and refresher course facilities' (2.12 each) have been placed higher than 'lack of facilities to travel abroad' and 'administrative difficulties' (1.75 each). On the other hand, Readers in this group have given the highest rank to 'lack of autonomy to the teachers' (4.16). This is followed by 'inadequate housing accommodation' (4.00), 'competing claims of research and teaching,' 'inadequate physical surroundings' and 'competing claims of teaching and family role' (3.83 each). Further, 'competing claims of students' work and one's own work' as well as 'lack of incentives such as promotional avenues' (3.50 each) have been given more importance than 'conflicting claims of profession' 'conflicting claims of reading, teaching and writing' and 'administrative difficulties' (3.33 each). Even, 'lack of orientation and refresher course facilities' (2.83) finds a higher place than 'lack of facilities to travel abroad' (2.60). On the other hand, Lecturers in this group have assigned the highest rank to 'lack of incentives such as promotional avenues' (4.25) followed by 'administrative difficulties' (4.00) as well as 'lack of facilities to travel abroad' and 'inadequate medical facilities' (3.50each). The above find a higher place than 'conflicting claims of profession,' 'competing claims of students' work and one's own work' and 'inadequate housing accommodation' (3.25each). This is followed by 'conflicting claims of reading, teaching and writing,' 'competing claims of teaching and family role,' 'inadequate salary structure' and 'lack of orientation and refresher course facilities' (3.00 each).

The above analysis suggests that among the university teachers, there are varied responses given to various types of problems by Professors, Readers and Lecturers belonging to different courses. For instance, as compared to Professors, Readers and Lecturers in all the three groups, have given more importance to 'lack of incentives such as promotional avenues'. This is understandable as Professors have already attained their maximum status in the university system while others have yet to achieve the same. Again, we observe that in all the three groups, in comparison to Professors; Readers and Lecturers have given more importance to 'competing claims of teaching and family roles'. This may be because of preponderance of female than male teachers in the category of Readers and Lecturers.

As regards, college teachers, it is observed that they have given importance to 'lack of incentives such as promotional avenues'.(3.92), 'inadequate physical surroundings' (3.74), 'lack of autonomy to teachers' (3.57), 'inadequate medical facilities'

(3.45), 'administrative difficulties' (3.32), 'competing claims of teaching and family role' (3.21) 'lack of orientation and refresher course facilities' (3.19) 'competing claims of students' work and one's own work' (3.15), 'competing claims of research and teaching' (2.99), 'inadequate salary structure' (2.99) 'inadequate housing accommodation' (2.97) 'lack of facilities to travel abroad' (2.95), 'conflicting claims of reading, teaching and writing' (2.88) and 'conflicting claims of profession' (2.85) in that order.

The college teachers as compared to those in the university have relatively given more importance to some of the organisational issues such as facilities and incentives than professional problems.

In respect of Government college teachers, it is observed that, apart from the first three ranks given to issues as stated in the overall analysis of college teachers, they have given more importance to 'competing claims of teaching and family role' than 'administrative difficulties,' 'lack of orientation and refresher course facilities' and 'inadequate medical facilities'. Further, 'competing claims of research and teaching,' 'lack of facilities to travel abroad' and 'inadequate salary structure' find a higher rank order than 'conflicting claims of profession'. The status-wise analysis in this college shows that Senior Lecturers have given highest importance to 'competing claims of teaching and family roles' (4.14) than 'lack of incentives such as promotional avenues,' and 'inadequate physical surroundings' (4.00 each). Further, they have rated 'competing claims of students' work and one's own work' and 'lack of autonomy to teachers' (3.71 each) higher than 'lack of orientation and refresher course facilities' (3.28) as well as 'administrative difficulties' and 'competing claims of research and teaching' (3.14 each). This is followed by 'inadequate medical facilities' and 'conflicting claims of reading, teaching and writing (2.85 each) while 'conflicting claims of profession' has been given the lowest rank order (2.42). On the other hand, Lecturers in this college have given a higher rating to 'administrative difficulties' (3.69) than 'lack of autonomy to teachers' and 'lack of orientation and refresher course facilities' (3.38 each). This is followed by 'inadequate medical facilities' (3.30), 'competing claims of research and teaching' (3.15), 'lack of facilities to travel abroad' (3.00) and 'competing claims of teaching and family role' (2.92) while 'conflicting claims of profession' and 'inadequate salary structure' (2.84) have been bracketed below them. Even, 'conflicting claims of reading, teaching and writing' (2.76) has been placed higher than 'inadequate housing accommodation' (2.69). The Guest Faculty has given more importance to 'competing claims of teaching and family role' and 'inadequate salary structure' (4.00 each) than 'conflicting claims of profession' and 'inadequate housing accommodation' (3.66 each). 'Lack of facilities to travel abroad' has been bracketed along with 'inadequate medical facilities' and 'lack of orientation and refresher course facilities' (3.33 each). Even, 'competing claims of students' work and one's own work' (3.00) has been placed higher than 'administrative difficulties' (2.66).

In the case of Private college, teachers have given a higher rating to 'inadequate medical facilities' than 'inadequate physical surroundings' and 'lack of autonomy to teachers'. This is followed by 'administrative difficulties,' 'competing claims of students' work and one's own work,' 'inadequate housing accommodation,' 'inadequate salary structure,' 'lack of orientation and refresher course facilities' and 'conflicting claims of reading, teaching and writing.' The 'conflicting claims of profession' clubbed together with 'competing claims of research and teaching' find a place lower than 'competing claims of teaching and family role' bracketed along with 'facilities to travel abroad'.

The status wise analysis in this college suggests that Senior Lecturers have given the highest rank position to 'inadequate salary structure' (3.90) followed by 'lack of autonomy to teachers' (3.80). Even, 'inadequate medical facilities' (3.70) 'inadequate housing accommodation' (3.60) have been rated higher than 'administrative difficulties', 'competing claims of students' work and one's own work' and 'competing claims of teaching and family role' (3.50 each). This is followed by 'inadequate physical surroundings' and 'conflicting claims of reading, teaching and writing '(3.40 each) while 'conflicting claims of profession' (2.50) has been given the lowest rank. As far as Lecturers in this college are concerned, they are giving more importance to 'inadequate medical facilities' (3.90) than 'lack of autonomy to teachers (3.36) and 'conflicting claims of profession' (3.18) than 'administrative difficulties,' 'competing claims of students' work and one's own work' and 'competing claims of research and teaching' (3.00 each). This is followed by 'lack of orientation and refresher course facilities,' 'lack of facilities to travel abroad' and 'inadequate housing accommodation' (2.90 each). Even, 'conflicting claims of reading, teaching and writing' (2.81) finds a higher placing than' competing claims of teaching and family role' (2.72). As regards the Guest Faculty in this college, he or she seems to be giving more importance to 'administrative difficulties,' 'lack of orientation and refresher course facilities' and 'conflicting claims of profession' (4.00 each) than 'inadequate medical facilities,' 'competing claims of students' work and one's own work, 'lack of facilities to travel abroad' and 'competing claims of research and teaching' (3.00 each). However, the 'competing claims of teaching and family role' in his or her case finds the lowest importance. This may be because the only female Guest Faculty was unmarried and had not yet entered into family role.

The above analysis clearly brings out that the nature of problems faced by college teachers are more organizational than professional. They are concerned more with facilities, incentives and reward system than professional issues.

The varied responses to these problems, according to the status or rank position of teachers in the university and colleges confirm that there is an influence of status of teachers on their opinions towards the problems faced by them while performing their duties and responsibilities.

12. Availability of Leisure Time with Teachers to Pursue their Interests

It is a well-known fact that all work and no play makes a person dull. As such, it is always desirable to utilize one's leisure time to pursue various interests for relaxation, recreation and play. These activities can contribute significantly towards the role performance of teachers. Leisure has social, psychological and cultural connotations in its conception. In common parlance, leisure implies free time available with a person to engage himself in activities that are basically non-economic but satisfies his or her aesthetic and cultural needs through recreation and play. However, in the sociological sense, it is essentially associated with the nature of social organisation in terms of relationships between various actors at a particular point of time, while the leisure activities get established in a society by its cultural and structural correlates (Modi, 1985).

The teachers in the university as well as in the colleges were asked to indicate whether or not they got adequate leisure time to pursue their various interests. Those who responded to 'most adequate' category were given a score of 5 while those who replied to the 'inadequate' leisure time availability were given a score of 1. Further, those who responded to 'fairly adequate', 'adequate' and 'just adequate' availability of time to pursue their interests were given a score of 4, 3 and 2 respectively. A mean score value was worked out separately for the university and college teachers sex-wise, academic level index wise and participation index of teachers in university bodies and associations, to find out if there was any relationship between these factors and the extent of leisure time available with the teachers to pursue various interests.

(i) Relationship between the sex of the teachers and the extent of leisure time available with them to pursue various interests

An examination of Table 5.7 shows that on the basis of the overall mean score values, as compared to the university teachers (3.30), the college teachers have a greater extent of leisure time available with them to pursue their various interests (3.90). Among the university teachers, we observe that the teachers in the professional group (3.38) have more leisure time available with them than the teachers in the science and social science groups (3.30 each). On the other hand, there is no difference observed in regard to availability of leisure time in between teachers belonging to the Government and the Private college.

However, the sex-wise analysis of teachers both in the university as well as in the colleges shows that as compared to female, male teachers have a greater extent of leisure time available with them to pursue their interests. However, the faculty-wise analysis of teachers in the university shows that in the social science group, females seem to be having more leisure time available with them (3.32) than males (3.29). On the basis of overall analysis for the university and college teachers, there appears some association between the sex of the teachers and the availability of leisure time to pursue various interests. Invariably, the female teachers apart from their professional role, have also to share their family obligations of bringing up children and managing the household. As such, they have less leisure time available with them.

Table 5.7

Relationship between the Sex of the Teachers and the Extent of Leisure Time available to pursue various interests.

S. No.	Sex of the Teachers	Extent of Adequacy of Leisure Time to Pursue various interests						
		University Teachers			Combined Mean	College Teachers		Combined Mean
		Science (Mean Score Value)	Social Science (Mean Score Value)	Professional (Mean Score Value)		Government (Mean Score Value)	Private (Mean Score Value)	
1.	Male	3.74	3.29	3.45	3.52	4.10	4.37	4.22
2.	Female	2.42	3.32	3.28	2.97	3.76	3.64	3.70
Overall Mean Score Value		3.30	3.30	3.38	3.30	3.90	3.90	3.90

Table 5.8

Relationship between the Academic Level Index of Teachers and the Extent of Leisure Time available to pursue various Interests

S. No.	Extent of Adequacy of Leisure Time to pursue various interests					
	Academic Level Index of Teachers	University Teachers (Mean Score Value)	Academic Level Index	College Teachers (Mean Score Value)		Combined Mean
				Government	Private	
1.	High (23 and Above Score)	3.28	High (8 and Above Score)	4.00	3.58	3.70
2.	Low (22 and Below Score)	3.09	Low (Upto 7 Score)	3.88	3.90	3.88
Overall Means Score Value		3.16	Overall Means Score Value	3.90	3.72	3.81

(ii) Relationship between the academic level index of teachers and the extent of leisure time available

It is possible that those teachers who have a high level of academic accomplishment may find more leisure time to pursue their interests than those who are still pursuing to accomplish their academic goals and are having a relatively lower academic level index.

An examination of Table 5.8 shows that on basis of overall mean score value as compared to the university teachers (3.16), the college teachers have a larger extent of leisure time available with them (3.81). In between the two colleges, the teachers in the Government college have more leisure time available (3.90) than those in the Private college (3.72). However, on the basis of the academic level index of teachers in the university as well as in the Government college, it is clear that teachers having a high academic level index have more leisure time available to pursue their interests than those with the low academic level index. But it is vice-versa the case with the teachers in the Private college.

In the case of university teachers, in respect of analysis pertaining to their gender and the academic level index, it is clear that most of the responses of teachers fall in between 'fairly adequate' and 'adequate' categories while that of college teachers in between 'most adequate' and 'fairly adequate' availability of leisure time.

(iii) Relationship between participation index of teachers in university bodies/associations and the extent of leisure time available to pursue various interests

It is assumed that teachers in the university as well as in the colleges who participate in university bodies/associations actively may have more time available to pursue their leisure time activities than those having low participation. It is found that teachers both in the university as well as in the colleges having a high participation index in university bodies and associations, have a greater extent of leisure time available to pursue various interests than those with low participation index, (university teachers High participation Index (H.P.I)–3.23, Low Participation Index (L.P.I.)– 3.13, college teachers -H.P.I-4.14, L.P.I-3.69). This may be due to the fact that teachers with high participation index in various bodies and associations may be more adventurous, outgoing and extrovert in personality than those with the low participation index who may be passive, academically oriented and having introvert personality. As such the latter type of teachers may have less time available to them to pursue their leisure time activities.

The teachers were asked to specify the type of leisure time activities in which they were involved. In most of the cases, it was mentioned that they utilized their leisure time in activities related to gardening, reading, sport, travel, listening to music, going for long drives, family get-together, picnics, cooking, visiting places and friends, keeping physically fit, contemplating, observing and enjoying nature and having intellectual conversation with other people regarding socio-economic problems.

13. Role of Teacher's Association in Improving the Working Conditions of Teachers

Over the years, the unions of the teachers have become instrumental in getting many of their demands met. These have telling effect on the role performance of teachers. In this regard, the teachers in the university as well as in the colleges were asked to indicate whether or not their associations can play a role in improving their working conditions.

Out of 132 teachers in the university, as many as 103(78.03 per cent) state that the association of the teachers can play a role in improving their working conditions while the rest of them do not think so. The faculty-wise analysis in the university brings out that a higher proportion of male (79.49 per cent) teachers in science and female (85.72 per cent). teachers in the professional group as compared to their counterparts in these two stream of courses consider that their union can bring about improvement in their working conditions. However, in the case of social science group, nearly an equal proportion of male and female teachers feel so.

On the other hand, in the case of colleges, out of 45 teachers, as many as 37(82.20 per cent) consider that the association of teachers can bring about improvement in their working conditions whereas the remaining 8(17.78 per cent) do not think so.

In view of a small number of responses of multiple nature as reasons given by teachers in regard to the role of the association in improving their working conditions, these have been clubbed together for male and female teachers and are presented below separately for the university and colleges.

(1) University Teachers

It is suggested by many (35) that a teacher's association provides a link between university authorities and teachers for improvement in teaching as well as for salvaging their problems. According to some (30), an association is a forum for expression of views in a proper manner and for building pressure on the university authorities to get the demands of teachers met. It is also argued by some (25) that organized efforts are always helpful for safeguarding the interest of teaching community. However, a few (6) have cautioned that united efforts and team-work may produce results only if leadership is dynamic and moves in the right direction. It is also suggested by some (4) that unionism serves as a shield against victimization. It is also mentioned by a few that democratization of functioning of departments, rotation of headship and the merit promotion schemes have all been achieved with the efforts of the teacher's association. However, quite a few (8) are vocal in suggesting that the teacher's association is not an effective body as politics reigns supreme over academics due to personal interest of members of the executive body.

(2) College Teachers

The college teachers, by and large, (12) feel that the teacher's association can properly project their problems related to teaching and fight for their rights. Further, some of them (7) feel that an association can point out to the authorities about the lack of facilities for effective teaching, welfare and development. A few of them (6) also feel that it provides a link between the teachers and the university authorities for tackling their problems because it has bargaining power and can put pressure on the authorities. However, some of them (3) express that a teacher's union can improve conditions of teachers but is not playing any positive role due to politicization and disintegrity of its members.

6

Views of Teachers on Crisis in Higher Education

In the wake of crisis in higher education observed during the last couple of decades, the question often raised is how to make the role of a teacher more effective in the university system. There are a number of problems confronted by teachers and these have contributed towards generating crisis in higher education. Broadly, we can classify these problems as socio-political, financial, organizational, academic including autonomy of teachers, their role commitment and dedication and unionism among them. Besides, issues such as hike in fee structure, reservation of seats in admission, favouritism, and double standards exhibited by academic administrators in the selection of various incumbents in the university system, further add fuel to the fire in creating crisis in higher education. How do we go about in tackling some of these problems, is the key question faced by educational policy planners and administrators. Perhaps, the solution to some of these problems may lie in the ways and means suggested by teachers to make their role more effective.

Before we take up the above issues as perceived by university and college teachers, it may be worthwhile examining the problems of higher education in general.

In conceiving education in the cultural context, it is observed that an educational system is both the product of cultural goals determined by a society and that of the distribution of knowledge delivered by the politico-economic structure of the nation. Moreover, it takes into account the spatial-cultural uniqueness empirically expressed through social structure at a given point of time. This approach helps us in providing a synthesis between the macro and the micro levels of expectations that one may have from education and its functional outcomes. It is observed that at a general level, this view recognizes the non-economic attributes of knowledge (macro level). However, at the operational level, it gets manifested through its day to day mode of translation of cultural goals of education (micro level) and its functional means towards the accomplishment of the desired objectives. This operational mode is determined by the national experience of each nation (Basu, 1986).

Our national experience with higher education has not been very satisfactory. It is observed that higher education in our country suffers from four major maladies namely inadequate budget for education, less grants for universities and institutes of higher education, unemployables of university/college products and steep deterioration in the quality of teachers. The salvation suggested is mainly two-folds. First, there is a need to revamp and consolidate the educational processes at all stages, since we have had enough of expansion particularly in the fields of tertiary and university education. There is a need to encourage private initiatives and open learning systems in certain areas and even we should try out the concept of private universities as pilot projects. Secondly, optimum attention to the resources and energy should be directed to elementary education to make the basics of our educational system strong. In short, our strategy as a developing nation should be clear and meaningful, primary education for all, secondary education for many and higher education for a few (Rani, 1998).

Further, an eminent Indian sociologist, after providing a critical review of the New Education Policy (1986) argues that education is a fundamental human right, a pre-requisite for any State and its government to claim itself as democratic. According to him, the formal education system in India has expanded enormously at all levels, that is, elementary, secondary and higher education (about 700,000 institutions, 3.5 million teachers, 100 million students and an annual expenditure of Rs.25,000 million), yet it hardly benefits the common people who are poor or very poor. He points out various contradictions in the education policy. These pertain to first, education not being treated as a fundamental right. Secondly, it fosters and accentuates inequality through its anti-poor approach. Further, there are gaps observed between expected functions and real functions and its approach is regulatory in nature rather than based on problem solving. These contradictions affect the underprivileged adversely. As such, he makes a plea for the pedagogy of the oppressed and desires that scholars, researchers and academicians should focus their studies on the problems of the underprivileged (Desai, 1994).

Notwithstanding the issues raised by scholars on higher education, the role of the teacher is prominent in proper functioning of the university system. The intellectual preparation of teachers is an important prerequisite for preparing students adequately so that they could expand their resources and have better control of their socio-cultural environment. In this connection it may be appropriate to refer to a portion of convocation address given by Pandit Jawaharlal Nehru at the University of Allahabad in 1947 (as cited in the report of Education commission, 1964-66, p.274). 'A teacher's principal object is to deepen man's understanding of universe and of himself in body, mind and spirit, to disseminate this understanding throughout society and to apply it in the service of mankind. Teachers are the dwelling places of ideas and idealism, expected to have high standards of conduct and integrity. Theirs is the pursuit of truth and excellence in all its diversity, a pursuit which needs, above all, courage and fearlessness" (Rani, 1998).

In this section, an attempt has been made to ascertain the views of teachers both in the university as well as in the colleges regarding crisis in higher education. They were asked to specify whether or not, in their opinion, the higher education at the university/college level is in crisis.

1. Views of Teachers on Higher Education being in Crisis or Not

It is observed that in the university, out of 132 teachers in our sample, a majority of them 112 (84.85 per cent) express that higher education is in crisis whereas the remaining 20 (15.15 per cent) do not think so. The faculty-wise analysis in the university shows that as many as 77.59 per cent teachers in science, 89.29 per cent in social science and all except one teacher in the professional group feel that the higher education is in crisis. Again, a higher proportion of females (84.21 per cent) than males (74.36 per cent) in science group and all female teachers (7) as well as 10 out of 11 male teachers in the professional group, have stated that the higher education is in crisis. However, a higher proportion of male (93.55 per cent) than female teachers (84.00 per cent) think so in the social science group.

On the other hand, in the case of colleges, it is observed that out of 45 teachers in our sample, with the exception of 3, all of them are of the opinion that the higher education is in crisis. There appears no difference in the response pattern of teachers in the Government and the Private college. However, out of the 3 teachers who have stated that higher education is not in crisis, one each of male and female category, belongs of Government college while the third is a female teacher in the Private college.

2. Relationship between the Sex of the Teachers and the extent of their agreement on issues related to Crisis In Higher Education

All those teachers in the university (112) and in the two colleges (42) who responded that there was crisis in the higher education, were asked to reflect their opinion on a set of statements provided to them in terms of agreement-disagreement. These statements focused on issues related to socio-political, organizational, financial, academic and personal commitment and dedication of teachers affecting crisis in higher education. The extent of agreement-disagreement on these statements was determined on the basis of a five point scale. Those teachers who responded 'strongly agree' to a statement were assigned a score of 5 while those who mentioned 'strongly disagree' were given a score of 1. Further, those who replied to 'agree,' 'undecided' and 'disagree' categories were given a score of 4, 3, and 2 respectively. A mean score value was worked out for each of these statements sex-wise within science, social science and professional groups of teachers in the university as well as in the two colleges. Again, a combined mean score was worked out for teachers of both the sexes in the three faculties in the university as well as in the two colleges. An overall mean score value for these statements was also worked out for teachers in the university and the two colleges for comparative purposes.

An examination of Table 6.1 highlights the relative extent of agreement-disagreement on these statements on the basis of the mean score values, the higher the mean score value for a statement, the greater is the extent of agreement to it shown by the teachers. These have been arranged in the descending order to indicate the relative extent of agreement-disagreement by teachers on various issues related to crisis in higher education.

On the basis of the overall mean score values, the teachers in the university have shown extent of agreement-disagreement on various statements in the order given below; 'over the years there is increasing politicization and bureaucratization of higher education' (4.43), 'a teacher needs to rise above his self interest and work more towards the common good of students and society' (4.35), 'faulty examination and evaluation system have failed to raise the academic standard of students' (4.18) 'inadequate participation of teachers in academic decision making bodies has led to lop-sided development of educational institutes' (3.96), "financial constraints have arrested the growth, development and creativity of teachers' (3.95), 'outdated course syllabi for various examinations have led to deterioration in the education system' (3.90), 'educational system in our country even after more than fifty years of independence is still on western pattern (3.74), 'stress on liberal arts rather than on vocational courses has increasingly put pressure on university/college education (3.60), 'inadequate or lack of autonomy to teachers make them less creative in work' (3.27) and 'confrontational and agitational attitude of students through unions has reduced the influence of teachers on them' (3.21).

The faculty wise analysis shows that the teachers in the science group have shown a greater extent of agreement with 'a teacher needs to rise above his self-interest' and 'financial constraints' than 'increasing politicization and bureaucratization of higher education'. Even, the 'confrontational and agitational attitude of students' finds a higher rank order than 'inadequate or lack of autonomy to teachers'. The sex-wise analysis of teachers in this group shows that the male teachers exhibit a greater extent of agreement with 'a teacher needs to rise above his self-interest' (4.41) and 'financial constraints' (4.37) than 'increasing politicization and bureaucratization of higher education' (4.31). Even, 'inadequate participation of teachers in academic decision making bodies' (4.17) finds a higher place than 'faulty examination and evaluation system' (4.10). Further, 'educational system on western pattern' (3.68) and 'confrontational and agitational attitude of students' (3.58) have been given higher extent of agreement than 'outdated course syllabi' (3.51). The female teachers in this group seem to be also in greater

Table 6.1 Relationship between sex of the Teachers and the Extent of their Agreement on crisis in Higher Education on the provided statements

S. No.	Statements related to crisis in Higher Education	Overall Mean Score Value	Rank	Extent of Agreement								
				University Teachers								
				Science (Mean Score Value)			Social Science (Mean Score Value)			Professional (Mean Score Value)		
				Male	Female	Combined Mean	Male	Female	Combined Mean	Male	Female	Combined Mean
1.	Over the years there is increasing politicization and bureaucratization of higher education.	4.43	1	4.31	4.12	4.24	4.48	4.42	4.45	4.80	5.00	4.88
2.	A teacher needs to rise above his or her self interest and work more towards the common good of students and society	4.35	2	4.41	4.37	4.39	4.37	4.19	4.29	4.80	4.00	4.47
3.	Faulty examination and evaluation system have failed to raise the academic standards of students	4.18	3	4.10	3.68	3.95	4.20	4.66	4.39	4.40	3.85	4.17
4.	Inadequate participation of teachers in academic decision-making bodies (university/college) has led to lop-sided development and creativity of teachers	3.96	4	4.17	3.56	3.95	3.68	4.42	3.99	4.00	3.85	3.93
5.	Financial constraints have arrested the growth, development and creativity of teachers.	3.95	5	4.37	4.31	4.34	3.75	3.61	3.69	3.50	4.00	3.70
6.	Outdated course syllabi for various examinations have led to deterioration in the education system	3.90	6	3.51	3.87	3.63	4.17	4.19	4.18	3.60	4.14	3.82

(Contd.)

(Contd. Table 6.1)

S. No.	Statements related to crisis in Higher Education	Overall Mean Score Value	Rank	Extent of Agreement								
				University Teachers								
				Science (Mean Score Value)			Social Science (Mean Score Value)			Professional (Mean Score Value)		
				Male	Female	Combined Mean	Male	Female	Combined Mean	Male	Female	Combined Mean
7.	Educational system in our country even after more than fifty years of independence is still on western pattern	3.74	7	3.68	3.56	3.63	4.00	3.90	3.95	3.60	3.28	3.46
8.	Stress on liberal arts rather than on vocational courses had increasingly put pressure on university/college education	3.60	8	3.51	3.50	3.50	3.41	3.80	3.57	3.80	4.28	3.99
9.	Inadequate or lack of autonomy to teachers make them less creative in their work	3.27	9	3.41	3.12	3.30	3.06	3.38	3.19	2.90	4.28	3.46
10.	Confrontational and agitational attitude of students through unions has reduced the influence of teachers on them.	3.21	10	3.58	3.31	3.48	3.00	2.80	2.91	2.80	4.28	3.40

(Contd.)

(Contd. Table 6.1)

S. No.	Statements related to crisis in Higher Education	Overall Mean Score Value	Rank	Extent of Agreements					
				College Teachers					
				Government (Mean Score Value)			Private (Mean Score Value)		
				Male	Female	Combined mean	Male	Female	Combined mean
1.	A teacher needs to rise above his or her self interest and work more towards the common good of students and society	4.66	1	4.88	4.66	4.75	4.75	4.46	4.57
2.	Over the years there is increasing politicization and bureaucratization of higher education.	4.54	2	4.55	4.83	4.71	4.25	4.46	4.38
3.	Faulty examination and evaluation system have failed to raise the academic standards of students	4.46	3	4.33	4.58	4.47	4.37	4.53	4.46
4.	Outdated course syllabi for various examinations have led to deterioration in the education system	4.44	4	4.55	4.08	4.28	4.75	4.53	4.61
5.	Inadequate participation of teachers in academic decision-making bodies (university/college) has led to lop-sided development of educational Institutes	4.09	5	4.33	4.25	4.28	3.50	4.15	3.90

(Contd.)

(Contd. Table 6.1)

S. No.	Statements related to crisis in Higher Education	Overall Mean Score Value	Rank	Extent of Agreements					
				College Teachers					
				Government (Mean Score Value)			Private (Mean Score Value)		
				Male	Female	Combined mean	Male	Female	Combined mean
6.	Financial constraints have arrested the growth, development and creativity of teachers.	3.96	6	4.22	3.91	4.04	4.37	3.61	3.89
7.	Inadequate or lack of autonomy to teachers make them less creative in their work	3.92	7	4.55	3.66	4.04	4.25	3.53	3.80
8.	Stress on liberal arts rather than on vocational courses had increasingly put pressure on university/college education	3.68	8	3.77	3.41	3.56	4.12	3.61	3.80
9.	Educational system in our country even after more than fifty years of independence is still on western pattern	3.66	9	3.22	3 33	3.28	4.12	4.00	4.04
10.	Confrontational and agitational attitude of students through unions has reduced the influence of teachers on them.	3.18	10	2.66	3.83	3.32	3.25	2.92	3.04

agreement on the above statements in the same order. Again, they are in more agreement with 'outdated course syllabi' (3.87) than 'faulty examination and evaluation system' (3.68). The 'confrontational and agitational attitude of students' (3.31) also finds a higher place than 'lack of autonomy to teachers' (3.12).

In the case of social science group, teachers have shown greater extent of agreement with 'faulty examination and evaluation system' than "a teacher needs to rise above his self-interest'. Again, they have shown a greater extent of agreement with 'outdated course syllabi' than 'inadequate participation of teachers in academic decision making bodies'. The sex-wise analysis in this group shows that male teachers have exhibited more agreement with 'outdated course syllabi' (4.17), 'educational system still on western pattern' (4.00) and 'financial constraints' (3.75) than 'inadequate participation of teachers in academic decision making bodies' (3.68). On the other hand, female teachers in this group are in more agreement with 'faulty examination and evaluation system' (4.66) than 'increasing politicization and bureaucratization of higher education' and 'inadequate participation of teachers in academic decision making bodies' (4.42 each). Even, they have assigned a high rank order to 'outdated course syllabi' (4.19), 'educational system still on western pattern' (3.90) and 'stress on liberal arts rather than on vocational courses' (3.80) than 'financial constraints'(3.61). As compared to male teachers in this group, female teachers are giving the highest rank to 'faulty examination and evaluation system'. This may be because of their greater sensitivity towards this issue based on personal experiences.

In the case of teachers in the professional group, they have shown greater extent of agreement with 'stress on liberal arts rather than on vocational courses' than 'inadequate participation of teachers in academic decision making bodies'. Even, the 'outdated course syllabi for various examinations', has been placed higher than 'financial constraints'. The, sex-wise analysis in this group shows that male teachers have shown greater extent of agreement with 'stress on liberal arts rather than on vocational courses' (3.80) and 'outdated course syllabi for various examinations' along-with 'educational system still on western pattern' (3.60 each) than 'financial constraints' (3.50). However, female teachers in this group have expressed greater extent of agreement with 'stress on liberal arts rather than on vocational course,' 'inadequate or lack of autonomy to teachers' 'confrontational and agitational attitude of students (4.28 each) and 'outdated course syllabi' (4.14) than 'a teacher needs to rise above his self-interest' and 'financial constraints' (4.00 each). The female teachers seem to be showing greater extent of agreement with the above mentioned statements than the male teachers.

In the case of colleges, it is observed that teachers as compared to those in the university have given somewhat a different pattern of agreement-disagreement to various statements. In their opinion, the statements pertaining to crisis in higher education have been mentioned in order of agreement-disagreement as below; 'A teacher needs to rise above his or her self-interest' (4.66), 'increasing politicization and bureaucratization of higher education' (4.54), 'faulty examination and evaluation system' (4.46), 'outdated course syllabi for various examination' (4.44), 'inadequate participation of teachers in academic decision making bodies' (4.09), ' 'financial constraints' (3.96), 'lack of autonomy to teachers' (3.92), 'stress on liberal arts rather than on vocational courses' (3.68), 'educational system still on western pattern' (3.66) and 'confrontational and agitation attitude of students' (3.18).

In respect of teachers in the Government college, it is observed that they have given a greater extent of agreement to 'confrontational and agitational attitude of students' than 'education system still on western pattern'. The sex-wise analysis in this college shows that male teachers are more in agreement with 'outdated course syllabi' for various examinations' and 'lack of autonomy to teachers' alongwith 'increasing politicization and , bureaucratization of higher education' (4.55 each) than 'faulty examination and evaluation system' and 'inadequate participation of teachers in academic decision making bodies' (4.33 each). However, female teachers in this college have emphasized more on 'increasing politicization and bureaucratization of higher education' (4.83) than 'a teacher needs to rise above his or her self-interest' (4.66). Even, 'inadequate participation of teachers in academic decision making bodies' (4.25) has been placed higher than 'outdated course syllabi' (4.08). They also seem to be more in agreement with 'confrontational and agitational attitude of students' (3.83) than 'lack of autonomy to teachers' (3.66).

On the other hand, in the case of Private college, teachers are in more agreement with 'outdated course syllabi for various examination' than 'a teacher needs to rise above his or her self-interest'. Even, 'faulty examination and education system' finds a higher place than 'increasing politicization and bureaucratization of higher education'. Further, 'education system still on western pattern' is given a higher rank order than 'inadequate participation of teachers in academic decision making bodies'. The sex-wise analysis of teachers in this college shows that male teachers are in more agreement with 'outdated course syllabi for various examination' (4.75) than 'faulty examination and evaluation system' and 'financial constraints' (4.37 each). Further, they seem to be in more agreement with 'increasing politicization and bureaucratization of higher education, 'lack of autonomy to teachers' (4.25 each) as well as 'stress on liberal arts rather than on vocational courses' and 'educational system still on western pattern' (4.12 each) than 'inadequate participation of teachers in academic decision making bodies' (3.50). The female teachers in this college have shown greater extent of agreement with 'outdated course syllabi' for various examination and 'faulty examination and evaluation system' (4.53 each) than 'a teacher needs to rise above his or her self-interest' and 'increasing politicization and bureaucratization of higher education, (4.46 each). Even, 'educational system still on western pattern' (4.00) has been placed higher than 'financial constraints' and 'stress on liberal arts rather than on vocational courses' (3.61 each).

Although, on the basis of overall analysis, teachers in both the colleges seem to be emphasizing on role commitment, socio-political setup and inadequacies in the academic system; yet more male than female teachers are concerned about 'lack of autonomy to teachers,' 'financial constraints', 'stress on liberal arts rather than on vocational courses' as well as on 'educational system still on western pattern' especially so in the Private college.

However, in the case of university teachers, there is greater agreement shown on 'increasing politicization and bureaucratization of higher education, greater role commitment of teachers and inadequacy in academic system. But both male and female teachers are also concerned about 'financial constraints,' 'educational system still on western pattern' and 'inadequate participation of teachers in academic decision making bodies'.

The varied responses of the university and college teachers to various statements on agreement-disagreement scale may be due to different role orientation, personal experiences, exposure to mass-media and family socialization based on their gender status.

2. (a) Relationship between Academic Level Index of Teachers and the Extent of their Agreement on. Issues Related to Crisis Higher Education

An attempt was also made to relate the academic level index of the university and college teachers with the statements provided to them on crisis in higher education. The procedure for working out the mean score values for each of these statements on the agreement-disagreement scale is same as stated in the earlier table.

An examination of Table 6.2 shows that on the basis of the overall mean score values for these statements, teachers in the university have given the same rank order to these statements as mentioned in the previous table. These in order are 'increasing politicization and bureaucratization of higher education,' (4.39), 'a teacher needs to rise above his or her self interest (4.32), 'faulty examination and evaluation system' (4.17), 'inadequate participation of teachers in academic decision making bodies' (4.00), 'financial constraints' (3.95), 'outdated course syllabi for various levels of examinations' (3.90), 'educational system still on western pattern' (3.71), 'stress on liberal arts rather than on vocational courses, (3.55), 'lack of autonomy to teachers' (3.28) and 'confrontational and agitational attitudes of students' (3.22).

However, the analysis on the basis of a high and a low level index of teachers faculty wise suggests that teachers in the science group in the combined form have shown greater agreement with ' a teacher needs to rise above his self-interest' and 'financial constraints' than 'increasing politicization and bureaucratization of higher education'. Even, 'inadequate participation of teachers in academic decision making bodies' has been placed higher than 'faulty examination and evaluation system'. Further, they are showing more preference for 'educational system still on western

Table 6.2 Relationship between Academic Level Index of Teachers and Extent of Agreement on crisis in Higher Education on the provided statements

S. No.	Statements related to crisis in Higher Education	Overall Mean Score Value	Rank	Extent of Agreement — University Teachers								
				Science (Mean Score Value)			Social Science (Mean Score Value)			Professional (Mean Score Value)		
				Male	Female	Combined Mean	Male	Female	Combined Mean	Male	Female	Combined Mean
1.	Over the years there is increasing politicization and bureaucratization of higher education.	4.39	1	3.84	4.42	4.17	4.18	4.64	4.43	4.80	4.91	4.87
2.	A teacher needs to rise above his or her self interest and work more towards the common good of students and society	4.32	2	4.31	4.42	4.37	4.13	4.25	4.19	4.60	4.58	4.58
3.	Faulty examination and evaluation system have failed to raise the academic standards of students	4.17	3	3.73	4.07	3.92	4.27	4.50	4.39	4.60	4.00	4.17
4.	Inadequate participation of teachers in academic decision-making bodies (university/college) has led to lop-sided development and creativity of teachers	4.00	4	4.10	3.88	3.97	3.86	4.10	3.99	4.20	4.08	4.11
5.	Financial constraints have arrested the growth, development and creativity of teachers.	3.95	5	4.31	4.38	4.35	3.22	4.07	3.69	3.60	3.75	3.70
6.	Outdated course syllabi for various examinations have led to deterioration in the education system	3.90	6	3.10	3.96	3.59	3.81	4.46	4.17	4.40	3.83	3.99

(Contd.)